AFTER THE BUFFALO WERE GONE
THE LOUIS WARREN HILL, SR., COLLECTION OF INDIAN ART

ANN T. WALTON
JOHN C. EWERS
ROYAL B. HASSRICK

a publication of the Northwest Area Foundation
in cooperation with the Indian Arts and Crafts Board
of the United States Department of the Interior, Washington, D.C.,
and the Science Museum of Minnesota, St. Paul, Minnesota

Catalogue Design: Patricia Hemmis Osthus
Artifact Photography: David John Oakes
Drawings: Anne Hassrick Morales and Patricia Hemmis Osthus
Copy and production editing: Ellen B. Green
Printing: Sexton Printing, Inc.

Cover illustration: Pictographic canvas showing war record of White Quiver,
the most successful Indian horse raider. See Plate 5,
Cats. 297a and b, and discussion, pages 222–28.
Burlington Northern Collection

Sepia illustrations: Courtesy of Northwest Area Foundation

"... SO LONG AS THERE WERE BUFFALO, the Blackfeet lived well and happily; but with the buffalo's extermination came dire trouble, then for two or three years they starved, and of those living in the United States, one quarter of the people died from lack of food. Later, better times came. Some cattle were given to them and at one time, they seemed on the way to self-support and independence; but incompetent agents, handling their cattle badly, threw them back into poverty. Their cattle disappeared; cold and drought carried off more and more of their live stock; and today the Blackfeet are poor and suffering; for on their cold and bleak reservation there is no work — no way by which they may earn money to buy food.

"... We must all sympathize with the hard conditions that the Blackfeet are facing today. They need help, but they do not need and should not have charity. If work can be furnished them, by which they may earn food and support for their dear ones; or if people are willing to buy the examples of their ancient arts and industries which they offer for sale, these things will help them far more than will gifts of money.

"I could wish that the officials of the Great Northern Railroad, who collected the material of Indian manufacture to be shown with Mr. [Langdon] Kihn's pictures, might have sent on more of it, as each article is to be sold for the benefit of its maker.

"... I feel that the pictures of these people will interest not only all artists and those who know something about Indians, but also all who possess a real love for the life out of doors — the widespread spaces of their own prairies and mountains."

George B. Grinnell in *Portraits of American Indians: W. Langdon Kihn* (1922)

AFTER THE BUFFALO WERE GONE, the reservation-bound Blackfeet Indians were deprived of their traditional source of food, clothing, and cultural identity. For a Plains Indian warrior, the transition to agricultural life was difficult, if not impossible. The perception by Grinnell and others that Blackfeet civilization was changing became tragically accurate.

Louis W. Hill became involved with the Blackfeet Indians and Glacier Park early in his life. Thereafter, he sought to the best of his ability to do something about the plight of the Indians. With significant success, he brought about a symbiosis between Glacier Park and the Blackfeet Indians; as the park became a national playground, the Indians derived economic benefit from the vacationers.

In terms of today's sensibilities, the concept that once-proud warriors should pose for tourists may seem insensitive and demeaning. But, as Grinnell pointed out, survival took more than sympathy, more than charity — it took jobs.

As we peruse the literature of these times, there may be terms and expressions that are jarring to us today. We should remember that we are reading about a period of history through which our nation has lived and that this is a record from that time. Throughout his life, Louis W. Hill sincerely strove to create a better life for the Blackfeet Indians.

ANN T. WALTON

Introduction

Collections of American Indian material can be traced back as far as the sixteenth century. They show great variety in size, scope, and quality. Interest in the American Indian was great during the nineteenth century — first as explorers and fur traders encountered various tribes and collections were formed, then as westward expansion brought settlers onto Indian tribal lands, which resulted in the removal of Indians to reservations. Finally, as "wild west shows" (such as the famous show put together by "Buffalo Bill" Cody) toured the United States and Europe, a romantic view of the Indian and "Old West" came into vogue. This interest in the Indians manifested itself in the formation of collections of objects that Indians had made for their own use. Eventually production shifted from things the Indians themselves used to things that they made to be sold, often bypassing any utilitarian function.

For many years these collections of Indian material culture were mostly the province of ethnologists and were often not thought of as having much artistic merit. Within our own lifetime, these beautifully designed and constructed objects have attained their rightful place as rare and distinguished works of art that have been collected and displayed by the world's great museums of history, science, and art. Each type of museum collects Indian material culture from a different point of view and applies a different set of criteria. These collections and the exhibits showing them have concentrated on surveying objects of the highest quality from Indian tribal art.

Because of the renewed interest in Indian art in the last ten years, a knowledgeable audience has been created, and Plains Indian scholarship is currently at an all-time high. The American Bicentennial spawned a new interest in Indian art with exhibits such as "Sacred Circles" in London and Kansas City. The need for "tribe-specific" rather than "general-survey" types of exhibitions is the direct result of a better-educated museum-going public.

Transition Period   The spreading European/American culture came into conflict with traditional Plains Indian tribal culture roughly around 1850. The resulting removal to reservations served to weaken the tribal art and traditions. Interaction with forms from other tribes encountered on the reservations often makes Indian art of the post-1850 period very difficult to identify by tribe. Indian exposure to non-Indian civilization further complicates the issue.

The latter half of the nineteenth century and early years of the present century may be referred to as the transition period. It is not regarded as the highest or classic phase of artistic development. The motivation, as well as the raw materials, changed during the transition period. For example, buffalo hides were no longer available for use in making clothing, shelter, and containers. The transition period of Indian art needs to be further explored and documented by scholars. *After the Buffalo Were Gone* concerns itself with this era of history.

The Hill Collection   The Louis W. Hill, Sr., Collection documents the interaction of Indians and non-Indians during the late period of westward expansion and development of the railroads. The collection offers a unique contribution to scholarship in that the effects of the transition period can be seen in a great range of objects and quality. As a collection, it must be viewed within the framework of its time, purpose, and the distinctive personality of its collector. Its time ranges approximately from 1880 to 1940. Its purpose, aside from the satisfaction realized by its collector, Louis W. Hill, Sr., was to enhance the public relations efforts of the Great Northern Railway Company, of which Hill was twice president and, for many years, chairman of the board. The Great Northern became the major concessionaire for the newly designated Glacier National Park in 1910. The promotion of Glacier Park vacations was accomplished through popularizing the image of the "Blackfeet Indian Chief" whose native habitat the park was thought to be. Blackfeet Indian objects, as well as other intermingled High Plains Indian art, were used by the railroad in connection with this campaign for more than fifty years, until the railroad stopped transporting passenger traffic.

In 1952 the collection was divided, when half of it was given by the Great Northern Railway to the Museum of the Plains Indian at Browning, Montana, as a memorial gift in honor of Louis W. Hill, Sr. The other half of the collection is owned by the Northwest Area Foundation, successor to the Hill Family Foundation, and is on loan to the Science Museum of Minnesota in St. Paul.

It is the wish of the Northwest Area Foundation and of Hill's son Louis W. Hill, Jr., that this catalogue serve to reunite his father's collection in order that scholars and the general public can see and enjoy its original continuity, exclusive of the artificial barriers placed on it by time and geography.

Both Louis W. Hill, Sr., and Louis W. Hill, Jr., have enjoyed the mutual friendship and respect of generations of Blackfeet Indians for almost a century. It is entirely fitting that this catalogue be dedicated to both Louis W. Hills and to their many Blackfeet friends.

The Louis W. Hill, Sr., Collection of American Indian Art

Ann T. Walton

Although there is no majestic, ice-crowned mountain or mirror-surfaced lake named for him, in a larger sense the entire area known as Glacier National Park is a product of the creative energy of Louis Warren Hill, Sr. (Fig. 1). He endowed this area on the border between Montana and Canada with every gift at his disposal. No detail was too small to escape his notice, and the sum total of his diligence was to make available to the ordinary American citizen a most extraordinary vacation experience in the American "Alps."

Prior to 1910, an Alpine vacation was generally the privilege of those wealthy enough to visit the inns and spas of Europe. Louis Hill believed in the slogan he coined: "See America First." He set about making the American vacation a family experience. He took his own family for vacations in Glacier National Park and tried to persuade American families to follow his example. Perhaps his greatest genius lay in the emerging enterprise called "Public Relations." His son, Louis W. Hill, Jr., has said that his father could take any promotional idea, "turn it around, enlarge upon it and make it better." After the "America First" slogan was well established, Hill instructed his publicity advisor, W. R. "Bob" Mills, to try to get it on the cover of the *Saturday Evening Post*. There is said to have been a *Post* cover showing an eagle soaring high above the glaciers, with the caption "I saw America first."

Louis W. Hill, Sr., was the second son of James J. Hill, founder of the Great Northern Railway, which linked St. Paul on the Mississippi River with Seattle on the Pacific Ocean. The line followed a northern route, via Montana, passing through the awesome Rocky Mountain terrain that would become Glacier National Park.

The fortunate discovery of Marias Pass, at the southeastern edge of today's Glacier Park, by engineer John F. Stevens, speeded completion of this northernmost transcontinental railroad. The event was celebrated at Scenic, Washington, on January 6, 1893, when the final spike was driven.

Louis Hill was then twenty years old and a student at the Sheffield Scientific School of Yale University. Soon after his graduation in June of the same year, he began to work for the Great Northern Railway in a series of jobs that carried increasing responsibility. These jobs began at the lowest level and included "hands-on" training in all phases of running a railroad. Much was expected of the son of a man who earned the name of "Empire Builder," and Louis Hill was diligent in the performance of his many assignments (*St. Paul Pioneer Press* 1948:2).

In 1904 James J. Hill wrote of his second son, "Louis is running the Great Northern, and while he is not quite so quick as Jim [James N. Hill, the eldest son] he is very sound and careful, and is doing the best railroad operation I have ever seen" (Martin 1976:575). In 1907, upon the retirement of his father from the presidency to become chairman of the board, Louis W. Hill became president of the Great Northern.

Aside from his business accomplishments, he was musically talented and had great skill as a painter and photographer. He loved strenuous outdoor life and in the early 1890s, he "began dropping off the Hill road where it reached the Rocky Mountains for the rugged holiday he loved. He would come into camp with the buck or goat he had climbed after all day, and changing rifle for violin, he would revenge himself on the walls and cliffs by teasing them with strains which they could only repeat over and over without ever seeming to grasp. Sometimes when he sat cross-legged on a summit commanding a vista such as popularly is supposed to exist only in the Alps, he would draw a color box, a roll of canvas and a folding easel from his knapsack and with facile strokes perpetuate his impression in oil" (Steele 1915:479).

Fig. 1 Louis Warren Hill, Sr., at St. Mary's Glacier, Glacier National Park, 1925. *Northwest Area Foundation*

Fig. 2 Louis W. Hill as shown in
Glacier Park Blazer, July 17, 1913.
Northwest Area Foundation

His friendship with the Blackfeet Indians who lived in the region began at this time. Blackfeet leaders of legendary greatness, Chief White Calf and his son Two Guns White Calf. Three Bears, Wades-in-the-Water and his wife, Julia, Johnny and Mary Ground, Lazy Boy, Black Boy, and Medicine Owl, became his lifelong friends. He was adopted into the Blackfeet tribe and given a name that translates as "Gray Horse Rider" (Fig. 2).

James Willard Schultz, who wrote about Blackfeet life and who was married to a Blackfeet woman, served as Hill's guide and became another lifelong friend. Schultz was the earliest to recognize the great contributions of Louis Hill when, in 1915, he dedicated his book *Blackfeet Tales of Glacier National Park* to him, as follows: "To LOUIS WARREN HILL, esq. True friend of my Blackfeet people and the one who has done more than any other individual, or any organization, to make the wonders of Glacier National Park accessible to the American people" (Hanna 1976:114).

Hill became a student of Blackfeet culture long before Glacier National Park came into existence in 1910. Throughout his life he was a tireless worker on behalf of the Blackfeet, an advocate of their rights and needs, and a true friend to all who knew him. His natural artistic bent combined with his love of the Blackfeet to make him a discerning collector. He did not limit himself to collecting only from the Blackfeet, but acquired interesting and handsome objects from other tribes of the High Plains, Northwest Coast, and southwestern tribes as well.

Hill had been able to draw quite well since childhood, and his course of study at Yale would have included many hours of engineering drawing. He always liked to paint, and in later life, when he had the time to develop this talent, his painting *Carmel Mission* won a prize at the Minneapolis Institute of Art (*St. Paul Pioneer Press* 1948:2). His son, Louis, remembers that his father would go next door to James J. Hill's Richardsonian Romanesque mansion on Summit Avenue after everyone had retired for the night. There he would spend the evening by himself in the art gallery, studying and copying the late Impressionist and Barbizon School paintings in his father's collection. At the end of his life, it was said of him, "If he had not been a railroader, he might have been a painter" (*St. Paul Pioneer Press* 1948:2).

Artistic ability played an important role in the life of Louis W. Hill. His second son, James Jerome Hill II, inherited his talent for music and art and became a renowned filmmaker, painter, and art collector in the years following World War II. In Jerome Hill's film *Family Portrait,* private footage from Louis Hill's films of family vacations in Glacier Park is used to create a glimpse of what was entailed in "Seeing America First." This included loading the touring car onto a private train car because the "rubber wheels" would be necessary for bumpy tours of many roadless parts of the park and the adjacent Blackfeet Indian reservation. The film also includes frames of Hill's sons, Louis, Jr., and Jerome, standing before an Indian tipi after their adoption into the Blackfeet tribe.

In retrospect, it seems as though the many interests and abilities of Louis W. Hill converged in his important role in realizing the full potential of Glacier National Park. It was a demanding and ongoing job, suitable for his temperament. The job required enthusiasm, responsibility, and steady guidance. As its president, Hill was also able to command the full support of the Great Northern Railway. It is difficult to imagine any other person filling his role.

Following completion of the railroad in 1893, the Great Northern sought freight for the line by encouraging agriculture, timber interests, and mining shipments. The opening of Glacier Park offered an opportunity to transport a new kind of traffic — vacationers. The Great Northern Railway's track formed the southern boundary of Glacier National Park, between Midvale and Belton.

From the time that the first Glacier Park bill was introduced in the U.S. Congress by Montana Senator Thomas Carter in 1907 until it became law in 1910, Louis Hill worked adroitly behind the scenes, reconciling the differing views of conservationists and preservationists and gathering the political support necessary to pass the bill. President William H. Taft signed the bill into law on May 10, 1910, and by June 7, 1910, William R. Logan, first superintendent of Glacier Park, wrote to Senator Carter, "Mr. L. W. Hill has an engineering force at work in Glacier Park laying out automobile roads. Later on he will put a construction force to work" (Sheire 1970). The road, completed in 1913, was funded by the Great Northern Railway Company, which became the major concessionaire of the new national park. (Later a subsidiary called the Glacier Park Hotel Company was formed.) The road led from the park's eastern entrance at Midvale (later changed to East Glacier), site of the Glacier Park Lodge, north to Many Glacier, site of a second great lodge. Although Glacier Park received a congressional appropriation of $15,000 in 1910, most unusual for the time, this amount was insufficient to launch a good construction program. Not only did the railroad throw its resources behind the development of the park from the earliest date, but Louis Hill committed his own considerable energies to the success of this venture.

Grand hotels had previously been built by railroad companies in national parks served by rail lines. The automobile was still too new and highway systems too primitive to make any sizable impact on vacation transportation. The Atchison, Topeka, and Santa Fe had opened the famous El Tovar Hotel at Grand Canyon soon after the turn of the century (Schwarz 1982:32). Both the Northern Pacific and the Union Pacific had interests in Yellowstone Park while the Southern Pacific was associated with Yosemite Park in California. The difference in Glacier was that never before had the president of a railroad taken the kind of interest that Louis Hill had in Glacier Park. He made the decision that a Swiss theme was in keeping with the mountains already designated as the Alps of America. With his background in engineering and the architectural experience gained from building his own residence on Summit Avenue, he sketched Swiss-chalet-inspired designs for the three main lodges and then turned them over to architects for completion.

The chalets were built first and were fairly Spartan in appointments. Except for the Granite Park chalet, they were all constructed on the same plan — a common dining room and service kitchen, a storehouse, and dormitories that contained wooden-frame beds strung with rope in place of bedsprings. Rugged outdoor activity was stressed; climbing, riding, boating, and pack trips were the means of appreciating the natural beauty of the park.

Belton Chalet, built at the western entrance to Glacier Park, ca. 1911, is typical of the design for the eight chalets that were eventually built by the railroad and operated by the Glacier Park Hotel Company (Fig. 3). The rendering and elevation of the Belton Chalet were executed by the Spokane firm, Cutter and Malmgren. Louis Hill also relied on the Great Northern Railway architect, Thomas D. McMahon, to realize his ideas. Hill's own house at North Oaks Farm, outside of St. Paul, bears a striking resemblance to the Belton Chalet rendering. He designed it and had it constructed in 1928, and after it burned in 1930, he rebuilt it in the same style (Johnston 1981:62).

The train stopped at the east and west entrances to Glacier Park. Belton Chalet served the west portal while the east portal, located at Midvale (the name was later changed to Glacier Park Station), was the site of Hill's most magnificent lodge, Glacier Park Lodge (Fig. 4). The architects were S. L. Bartlett of Chicago and Thomas D. McMahon of St. Paul, but the idea

Fig. 3   Drawing of Belton Chalet. *Northwest Area Foundation*

Fig. 4 Lobby, Glacier Park Hotel. *Great Northern Railway photograph by T. J. Hileman, courtesy of Burlington Northern Railroad*

Fig. 5 Glacier Park Hotel from Glacier Park Station. *Great Northern Railway photograph by T. J. Hileman, courtesy of Burlington Northern Railroad*

was Louis Hill's. He was inspired by the forestry buildings in the 1912 Portland Exposition (Hanna 1976:131), and he may well have been influenced by the monumental timber-post architecture of Japanese temples. The most striking feature of Glacier Park Lodge is its "forest lobby" lined with massive Douglas fir columns that rise majestically from the basement to the third floor and bear the weight of the heavy gabled roof. Both exterior and interior walls are essentially nonload-bearing curtain walls. The columns are from 36 to 42 inches in diameter and 40 feet long. Cedar timber columns of like dimensions were used on the exterior of the building. Sixty of the timbers were transported by rail, three to a flat car, from Oregon and Washington. Amazingly, this lodge was completed in just a year and a half. It contained 61 guest rooms and opened for business on June 15, 1913, in time to celebrate the seventy-fifth birthday of James J. Hill late that summer. An annex was added the next year (Steele 1915:480).

Midvale, on the eastern side of the Rockies, was the site of an Indian trading post prior to 1911: "The Glacier Park Hotel was built on 160 acres of land which, by special act of Congress, Louis W. Hill was authorized to buy from the Blackfeet" (Hanna 1976:137).

The Indian presence was expressed in certain well-defined forms. Indian tipis stood outside of the Glacier Park Lodge (Fig. 5); Blackfeet Indian "chiefs" greeted arriving guests and entertained them (Figs. 6 and 7). (Public relations releases of the Great Northern Railway were not always historically accurate. Occasional liberties were taken, especially with Indian names and dates. The title "chief" was often used inappropriately.) The decor made frequent use of Blackfeet pictographs, as for example on lampshades, and a Blackfeet Indian war record canvas hung outside on the lodge lining the walls (Glacier Park Hotel Company n.d.).

Fig. 6   Exterior, Glacier Park Hotel.
*Photograph courtesy of Burlington
Northern Railroad*

Glacier Park Lodge publicity relates:

> While the Lodge was being constructed,
> Indians of the Blackfeet tribe stood
> in awe as the gigantic fir and cedar
> columns were unloaded from flat cars.
>
> The Indians promptly pinned the
> name "Oom-Coo-La-Mush-Taw"
> on the mammoth new building.
> Translated, this is "Big Tree Lodge."
>
> The Indians had a right to be awed.
> There is no building quite like it in
> the entire world!
>
> Situated on Indian land, the hotel site
> was purchased from the Piegans, a tribe
> of the Blackfeet Nation, many years ago.

The architecture of these hotels is quite remarkable in its enduring simplicity, functional aspects, daring monumental scale, and overall harmony. The lodges are constructed of materials that were, for the most part, found near the site. They sought not to proclaim their own importance but rather to blend inconspicuously into their magnificent setting to become an extension of the outdoors brought inside. It is this conceptual unity that has made them classic examples of monumental wooden architecture from the turn of the century.

Curio shops selling Indian objects and clothing were built into the lobbies of the Glacier Park Lodge and the Many Glacier Lodge, which opened in 1915 on the east side of the park. The Swiss influence is more pronounced at Many Glacier; the staff is attired in lederhosen and dirndls,

Fig. 7 Glacier Park Station. *Photograph
courtesy of Burlington Northern
Railroad*

Fig. 8 Members of the Many Glacier
Hotel staff. *Photograph courtesy
of Burlington Northern Railroad*

Fig. 9 Waterton Lake from Prince of Wales
Hotel lobby. *Great Northern Railway
photograph by T. J. Hileman, courtesy
of Burlington Northern Railroad*

and the door to each room bears a Swiss crest. However, a fusion of Indian
and Swiss themes was attempted by using feathers in the women's
coiffures, thus achieving a pseudo-Indian "cuteness" that marks much of
the early publicity (Fig. 8).

Many Glacier Lodge, just as Glacier Park Lodge, used Indian
pictographs as an important element of the interior decor: "At Many Glacier,
more trophies of the hunt, twenty-four bearskins and twenty-four buffalo
heads, hung on the walls. But the real *piece de resistance* consisted of a
huge 180 foot canvas mural painted by Medicine Owl and no less than
eleven Blackfeet chiefs. Its winter court figures told the history of the
Blackfeet nation. It was a museum piece to accompany the living history
demonstration camped on the hotel grounds" (Sheire 1970:199).

In 1925, Louis Hill received permission from the Canadian government
to construct the third and last of his great hotels, the Prince of Wales Lodge
at Waterton Lakes Park in Alberta. This lodge has more stories than the
other two. It is dominated by a steep, gabled roof line and is encircled by
bracketed Swiss-type balconies. The lobby faces the lake and takes fullest
advantage of a magnificent view with a window wall two stories high. As in
other hotels, Indian pictographs stand out as the central decorative motif
amid less rustic, more streamlined furniture of the late 1920s (Figs. 9, 10
and 11). A travel guide entitled *The Call of the Mountains* describes the
lobby: "A unique and interesting feature of the Prince of Wales Hotel is the
lobby and lounge room decorations. Friezes around the walls of these
public rooms were made by the old chiefs of the Kainah or Blood Indians,

Fig. 10 Prince of Wales Hotel. *Photograph courtesy of Burlington Northern Railroad*

Fig. 11 Lobby, Prince of Wales Hotel. *Great Northern Railway photograph by T. J. Hileman, courtesy of Burlington Northern Railroad*

one of the Blackfeet Confederacy. The friezes are stories, in vividly colored pictographs, of battles and hunting exploits participated in by the elder chiefs when the country hereabouts was a rich hunting ground and the exciting buffalo chase and intertribal strife was the order of the day. The lobby and lounge are lighted by many large and small pendant lamps of parchment ornamented with the symbolic figures of Indian pictography" (Rinehart n.d.:30).

The image of a Blackfeet Indian, often identified as "chief," was the symbol used to publicize Glacier National Park from its earliest days. Indicative of this is the fact that among the first listing of "Concessions and Permits" in the *Report of the Superintendent of the Glacier National Park,* dated 1911, were photographic permits bought by F. H. Kiser for $50.00 and R. H. Marble for $10.00. Both Kiser and Marble took some of the earliest photographs the railroad used to promote Glacier Park, and they took hundreds of photographs each year of visitors with Indians, Indians living on the grounds of Glacier Park Lodge, and Indians involved in activities such as fishing, dancing, canoeing, and carrying firewood. The list is endless, and many of these scenarios were obviously inspired by the photographers' concept of Indian life rather than the reality. The pattern was established early with a small book produced by Great Northern, using Kiser photographs from the 1912–1913 season, titled *Glacier National Park "See America First":* "And a host of novel things—the mountain goats, the cutthroat trout, the Iceberg Lake, where ice-cakes float the summer through,

Fig. 13 Two Guns White Calf. *Glacier National Park "See America First" photograph by F. H. Kiser, courtesy of Burlington Northern Railroad*

Fig. 12. Medicine Owl. *Glacier National Park "See America First" photograph by F. H. Kiser, courtesy of Burlington Northern Railroad*

the Trick Falls and the picturesque camps of the gaily blanketed Blackfeet, for just a few of them — are within the Park beside."

Tinted photographs of Two Guns White Calf, Lazy Boy identified as an "old time Blackfeet Warrior," and Medicine Owl, "Blackfoot Indian Medicine Man," show each of the three costumed in the same "Sioux-type" feather bonnet. This bonnet is similar to Cat. 49. Two Guns wears a Crow-style necklace similar to Cat. 128. It is impossible to make positive identifications from these photographs (shown in black and white in Figs. 12 and 13). However, an obvious use of some items in the Hill Collection was for publicity purposes.

In an interesting switch of subject matter, Louis Hill is shown in Fig. 2, wearing a feather bonnet that is similar to the one above. His handsome shirt is Cat. 59. The circumstances of the acquisition of this gift were described in the same issue of the *Glacier Park Blazer:* "Hanging from one saddle bow was a mysterious bundle that soon proved to be the full dress of a chief and was destined for Mr. Hill. Into it he got and then, abandoning modern for more elemental modes of transit, he mounted a horse."

The event referred to in the *Glacier Park Blazer* was the last of the Glidden Tours, an automobile reliability competition held in July, 1913. Conducted by the American Automobile Association, the rally began in Minneapolis and ended in Glacier Park. Gift-giving was a common way of showing respect among the Plains Indians and it occasionally extended to Indian-non-Indian contacts, such as this one. The *Blazer* article further explains the reason for such a magnificent gift: "Another interesting side light was the devotion which the Indians showed Mr. Hill. To them he is a sort of 'pale-face' god because of his bounties — today he brought them beef — and when he arrived there was a scramble to shake his hand and also to ask him if he had anything to smoke." The *Glacier Park Blazer* was part of a well-planned public relations event or "booster trip" as these journeys came to be known. Louis Hill carefully orchestrated each of these trips to gain the maximum favorable publicity for Glacier Park. On the Glidden Tour: "Hill undertook to provide food, lodging, repairs [for the cars] and general hospitality along the entire route. Equipment for repairing automobiles and a newspaper car fitted out with a linotype machine, a photoengraving plant and mailing facilities were part of the special train that closely followed the cars across the route. With these, newspapermen accompanying the tour produced the Glacier Park Blazer, a daily four-page souvenir sheet reporting the events of the trip, the ceremonies with which the tourists were received along the way, and the jokes and gossip current among the party" (Waters 1963:206).

It is later related that the host, Louis Hill, appeared leading a band of mounted and costumed Blackfeet braves, "riding an Indian mustang with casual skill and the motorists were astonished to find [that] their host . . . had bypassed the calvacade by train" (Waters 1963:214). Hill also used these events and the resulting publicity to prod the government into recognizing the plight of the Blackfeet Indians and to suggest solutions to their problems: "The charm of the Indian life in Glacier Park is in itself a unique feature presented nowhere else in these latter days of the rapid passing of the red man. Nearly 2,000 members of the Piegan tribe establish their tepee cities in the Park during the summer months and they are the center of much interest to the tourist in consequence of their extreme friendliness toward the white traveler . . . The park abounds in game, but the forest rangers patrol it and prevent hunters shooting the animals. The reservation of the Blackfeet, many acres, will be thrown open to white settlers before long, before that time each Indian is to be allotted a farm. Since Blackfeet will then no longer be allowed to hunt extensively, there will be nothing left for them but to try to be farmers.

Fig. 14 Blackfeet Indians in Chicago. *Photograph
by Burke Atwell, courtesy of
Burlington Northern Railroad*

Fig. 15 Owen Heavy Breast and St. Paul booster, 1915. *Photograph by John Anderson, courtesy of Burlington Northern Railroad*

Fig. 16 Blackfeet Indians. *Photograph by R. E. Marble, courtesy of Burlington Northern Railroad*

"Great interest is taken in their welfare by Louis W. Hill, Chairman of the Great Northern Railway, and some time ago he sent a delegation of braves from the reservation to attend a land show in New York City. His idea was that the education which these representatives of this fast-passing race would derive from seeing the show would have great influence in simplifying the United States Government's process of civilizing the tribe" (*Glacier Park Blazer* July 17, 1913:3).

Great interest was taken in Blackfeet welfare by Louis Hill. He saw the promotion of Glacier Park and the survival of the Blackfeet in their native land as being part of the same problem. His solution was to create a symbiosis between the park and the Indians. Each one could enhance the other. That was the reason for the Louis Hill Collection and for his tireless efforts to publicize the park.

The trip mentioned in the *Blazer* was one of many promotional tours on which Blackfeet Indians were taken. Since the Great Northern ran through Browning, site of the Blackfeet Agency, the Indians could be "deadheaded" (taken along with paid freight as space allowed) to major eastern cities. Arrangements were made with hotels for them to set up tipis on the rooftops, resulting in publicity for the hotels as well (Fig. 14).

Mary Ground, a centenarian Blackfeet Indian, recalls such a trip to St. Paul. Tipis were set up near Minnehaha Park and many Twin Citians came to view the Indian settlement. Mary Ground said that they were asked if they would mind the visit of two blind boys from a nearby school. The boys came inside the tipi and felt their way around the interior of the conical structure. Mary said that she was cleaning moccasins, and the boys wanted to feel what she was doing. Fig. 15 shows Owen Heavy Breast being welcomed to the city, and Fig. 16 shows two Blackfeet on their return from St. Paul. A large souvenir pin proclaims "St. Paul Gateway . . . Always open to the world."

Fig. 18 Mike Little Dog, Blackfeet Indian. Great Northern Railway calendar subject, 1934. *Portrait by Winold Reiss, photograph courtesy of Burlington Northern Railroad*

Fig. 17 Sun Dance, Blackfeet Indian. Great Northern Railway calendar subject, 1937. This easel portrait once stood in the "forest lobby" of Glacier Park Hotel. *Portrait by Winold Reiss, photograph courtesy of Burlington Northern Railroad*

Publicity for Glacier Park always had a strong educational flavor. Lectures were given during the winter months in major cities on both coasts. In 1921 Larry Kitchel reported that the crowds attending his presentations and lectures in California represented the "highest class of gatherings — culture and travel folks . . . the audiences, in great measure tourists, are here from every part of the world" (Kitchel 1921).

In 1922 another of Louis Hill's ideas was realized when the Skyland Camps opened. They were operated by Culver Military Academy of Culver, Indiana. Skyland Camps offered the full spectrum of Glacier Park activities including nature walks, climbing, riding, and boating.

In 1918 and 1919, the railroads were still under federal control, as they were throughout World War I, and promotion had to be curtailed (McGillis 1942). However, in 1921 there was a national effort to promote the national parks. The campaign sought "to launch propaganda to enlarge and preserve the parks — and to start state parks." A proclamation by the president of the United States set aside the first week in April to advertise and popularize national parks. All communications agencies were involved, including chambers of commerce, automobile clubs, national magazines, churches, motion picture companies, the secretary of the interior, and all types of advertising promoters. H. B. Kaltenborn, associate editor of the *Brooklyn Eagle,* was one of the many people to be included in the organization committees. He went to Glacier Park on one of the "booster trips" and became a friend of Louis Hill's.

It could have been through Kaltenborn that Louis Hill first heard of the German-born artist, Winold Reiss, or he may have discovered him in 1920 when Reiss had his first exhibit of Blackfeet Indian portraits in New York, resulting from a 1920 study trip to Montana with W. Langdon Kihn, who was Reiss's student at the time. Kihn wrote Louis Hill on October 1, 1921, enclosing an article from a *New York World* magazine section, which mentioned Reiss. Kihn was able to interest Hill in lending material from his own collection and assembling Blackfeet crafts to be sold in conjunction with an exhibit of portraits by Kihn of 55 Blackfeet Indians. This exhibition was sponsored by the Art Museum of Santa Fe and was held at the Anderson Galleries in New York, March 20 to April 2, 1922.

By 1925 Reiss's brother, Hans Reiss, was working as a guide in Glacier National Park (Glacier Park Hotel Company 1925). Hans Reiss had been recommended by Kaltenborn. A letter from Hans Reiss to Louis Hill, dated January 7, 1926, suggests that since "you always have an artist up there in summer to paint pictures to advertise the park . . . I wonder if you have already made arrangements with an artist for the coming season and if not would you feel disposed to have my brother come with me." In 1927 Reiss did go to the park and thus began the famous Blackfeet Indian portraits that appeared on Great Northern calendars (Fig. 17) from 1928 to 1958, some five years after Reiss's death. Boys who are grandfathers today grew up with these calendar prints on their bedroom walls. The series was so popular that beginning in 1930 only Blackfeet portraits by Reiss were used. During that first season in 1927, Hill bought 51 Blackfeet Indian portraits, of which five were oil paintings. In 1928 Hill bought an additional 28 pictures and printed a catalogue designed by Reiss to accompany the exhibition of his collection.

There were always artists at Glacier. The magnificent landscape that attracted them soon absorbed them, until it was perfectly natural to see any number of artists perched in unlikely spots painting the glories of nature. Arrangements were made with artists and writers to live and work at Glacier in the summer in exchange for room, board, and various other considerations. Joseph Scheurle was among the first to be promoted by the Great Northern. A 1916 listing of Great Northern publications advertised

WINOLD REI//
ART /CHOOL

WINOLD REISS
Assistant Professor of Mural Painting
NEW YORK UNIVERSITY

THIRD ANNUAL

/UMMER
/E//ION

June 15 — September 15

/T. MARY'/
LAKE

These courses are given under the auspices of the
College of Fine Arts of New York University. Students
who meet the entrance requirements of the College and
register for these courses may submit their work for
academic credit. These courses will be conducted by
the College of Fine Arts through the division of General
Education of New York University.

GLACIER
NATIONAL
PARK
MONTANA

© G.N. Ry. Co.

BLACKFEET INDIAN BOY *portrait by* **Winold Reiss**

Fig. 19 Great Northern Railway
travel promotion brochure. *Courtesy
of Burlington Northern Railroad*

"*Glacier National Park Indian Portfolio* — 75 cents — A collection of 12 reproductions in full color of paintings of Blackfeet Indian chiefs by the noted artist, Joseph Scheurle." Among the April 27, 1927, list of "Artists who are going to Glacier Park this summer" one finds Oliver Dennett Grover, Guy Wiggins, Katherine W. Leighton, Langdon Kihn, Winold Reiss, and John Fery. It was the Blackfeet portraits of Reiss, however, that served to bond in the public mind Blackfeet Indians with Glacier Park.

During the 1928 season, Reiss painted Mike Little Dog (Fig. 18), whose portrait was used on the 1934 calendar. The background consists of pictographs invented by Reiss in imitation of the Blackfeet war record canvases that adorned the hotels. Kihn also took up the pictographic form that appears in the catalogue of his 1922 exhibit at Anderson Galleries. There was a natural affinity of artists who paint images to be attracted to the painted images of Indians.

Winold Reiss was an assistant professor of mural painting at New York University during the school year. He had long dreamed of establishing a summer art school, and in 1934 he offered, in conjunction with Great Northern, a three-month course in drawing, painting, and sculpture at St. Mary's Lake chalets in Glacier National Park (Fig. 19). Reiss was known to non-Indian friends by the nickname of "Profess" and to Indians as "Beaver Child" because of his prodigious industry. He once painted 34 portraits in thirty-one days (Reiss 1981:28). He worked in a rapid, flat, decorative style that was an outgrowth of his German education at the end of the *Jugendstil* period. Sketching rapidly on Wattman board he covered large, flat areas in tempera paint, using pastel to build up skin tones and textures. Using the flat length of the pastel crayon, he frequently suggested a shadow by outlining a portion of the figure. His line is bold and sure while his costume detail is impeccable in its accuracy. The symmetry of costume design made it possible to first fill in the pattern on one sleeve or one legging only because the other side would be identical.

Reiss designed the interiors of train cars as well as providing the Indian portraits that were the central focus of the cars. His portraits adorned playing cards, postcards, and train menus, and eventually 49 of the portraits were compiled in a commemorative volume issued in 1935 by Great Northern Railway in recognition of the twenty-fifth anniversary of Glacier National Park. The design of the book, its cover, wrapper, slipcase, and mailing case, show the telling hand of Winold Reiss. His interpretative use of Indian geometric patterns translated perfectly into the geometric *metier* of Art Deco current in the 1930s. The prints from this book proved so popular that they were issued in two separate portfolios and distributed by mail to thousands of school children, as well as to other collectors, until 1960.

Reiss had ambitions beyond painting the Blackfeet Indians of Montana for the Great Northern Railway. On March 28, 1930, he wrote to Louis Hill suggesting that he be commissioned to paint an "Indian Monument . . . a collection of 300 to 350 pictures representing Indians of all the still-existing important tribes." It is indicative of his rapid style of work that he proposed to accomplish this in three years, working only four months of each year. The resulting "Indian Monument" would be the centerpiece of the Great Northern's exhibit in the Chicago World Fair of 1934. Still hopeful in 1931, Reiss was quoted in the March, 1931, *Dupont Magazine:* "This work I have done for Mr. Hill is part of my plan. It is my dream and desire to paint full-blooded representatives of every American Indian tribe. Altogether there will be three hundred and fifty when I have finished, and it will be the only accurate gallery of these people when they have suffered extinction, or lost bloodlines." Reiss did paint other tribes, particularly in the Southwest, but more's the pity that his ambitious project was never realized. We should have been greatly enriched as a nation by this modern-day George Catlin.

While photographers were always part of the Glacier Park scene, movie cameras were somewhat rarer, but nonetheless in evidence from time to time. Very early (ca. 1913, 1914) photographs exist of *Pathé Frères* camera crews (Fig. 20), who worked from dizzying heights to film the beauties of Glacier Park. On September 15, 1920, Marshall Neilan entered into an agreement with the Glacier Park Hotel Company to film a full-length feature after the tourists had left. The Hotel Company provided lodging, served meals, hauled freight, and maintained all necessary services during filming.

The film used the local Blackfeet Indians in the opening scenes, as well as cowboys and local "extras." Difficulty developed when it came to filming the Custer battle scenes that were part of the scenario. There just didn't seem to be the 500 or 600 Indians that the film required (Nobel 1920). The producers decided to shoot the final scenes of the Custer battle at Fort Peck Reservation in hopes of finding more Indians who wanted to take part in the movie. When Neilan and company left Glacier Park on October 11, 1920, Indians turned up en masse to give him a farewell ceremonial. The film was named *Bob Hampton of Placer.* It opened in 1921 with Blackfeet Indians provided by the Great Northern for publicity purposes. An interesting finale to all the excitement was provided in a letter to Louis Hill from Ralph Budd, then president of Great Northern Railway, in which he states: *"Bob Hampton of Placer* [opened] tonight here and [I] found it a delightful entertainment. The story is interesting and the scenes are beautifully staged, but there is no mention whatever of Glacier National Park. The following appears at the bottom of the title screen announcing the picture: 'Indians and authentic locations by courtesy of Louis W. Hill, Great Northern Railway Company.' There is nothing else to identify the Great Northern or Glacier National Park with the picture. I do not know what arrangements were made with Marshall Neilan, but except to those who are familiar with the scenery of Glacier National Park, there is absolutely nothing to indicate that the picture was not taken on the Custer battlefield in [sic] Wyoming."

Fig. 20 *Pathé Frères* camera crew at Glacier
National Park. *Photograph by R. E.
Marble, courtesy of Bulrington
Northern Railroad*

Later films were more effective than *Bob Hampton of Placer.* An agreement of August 16, 1921, between Outlook Photoplays, Inc., and the Great Northern Railway Company concerned a motion picture of Sinclair Lewis's novel *Free Air.* Several travel films were made in the early 1940s. Twentieth Century Fox filmed *Magic Carpet* in 1941, while MGM filmed a story of a typical vacationer's adventures in Glacier Park and Waterton Lakes Park the same year *(Great Northern Goat,* April, 1942). Ronald Reagan made a film with Barbara Stanwyck in Glacier Park during 1953, called *Cattle Queen of Montana.*

In addition to movie stars, important dignitaries came and went with impressive frequency. They were greeted by Blackfeet "chiefs" and on occasion were adopted by the Blackfeet into their tribe. A news release from May 1, 1922, by Hoke Smith of Great Northern describes the induction of members of the National Editors Association: "Welcoming the editors were tribal chiefs Two Guns White Calf, Eagle Calf, Wolf Robe, Many Tail Features, Heavy Breast, Turtle, Lazy Boy, Middle Rider, Big Springs and Curly Bear. This array of full bloods [was] attired in beaded buckskin and featured regalia. The paleface subjects stripped to the waist are arranged kneeling within a circle of Indians. Amid the tumult of beating tomtoms and solemn chanting of the adoption song, each chief paints his family hieroglyphics upon the bare back of the white man he is to sponsor with an Indian name . . .

"The Blackfeet Indian Council has written to L. W. Hill, Chairman of the Board of Great Northern Railway, one of the charter members of its tribe of 'Adopted Paleface Brothers,' asking him to issue formal invitations to all white men throughout the United States who have been taken into the Blackfeet tribe urging as many as can be present . .

"The Indians keep a record of all their adoptions, each accepted paleface member signing his own name and his Indian name with the historical mammoth Golden Eagle Quill that has been handed down through generations by the chiefs of the Blackfeet tribe. The tribal letter contains the names of several hundred white people, many of them men and women of distinction." (John Ewers says much of this adoption ceremony description is inaccurate, especially Golden Eagle Quill, which was not handed down through generations.)

Adoption *in absentia* was arranged for General Douglas MacArthur. A ceremony was held on March 18, 1942, in which a full-page newspaper photograph of MacArthur stood in his stead. He was given the name of Chief Wise Eagle. After World War II, 217 United Nations delegates and their aides from 16 countries stopped in Glacier National Park en route to the East Coast from the initial meeting of the organization in San Francisco: "Chief (George) Bullchild, interpreter for the Blackfeet Indians, presented each of the adopted delegates with deerskin certificates of their membership in the tribe, carrying legends of their Indian names" (*Great Northern Goat,* August, 1945:9).

President and Mrs. Franklin D. Roosevelt were inducted into the Blackfeet tribe on June 5, 1934 (Fig. 21). President Roosevelt then broadcast one of his celebrated fireside chats from Two Medicine Chalet (Hanna 1976:149). While all of these activities made news and that meant promotion for Glacier National Park, it also meant that important people from all over the world gained some knowledge of a culture other than their own. When the Blackfeet delegation traveled during the winter to promote park visitation through one event or another, they were also teaching a good number of men, women, and children something of Plains Indian life.

In 1930 the Glacier Park Hotel Company acquired the Lewis Glacier Hotel from John E. Lewis. It was the last of the Glacier Park hotels to be operated by the Great Northern and gave the company a lodge near the

Fig. 21 President Franklin D. Roosevelt at Glacier National Park in 1934. *United Press photograph courtesy of United Press International*

western portal. It was renamed the Lake McDonald Hotel. The hotel was built in 1913 while famous cowboy artist Charles M. Russell was still alive. Russell and "Trader Lewis" were good friends, and it is said that Russell scratched the Indian pictographs on the base of the hearth. Russell and his family occupied a cabin, studio, and camp at the south end of Lake McDonald. As in the other hotels, Indian pictographs adorned the lamp-shades and walls (Great Northern Railway Company 1957).

John Lewis ran a curio shop when he owned the hotel, and when the hotel was sold, a substantial number of Indian costumes and other artifacts was acquired by the Great Northern Railway. The *St. Paul Pioneer Press* stated, "The collection was begun by J. E. Lewis, who operated a hotel on Lake McDonald in the park area for many years" (October 18, 1959). It is this collection that formed the basis of the gift made to the Museum of the Plains Indian in Browning, Montana, by the Great Northern Railway Company in 1952. The collection was given as a memorial to Louis W. Hill, Sr., who died in 1948.

Dr. Claude E. Schaeffer was curator of the Museum of the Plains Indian when the collection was offered to the museum. Dr. Schaeffer drew up a list in October, 1951, giving a three- or four-word description of each item and indicating whether it was most desired, desired, or least desired by the museum. He was given the part of the collection that he requested. The remainder was retained by the railroad, along with a few other artifacts retained from the Glacier Park hotels after the railroad ceased to be a Glacier Park concessionaire in 1960. The most interesting and valuable portion of this remainder is the collection of war record canvases (Fig. 22), which tell individual Blackfeet histories in pictographic style and which were used to decorate both the interior and exterior of the Glacier Park hotels.

The bulk of the material actually collected by Hill and the Great Northern Railway remains in St. Paul. The sources of this part of the Louis W. Hill Collection are less clear. The collection as such is mentioned in print by George B. Grinnell in the 1922 exhibition catalogue *Portraits of American Indians: W. Langdon Kihn*. We know that gift-giving was a practice of the Plains Indians, and one recorded example of such a gift exchange is mentioned in the July 17, 1913, *Glacier Park Blazer*.

Louis W. Hill, Jr., recalls that parts of the collection were obtained from Frank and Joseph Sherburne, Browning merchants, as well as from Broadwater-Pepin Trading Company. J. J. Sherburne, father of the brothers, J. H. and Frank Sherburne, came up from Oklahoma. He was an "official of the Swiftcurrent Oil, Land and Power Company which drilled for oil in 1904" in what is today Glacier Park (Hanna 1976). In 1896 he opened the Sherburne Mercantile, which continues to the present time in Browning, and Lake Sherburne on the approach to Many Glacier Hotel bears his name. The Sherburnes' excellent collection of Blackfeet material is today in the University Museum, Spokane, Washington.

The Jack Carberry (an employee of the Broadwater-Pepin Trading Company) Collection was used for the Winold Reiss Blackfeet Indian portraits as related by Reiss's son Tjark: "Usually the Indians posed in their own ceremonial robes. However, if they didn't have any, we would borrow a fine one from Margaret Carberry who ran the trading post in Glacier Park station. Her father had collected some magnificent Indian clothing and gear; Margaret added to the collection until it was one of the greatest of its kind" (Reiss 1981:37). A portion of the Carberry Collection has also been given to the Museum of the Plains Indian, where it is on display today with many of the best pieces of the Hill Memorial Collection.

Fig. 22 Blackfeet Indian War Record Canvas A, Cat. 295 detail. *Burlington Northern Collection*

E. T. Broadwater arrived at Montana in 1881, and in 1891 he started a general mercantile business with Simon Pepin in what is now the city of Havre: "They conducted business in a tent for a time on the ground where the Great Northern Railway yards now are, but donated the ground to the railway company on the condition that the point should be made a division headquarters, and this was the real start of the city" (*Progressive Men of the State of Montana* n.d.: 550). The Havre store was such a success that it soon expanded into Browning. It is possible that items in the collection obtained from Broadwater-Pepin go back to the early days of the railroad in Havre.

The *Great Northern Goat,* a magazine published by the Great Northern Railway for travel agents, as well as for its own employees, discusses the material in this collection as follows: "In Great Northern's collection of Blackfeet Indian craftwork consisting of some five hundred articles are Indian costumes, war clubs and hunting paraphernalia. The articles, some of which are more than three hundred years old, were acquired from the Blackfeet whose reservation adjoins the Glacier National Park in Montana on the east. The craftwork has been classified and placed in storage until after the war when it will be assembled and installed as a permanent educational and historical exhibit in the company's museum in its general office building in St. Paul, Minnesota" (April, 1945:9).

The article points up some of the difficulties in determining the origins of the collection. The exaggeration that some items go back more than three hundred years may actually have been believed by both Blackfeet and railway personnel in 1945. The collection notes are generally unreliable and often totally incorrect. At the time that he accepted the gift to the Museum of the Plains Indian, Dr. Claude Schaeffer agreed to the stipulation that a collection history be written. It is indeed unfortunate that he was not able to complete this task. A survey of the collection was undertaken by Dr. Louis H. Powell, director, and Dr. Elden Johnson, curator (later chairman of the anthropology department of the University of Minnesota), and James H. Howard, research assistant at the Minnesota Science Museum (now the Science Museum of Minnesota), in May, 1953. The survey states that "it rapidly became apparent that the identification (functional occasionally and

tribal more frequently) on the tags attached to the specimens in the Louis W. Hill Memorial Collection at Browning were unreliable and often grossly misleading." Dr. Johnson recalled in a conversation with this author on December 13, 1983, the problem of inadequate and inaccurate collection history, but also indicated that the group was there only one month, and it worked very hard just to classify and organize the items and had no time for anything else.

Almost all those who owned, traded, and made the articles in the collection are dead. The sources of this collection are listed when they can be determined with any accuracy. For the most part, we simply do not have reliable information.

After the deaths of Louis W. Hill, Sr., in 1948 and Winold Reiss in 1953, an exhibit called "Indian Summer" was held in the lobby of the First National Bank of St. Paul in October, 1959. This exhibit "presented together for the first time elements of two outstanding collections historically identified with St. Paul through the Great Northern Railway and its second president, Louis W. Hill, Sr." The two collections were the paintings of Blackfeet Indians commissioned by Louis W. Hill, Sr., and by the Great Northern Railway and the collection of Indian art that is in this catalogue. The portraits made it possible to visualize just how some of the objects in the Louis W. Hill, Sr., Collection were worn and used by Blackfeet Indians. The artistry of Winold Reiss gave verve and vitality to the artifacts.

The inspiration of Louis Hill in putting together his collections was his longtime admiration for and appreciation of the Blackfeet Indians (Fig. 23). His two collections, the Indian art and the art of Winold Reiss, record for all to see the passing of an era when the buffalo were gone and Glacier National Park was born.

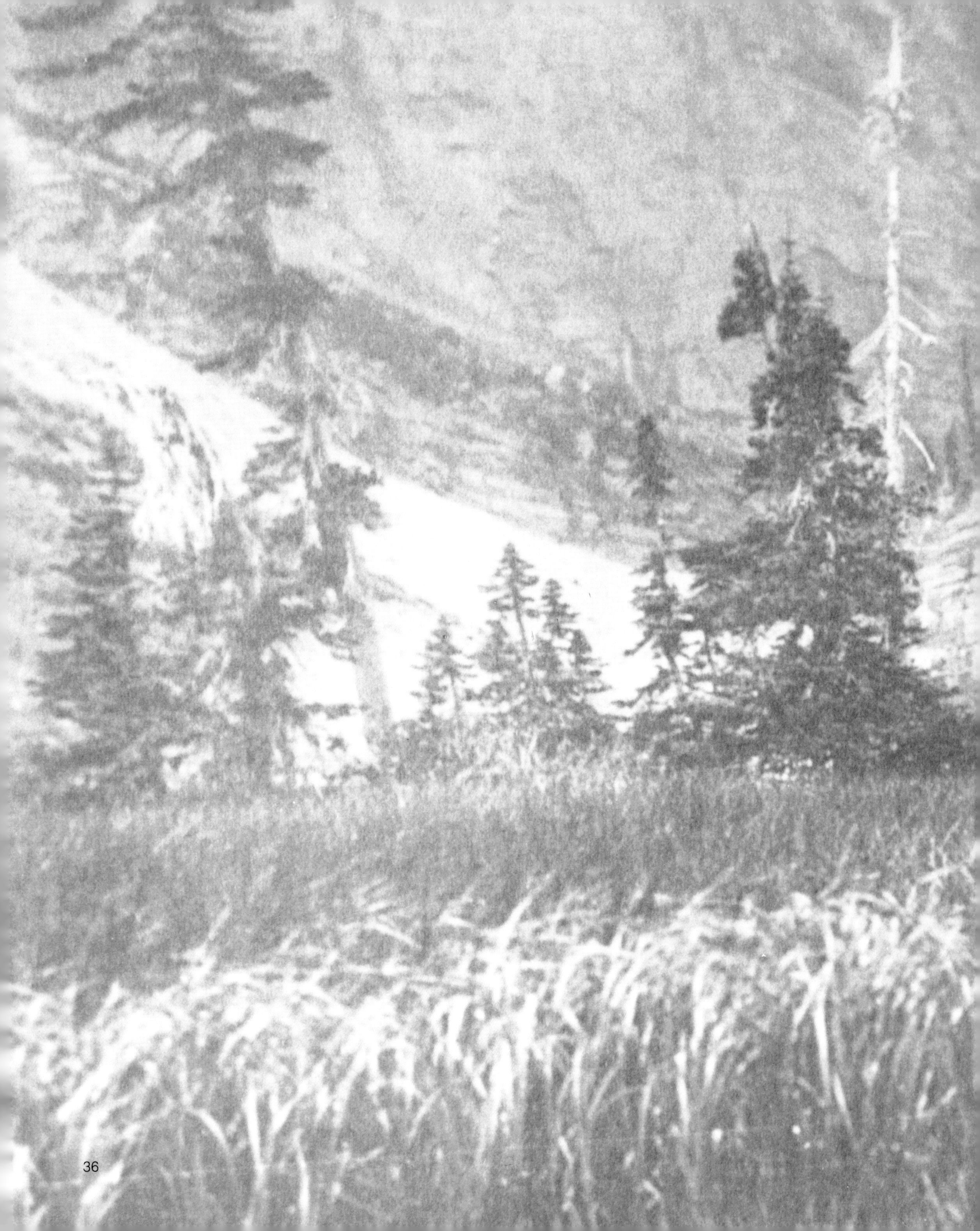

The Persistent Tradition:
The Hill Collection from the Viewpoint of a Student of Blackfeet Indian Arts and Crafts

John C. Ewers

Fig. 24 Group of young warriors at Blackfeet Old
Agency, 1888. *Photograph courtesy of
Montana Historical Society*

Fig. 25 White Calf at Old Agency, ca. 1888.
*Photograph courtesy of the Museum
of the Plains Indian*

Early in the year 1941 I was privileged to become the first curator of the new Museum of the Plains Indian, which was then under construction on the Blackfeet Reservation just west of the little town of Browning and less than 20 miles east of Glacier National Park. I had developed my exhibition plan with the advice of René d'Harnoncourt, then manager of the Indian Arts and Crafts Board in Washington, before going west to collect the specimens needed to fulfill it. The museum opened to the public in June, 1941, and it remained open through the summer months during the three years I was its curator.

Happily my employer, the Division of Education of the Indian Office, encouraged me to devote a good portion of my time during the intervening winters to the study of Blackfeet Indian history and arts. I read the pertinent literature in libraries and archives and examined Plains Indian collections in other museums. Even more important, I conducted extended interviews with elderly Blackfeet Indians who had been born and had grown to adulthood during "buffalo days." They had participated actively in hunting and warfare, as well as in the camp life of those times. They also possessed lively memories of the changes and the continuities in Blackfeet life since buffalo days ended, and these Indians were settled on reservations during the early 1880s.

Many hours of listening to these old people impressed me that despite the very traumatic experience of being quickly transformed from an independent, nomadic, hunting people, into a sedentary one dependent on government rations for their survival, a strong thread of continuity persisted in the lives of tribal members who survived this shock but stubbornly clung to their traditional beliefs and values after the buffalo were gone.

Intertribal warfare in the form of raiding for the horses of enemy tribesmen continued for a few years after the buffalo became extinct. A photograph of a group of young warriors taken at Old Agency in 1888 shows one of them, Stabs-by-Mistake, holding a repeating rifle, which had rendered both bows and arrows and muzzle-loading flintlocks obsolete as war weapons. Their clothing shows a mixture of traditional garments — moccasins, leggings, and breechclouts — with shirts obtained from white traders or received in government annuities (Fig. 24). At that time only the uniformed Indian policemen and some of the Blackfeet chiefs had fully adopted white men's clothing for daily wear. A portrait of White Calf (Fig. 25), head chief of the Piegan, taken at the same time, showed him clad in what was then called "citizen's dress" — coat and trousers. But he still wore moccasins on his feet. In one hand he carried a pipe and a tobacco pouch. The tobacco pouch was of traditional Blackfeet form, with a side panel of beadwork decorated in mountain designs, but the bowl of the pipe was a typical Siouan calumet, carved of the red stone known as catlinite and quarried by the Sioux at the famous pipestone quarry in southwestern Minnesota. It was traded widely to tribes on the Northern Plains and beyond.

Evidence of Blackfeet possession and use of objects made by Indians of other tribes may be found in the observations of literate white men who knew the Blackfeet earlier in the nineteenth century. As early as 1833 the German scientist, Prince Maximilian of Wied, noted, during a month's observation of Blackfeet Indians in the vicinity of Fort McKenzie on the Missouri River, that the Blackfeet were using Sioux pipes. He also reported their preferences for Flathead war clubs and Crow shields, and that they had but recently begun to borrow from the Assiniboine the custom of decorating their dress shirts with large circular ornaments in porcupine quills. He stated that some Blackfeet men were following Mandan and Hidatsa customs in their use of hair ornaments (Maximilian 1906: XXIII, 99–101, 118–19, 161).

Fig. 26 Rides-at-the-Door, age 84, 1947.
*Photograph by Donald Schmidt,
courtesy of John C. Ewers*

During the summer of 1891 Charles H. Stephens, an artist from Pennsylvania, visited the Blackfeet on their Montana reservation and filled a sketchbook with pictorial observations of the objects he saw in use among them. His sketchbook, preserved in the University of Pennsylvania Museum in Philadelphia, pictures a number of objects from the tribes west of the Rockies, including a pair of Pend d'Oreille moccasins, some beaded Flathead cradleboards, and several decorated flat pouches from the Nez Perce as far distant as Idaho.

My elderly Blackfeet informants told me that friendly visits back and forth with formerly hostile tribes were common after the Indian wars ended. The Blackfeet not only exchanged visits with the "overmountain tribes" to the west but with the Assiniboine, Cree, Crow, and other tribes on the Plains to the east and south. These old Indians stated that during these visits, gifts were given to and exchanged with individuals of the other tribes. During fieldwork among the Assiniboine on Fort Belknap Reservation in 1953, elderly members of that tribe confirmed the Blackfeet testimony regarding those exchanges of valuable possessions. Older informants of both tribes stressed the desire of the horse-poor Assiniboine for Blackfeet horses, as well as Blackfeet interest in obtaining men's dress shirts of buckskin, tastefully decorated with porcupine quills from the Assiniboine. They agreed that the Assiniboine first brought hairpipe breastplates and women's necklaces of the same trade materials early in the 1890s and introduced the Sioux type of flowing feather bonnet to the Blackfeet during the decade. But it was not long thereafter that some Blackfeet craftsmen were fashioning those bonnets quite skillfully.

It is not easy and sometimes not possible to determine whether some items collected among the Blackfeet, but of styles known to have been developed by neighboring tribes, were imported from the originating tribes or were copied by Blackfeet men or women from alien models. In some cases there were differences in techniques in construction or decoration that reveal Blackfeet adaptations from the other tribes. For example, by the early years of the present century, Blackfeet women were copying the tall triangular designs of Assiniboine quill and beadwork on the beaded panels on men's shirts. However, the Blackfeet rendered these designs in the overlay stitch, while Assiniboine and Sioux used the lazy stitch. A striking photograph of a Piegan, Rides-at-the-Door, taken by Donald Schmidt in 1947 portrays him wearing a beaded shirt bearing designs adopted from the Assiniboine (Fig. 26). This was a shirt he wore only on dress occasions. Rides-at-the-Door was pictured on the far right in the group of young Blackfeet at Old Agency sixty years earlier (Fig. 24). He was then a young man portrayed in everyday clothes. But at that earlier time it is doubtful whether young Rides-at-the-Door could have afforded a handsome dress shirt of buckskin decorated with beaded panels.

By the 1940s there were fewer than 40 men living on the Blackfeet Reservation in Montana who owned quilled or beaded buckskin shirts and leggings. Even fewer women owned beaded buckskin dresses. Yet there were some men and women participating regularly in the entertainment of tourists at the hotel in East Glacier who possessed more than one such Indian costume.

I had no part in the acquisition of a major portion of the Louis W. Hill Collection by the Museum of the Plains Indian in 1954, a decade after my service at that museum ended. I did not begin to study the portions of the Hill Collection in St. Paul and in Browning until 1982.

Any scholar who studies the Louis W. Hill Collection must be impressed with the artistic quality of most of the pieces in it. This may be, at least in part, due to Louis Hill's highly developed artistic taste. To an extent the content of the collection reflects the period during which the collection was made. Had Hill begun to collect thirty years earlier, in the 1880s, this collection surely would have contained a goodly number of Indian weapons and a considerable number of items decorated with the larger-sized embroidering beads the Blackfeet called "big beads," the use of which antedated seed beads. Had he begun to collect thirty years later, the collection probably would have included a number of medicine bundles, which were no longer used in the families of their owners by the 1940s.

At the same time, the scholar who studies this collection must wish that the individual pieces were better documented with accompanying written information about their history — who made them and when, who used them and how, and how they were acquired for the Hill Collection. A few of the specimens do have very helpful documentation. One of the several very fine men's suits is known to have been given to Wades-in-the-Water by his wife, Julia, to represent a decorated shirt he was given in a dream. Other evidence, not accompanying the specimen, can be found to show when this suit was made within a brief span of years. The Wades-in-the-Waters were married in 1915, and he was pictured wearing this shirt in a portrait executed by W. Langdon Kihn, known to have been exhibited in New York City early in 1922. Putting this evidence together, we can be sure that this beaded shirt of atypical Blackfeet design was given to Wades-in-the-Water in a dream and was made by his wife, Julia, between 1915 and 1922 (Cat. 82 and Fig. 30).

We know also that some of the other specimens in this collection bear tags indicating that they were purchased from the Broadwater-Pepin Trading Company and listing the names of their former owners. From that company's business records in the Montana Historical Society, we learn that it was licensed to trade on the Blackfeet Reservation in Montana from 1899 to 1920, and from tribal census records and other sources, we learn that the former owners named were Blackfeet Indians. An employee of the Broadwater-Pepin Trading Company was Jack Carberry, a very judicious collector of Blackfeet-owned material whose daughter Margaret deposited that collection in the Museum of the Plains Indian in 1941. Like the Hill Collection, the Carberry Collection was also rich in articles of clothing and clothing accessories, but it contained few weapons or sacred objects. My studies of the Carberry Collection, with the aid of elderly Blackfeet Indians who remembered many of the pieces, indicated that it was largely a turn-of-the-century collection.

For the great majority of specimens in the Louis W. Hill Collection, we have no close dates of creation or record of Indian ownership and use. We have no positive evidence, certainly, that any of them were collected elsewhere than on the Blackfeet Reservation. And Louis W. Hill's known close relationship with the Blackfeet, the Indians who lived nearest to his beloved Glacier National Park, makes it seem logical that he would have collected primarily, if not entirely, from those Indians.

Yet we find in this collection numerous objects whose form and/or decoration indicate that they were made by or copied from other tribes — in some cases Sioux, in other Crow, Flathead, Kutenai, or Nez Perce. Other pieces cannot be definitely assigned to any tribal style but make extensive use of floral designs used by the Metis, of mixed Indian and white descent, who had sizable settlements of their own on the Northern Plains, and who settled among and influenced the craftwork of all of the Indian tribes of the region. Seeing these pieces of non-Blackfeet style in this collection reminds me of the extensive and irrefutable evidence of the gift and exchange of objects to the Blackfeet from other tribes found in the writing of earlier white observers and in the verbal testimony of elderly Indians I have cited earlier.

Archaeologists have long recognized the occurrence of a few types of potsherds of types more typical of other sites than of the one under investigation as indicators of cultural influences of one Indian group upon another. But studies of the arts and crafts of the tribes on the Northern

Great Plains have been handicapped by scholars' tendencies to attribute to the tribe inhabiting a particular reservation all specimens of late nineteenth- or twentieth-century origin known to have been collected on that reservation. Adherence to such a rigid concept led to the erroneous identification of many objects in collections of large as well as small museums. We hope this study may help to correct such misunderstanding in a positive way by bringing to bear knowledge of particular objects. This knowledge has been obtained from the literature, from well-identified pictorial sources, and when available from the verbal testimony of Indians who were living during the years such objects were made. These Indians remembered the artistic creations of their fellow tribesmen and of neighboring tribes of Indians.

Knowledge of the history of the Indian use of certain classes of objects represented in this collection, obtained from sources other than an examination of the specimens themselves and the meager documentation accompanying them, can provide answers to some questions that at first blush appear to be unanswerable. For example, if the specimens in the Hill Collection were indeed collected among the Blackfeet, why should there be a high proportion of women's dresses of Sioux style in this collection? We don't know whether or not Hill preferred the more heavily beaded Sioux dresses to Blackfeet ones, but from other sources we can find that a number of Blackfeet women did prefer to wear Sioux-style dresses on occasions when it was most appropriate for them to appear in traditional Indian costume. Surely an Indian woman's selection of a dress for such occasions was a personal, not a tribal, decision. All Blackfeet women were not compelled to wear dresses of Blackfeet style and make.

On several occasions during the 1940s, I saw Julia Wades-in-the-Water, the fullblood wife of a prominent fullblood leader on the Blackfeet Reservation, wearing a Sioux dress with a solidly beaded yoke on which typical Sioux geometric designs stood out clearly against a background of blue beads. She wore this dress when she rode horseback in the Fourth of July parades in the town of Browning and when she was part of the group of elderly Blackfeet Indians who ceremonially bestowed a Blackfeet name upon some prominent white man or woman visitor to Glacier National Park. She also wore it when she attended Indian dances or ceremonies on the reservation. She further wore that dress when she sat for her portrait by Winold Reiss in 1943 (Fig. 27). Her niece, Mrs. Mae Williamson, for many years president of the Blackfeet Indian Arts and Crafts Cooperative on the reservation, wore a Sioux dress with a background of blue beads also. I photographed her in it at a ceremony honoring several officers from the Malmstrom Air Force Base in Great Falls, Montana, when they visited the reservation and were given Blackfeet names during the early 1940s.

Julia Wades-in-the-Water's daughter, Mrs. Nora Spanish, who served for more than forty years as the business manager of the Blackfeet Indian Arts and Crafts Cooperative, also owned a beautiful Sioux dress with a background of brown beads. She had worn it when she was introduced to President and Mrs. Calvin Coolidge at the White House in 1927. She also wore it when she welcomed Eleanor Roosevelt to the Indian Arts and Crafts Exhibit at the Golden Gate International Exhibition in San Francisco in 1939. I saw her wear it on rare occasions on the reservation when she deemed it desirable to appear in formal Indian dress.

Mrs. Spanish's dress became a prized family heirloom. It was worn by her granddaughter, Delores Racine, as a representative of the Blackfeet tribe, when she won the title of Miss Indian America 1959 at Sheridan, Wyoming. Fig. 28 portrays her wearing this dress and standing by Winold Reiss's portrait of her great-grandmother, Julia Wades-in-the-Water, in that lady's Sioux dress. Notice, however, that the handbags carried by both women are much alike and are definitely of Blackfeet design. The women did not mind mixing dresses of one tribal style with accessories of another.

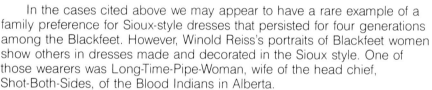

Fig. 27 Wades-in-the-Water wore an Assiniboine
shirt and his wife, Julia, wore a Sioux
dress for these Winold Reiss portraits,
later reproduced on playing cards.
*Great Northern Railway Company
Records, Minnesota Historical Society*

Fig. 28 Delores Racine in front of her
great-grandmother's portrait.
*Photograph courtesy of the Montana
Highway Commission*

In the cases cited above we may appear to have a rare example of a family preference for Sioux-style dresses that persisted for four generations among the Blackfeet. However, Winold Reiss's portraits of Blackfeet women show others in dresses made and decorated in the Sioux style. One of those wearers was Long-Time-Pipe-Woman, wife of the head chief, Shot-Both-Sides, of the Blood Indians in Alberta.

When dressed in their traditional Indian costumes, Julia and her husband, Wades-in-the-Water, made one of the handsomest Blackfeet couples. During the 1930s and 1940s, Wades-in-the-Water also preferred to wear clothing of non-Blackfeet origin. When he posed for his portrait by Winold Reiss in 1943, he wore a Sioux-type feather bonnet and a finely worked porcupine-quill buckskin shirt of Assiniboine make (Fig. 27). My wife and I recall that Wades-in-the-Water wore that shirt when a group of elderly Blackfeet gave us Indian names in a ceremony in the lobby of the Museum of the Plains Indian on September 21, 1941.

Perhaps it was the sight of such picturesque, tastefully, and colorfully clad Indians as the Wades-in-the-Waters that inspired Louis W. Hill to adopt the Blackfeet Indians as symbols for attracting tourists to travel over his Great Northern Railway to his hotels in glorious Glacier National Park. Repeatedly during the 1910s and 1920s, he sent delegations of Blackfeet men, clad in feather bonnets and colorfully decorated buckskins, along with their well-dressed wives, to visit major cities in both East and West and to encourage white Americans to visit Glacier National Park — the romantic homeland of these attractive people.

Soon after Hill built the impressive hotel at East Glacier near the railway station, he employed a group of these same Indians to greet tourists as their trains arrived and to entertain them in the evenings in the awesome, spacious hotel lobby, which was flanked by tall columns of huge tree trunks.

Fig. 29 Dolls representing Two Guns White
Calf and his wife, *Cat. 188.*

There, these Indians recited Indian legends, demonstrated the Indian sign
language, performed Indian dances, and invited tourists to join in their
dances.

One of the last items to be added to the Louis W. Hill Collection
probably was a pair of Indian dolls purchased by Hill's son, Louis W. Hill,
Jr., in the craft shop of the newly opened Museum of the Plains Indian
during the summer of 1941. These dolls were made by one of the most able
and versatile craftswomen among the tribes of the Northern Plains, Juanita
Tucker, an Assiniboine of Fort Belknap Reservation (Fig. 29). Her dolls,
however, were intended to represent a very prominent Blackfeet couple
dressed in their best Blackfeet-style clothing. The male doll is Two Guns
White Calf, a son of the tribal head chief, White Calf (Fig. 25). Possessed of
a striking, classic Indian profile, Two Guns White Calf has been a very
popular subject for Winold Reiss and other portraitists as well as for
photographers. He had been the center of attraction in many of the Indian
delegations dispatched by the elder Louis W. Hill to lure tourists to Glacier
National Park. He was one of 40 Blackfeet sent to Baltimore in 1927 to take
a prominent part in the Pageant of the Iron Horse commemorating the
centennial of the railroad in the United States. Juanita Tucker may never
have seen the Two Guns White Calfs. The dolls probably were made from
photographs several years after the Two Guns' deaths. But they represented
two of the elder Hill's best-known Indian friends and so provided a very
appropriate capstone to the Louis W. Hill Collection.

Fig. 30 Wades-in-the-Water, right, wearing his dream shirt. *Photograph courtesy of the Museum of the Plains Indian*

It is doubtful that any other twentieth-century collector of Indian artifacts had a more extended, more mutually helpful relationship with the Blackfeet than did Louis W. Hill. His influence upon Blackfeet arts during the 1910s and 1920s may have been greater than we can determine with any degree of certainty today. At a time when the traditional arts of the Blackfeet were in the doldrums, Hill provided encouragement and opportunities to a variety of artists and craftworkers. He employed Indian veterans of the intertribal wars to record their most important war honors in picture writings to decorate the walls of his hotels in Glacier National Park. The demand for fine examples of traditional clothing and accessories, for use by the many Indians who were sent to attract tourists to Glacier National Park and who entertained the tourists on arrival, must have encouraged the production of these articles. In addition, some Indian-made objects were sold in the shops of the hotels. On at least one occasion — during an exhibition of W. Langdon Kihn's portraits of Blackfeet and other Indians at the Anderson Gallery in New York in 1922 — Hill provided examples of Blackfeet arts and crafts to the gallery shop for sale directly to sophisticated New Yorkers.

As we look back upon the period of Louis W. Hill's close association with the Blackfeet Indians, we must now be aware that at the same time he was stimulating Indian artistic production he was seeking to preserve fine examples of traditional arts and crafts known to the Blackfeet through his extensive activity as a collector. Thus he played a dual role in his relations with Indian craftworkers during the two decades preceding the establishment of tribal and federal sponsorship of the arts on Indian reservations, under the Indian New Deal of the 1930s. It seems very appropriate to me that a major portion of the Hill Collection should be preserved in the Museum of the Plains Indian on the Blackfeet Reservation, where it can be seen, studied, and appreciated by the descendants of the Indians who created and/or used these cultural objects three or more generations ago.

After the Buffalo Were Gone

Royal B. Hassrick

Fig. 31 *Buffalo Chase, A Surround by the*
Hidatsa (1832–1833) by George
Catlin. *Photograph courtesy of the*
National Museum of American Art
(formerly National Collection of Fine
Arts), Smithsonian Institution; gift of
Mrs. Joseph Harrison, Jr.

In 1800 the Northern Great Plains were the homeland of both roving bands of buffalo hunters and sedentary agriculturalists. Warrior societies like the Blackfeet, Cheyenne, and Sioux moved their tipi camps to follow the vast herds of buffalo, for their life way was completely dependent on these great animals (Fig. 31). The farming people, such as the Mandan and Hidatsa, raising crops of corn, beans, and squash, lived in huge stockaded earth-lodge villages. Even for them, the buffalo was an important source of food and raw material. In a word, they were all buffalo people and their world view revolved around this great animal's presence.

The artistic expression of the Plains Indians was at once bold and dramatic. It was evident in everything they produced. From their painted buffalo robes to their porcupine-quill-embroidered moccasins, the dramatic flair of these people was apparent. Moreover, it was both functional and ornamental. A simple horn spoon became a graceful, decorative object with the carving of an animal's head on the handle. A rather mundane shirt became a striking costume with the application of colorful quilled bands covering the shoulder and arm seams. The simple garment was transformed into dazzling attire by adding quilled medallions, paint, and trimmings of hair locks or ermine tails. These people seemed to possess an inherent sense of good taste, an unfailing ability to combine color, form, and balance creating a work of art in nearly all things. Their stone-carved pipe bowls with long slender stems decorated with braided quills and dyed horsehair were as striking as their painted tipis. Only their tub-shaped bullboats could be said to have been ugly.

European trade goods were introduced early, at first indirectly from the French through intermediary tribes such as the Cree and Mandan, and later from fur trading posts established in Indian territory. Firearms, brass and copper kettles, knives, tomahawks, and trade cloth were highly desirable utilitarian items, but so too were such non-essentials as glass beads, colored pigments, bells, mirrors, and ribbons. Even brass upholstery tacks were bartered for furs. It was with these latter items that the Indians embellished their clothing, utensils, and weapons. Originally the color range of pigments available to these people was principally red, white, and black. When traders brought blues, greens, and yellows, the wider color spectrum was at once applied by the artisans. Beads found ready acceptance among the quillers and gradually replaced the porcupine quill as the principal form of decoration. As early as 1800 large "pony" beads were introduced primarily in white, black, blue, and red. Later, around 1850, the small "seed" beads found popularity with many more colors available. The Indian craftworkers were adept at incorporating new media to the existing native forms in a most pleasing and effective way.

The art forms of the Plains Indians, aesthetic expressions of their culture, were an integral part of the entire way of life. Never were they conceived as "art for art's sake." Rather, they were found in the decoration of skin clothing, the embellishment of war clubs; more significantly they were the actual form of the entire object whether it be a ceremonial pipe or feather bonnet.

The close of the nineteenth century was a period of catastrophic cultural upheaval for the Indians of the Great Plains. Where once there had been countless herds of buffalo upon which these people's very livelihood depended, now only a handful of the animals remained. Systematically decimated by professional hunters as food for mining towns and railroad gangs and as robes for the eastern markets, the buffalo by 1880 were nigh to extinction. The last Blackfeet hunt was held in 1883, and the Sioux had held their last hunt the year before. And so it was that with the passing of the buffalo the Indians' way of life came to an end. (Ewers 1938:92; 1958:290).

At the same time that the buffalo disappeared, the Indians were faced with an equally disastrous threat — the onslaught of advancing white immigration. During the first half of the century most relations with the white man had been marked by wary trade; major military conflicts occurred only after the 1850s. After this time the surge of immigrants and miners, accompanied by U.S. troops, aroused the Indians to the effects of encroachment. This was particularly true for the Sioux, Cheyenne, and Arapahoe, who fought valiantly to protect their domains and halt the flood of white men. Tribes to the north, such as the Crow, Blackfeet, Assiniboine, and Gros Ventre were out of the mainstream of western migration and were spared the cost of heavy bloodshed. Nonetheless, with the power of Manifest Destiny, which the United States government enforced, and with a depleted food supply, the Indians were confined to reservations and put on rations. Now, by the 1870s, if the people were not militarily subjugated, they were surely culturally defeated.

For nomadic hunters accustomed to moving their tipi villages at will in search of buffalo, reservation life was both confining and boring. For men whose wealth and status depended upon capturing enemy horses and accomplishing heroic exploits in battle, reservation life was hollow and empty. For these Indians, the buffalo not only had been the primary source of food, but also the principal raw material for dwellings, robes, and for many utensils, containers, and accoutrements of war. Nearly every part of the animal was utilized: sinews for threads, horns for spoons, hair for robes. In addition to the worldly aspects of the buffalo's place in the daily life of the Plains Indian, the animal played a most important role in the religious and ceremonial world. Among the many gods, the buffalo was among the most significant. Men, attired in horned buffalo masks, danced in emulation to secure his favor so the herds might be plentiful. Girls coming of age were honored with special rites in deference to the buffalo and were referred to as Buffalo Maidens. The sacred pipe of the Sioux nation was given them by the White Buffalo Woman. Priests made offerings and supplications to the Buffalo God to lure the herds to their villages. The Plains people were quick to recognize their dependence on this animal and acknowledged it wholeheartedly with prayers and acts of gratitude. For, indeed, these were people of the buffalo. When it was gone, so was their lifestyle.

War for the Plains Indian was the means to wealth and status. The horse, introduced to the Northern Plains in the mid-eighteenth century, markedly increased the Indians' mobility, making the hunters much more effective and the warriors much more audacious. As one patriarch explained it, "The men with the fastest horses lived in the largest tipis." Moreover, the foot soldier now became a cavalryman. So important was the horse that it immediately became a medium of exchange and a measure of wealth. Men constantly went on forays to capture horses from enemy camps, thereby increasing personal prestige and wealth.

In addition to horse-stealing parties, men took to the warpath to avenge the death of a relative or society brother and to collect "coups" or points achieved for striking an enemy. Men boasted of their war records by publicly recounting their acts of prowess. Warriors with the greatest number of valorous deeds were most highly esteemed. For the Plains Indian, warfare was the *raison d'etre*. The ways of the warpath ended with the establishment of reservations, and with it the Indian men lost the means for wealth and status. Moreover, no longer able to hunt, the men were deprived of their occupation. Life on a reservation was a life of studied idleness and ennui. Its meaning had vanished like the buffalo.

The federal government's Bureau of Indian Affairs, charged by the U.S. Congress to oversee the lives of Indians, issued beef that the people might not starve. Herds were driven to the reservations where they were corralled and then shot by the men. Sometimes the cattle were turned loose so that

Fig. 32 Tipi by cabin. *Photograph by John Anderson, courtesy of Jack R. Williams*

Fig. 33 *Red Thing That Touches in Marching, Daughter of Black Rock,* (1832) by George Catlin. *Photograph courtesy of the National Museum of American Art (formerly National Collection of Fine Arts), Smithsonian Institution; gift of Mrs. Joseph Harrison, Jr.*

the mounted horsemen might chase them in a mock hunt, bringing back memories of the days gone by. After butchering, the women prepared the meat much as they had always done, drying most of it for future use, boiling some for more immediate consumption. But the beef was too sweet and not to their liking. However, there was no choice.

In addition to beef, the government provided bacon, flour, sugar, and coffee, rationed out on a monthly basis. Each family was given a ticket that indicated the number of people entitled to receive groceries. While cow hides were now tanned for making clothing and robes, trade cloth and European garments were distributed, and Indian costumes, except for dress-up occasions, were lost forever. Canvas was introduced, replacing buffalo hide to tipi covers, and by 1900 the one-room log cabin had all but displaced the tipi (Fig. 32). It was mostly the old folks, unhappy with the confinement of a house, who pitched a tipi next to a cabin in which the children lived.

The Bureau of Indian Affairs, in its omniscience, parcelled the reservations into individual allotments and encouraged the men to farm in order that they might be self-sufficient. But that, at best, met with desultory success. Farming to the Plains Indian was woman's work, a task beneath the dignity of warriors. As an alternative, the bureau, as trustee, leased the allotments to white farmers and ranchers, collecting the monies and doling them out to the allottees. And so the men sat around reminiscing as they smoked their pipes — there wasn't much else to do.

The women's lot was considerably better. They carried on with their daily chores of preparing meals, minding children, and making clothes. In their spare time they continued with their handicrafts. Because these people generally found shoes to be especially uncomfortable, women were continually busy making moccasins. But they found time for other things, too. They still made painted rawhide parfleches, quilled and beaded "possible bags" (meaning it's possible to put anything in them), fancy clothes, and highly ornamented baby carriers. Among the Sioux, these carriers were a token of respect and one Sioux mother received 20 at the birth of her daughter, who was subsequently named They Love Her (Hassrick 1964:272).

The passing of the buffalo, the absence of war, and the confinement on a reservation would appear to have been ample reason for a decline in the artistic accomplishments of the Plains Indians. And yet the opposite effect seems to have taken place. Instead of a diminution in production, an actual flowering seems to have ensued. There appears to have occurred a significant increase both in the quantity of objects and in the complexity of embellishment. And the cause of this may have been twofold. The artisans had more time. Relieved of the constant moving that nomadism demanded and given the time that otherwise had been spent in hunting and warfare, the people were free to devote their energies to producing their arts and crafts. Moreover, they were now in close proximity to the traders and could more easily acquire and store larger quantities of the white man's products.

An example of this blossoming occurred among the Sioux. The embellishment of women's dresses at the time when George Catlin painted his Sioux portraits in 1833 (Fig. 33) was confined to narrow bands of what appear to be pony beads across the throat and along the sleeve seams, augmented by brass buttons (Ewers 1958:102). In a photograph of Spotted Tail's wife attributed to W. H. Jackson in the 1870s, the entire yoke of her dress is covered solidly with seed beads (Fig. 34). So taken were the Sioux women by the beauty of broad expanses of beadwork that they lavished their young girls in dresses beaded from neck to hemline, their boys in full beaded jackets and trousers. While the Sioux were the most extreme in the profuse use of beads to decorate their dresses, the Blackfeet and other

Fig. 34 Spotted Tail's wife. *Photograph by W. H. Jackson, courtesy of Royal B. Hassrick*

Fig. 35 Women scraping hides. *Photograph courtesy of the W. H. Over Museum, University of South Dakota*

tribes were no less flamboyant. The Crow women, for example, favored elk teeth, sometimes covering an entire dress with them. When genuine teeth became scarce, men carved imitations from bone.

The idea of covering certain objects completely with beads was popular among all the tribes. The possible bags, always made in pairs, became objects to display a woman's handiwork. Originally utilitarian with little or no embellishment, they now were fully beaded in colorful, geometric patterns. This was also universally true of men's vests. The Cheyenne, Arapahoe, and Sioux were particularly partial to fully beaded cradles; the Crow, to a lesser degree. The Blackfeet women say they preferred to carry their infants over their shoulders supported by a robe or blanket, probably because cradles were such a rare luxury (Ewers 1958:102).

With respect to the quantity of items made, the Sioux gift of 20 baby carriers to They Love Her is an example of overproduction. Only with a sedentary life could a recipient possibly store this many articles, and certainly the family could not be burdened with transporting them under nomadic conditions. But the reservation life provided time and space for these luxuries, and the environment was ideal for nurturing the arts.

The arduousness and dexterity required for the making of articles attest to the diligence of these Plains Indians: "Preparing a buffalo hide was a strenuous and tedious task that demanded strength, skill and patience. The first step was the removal of the flesh and gristle by staking the hide out and scraping away the tissue with a chisel-like implement fashioned from a bone and tipped with a blade. Stooping over the skin, the woman pulled the blade toward her, removing the particles. The hide was then allowed to dry in the sun, perhaps for several days, before being scraped to an even thickness with the short hoe-like tool. The hide was then turned over to remove the hair, a process usually carried out with a scraper. At this point the rawhide was stiff and hard. After soaking in water for about two days, the hide became soft and pliable and was ready for final curing. Mixtures of brains, liver, fats and sometimes red grass were rubbed thoroughly into the skin, and then allowed to dry. Next the skin was stretched and finally worked back and forth over a twisted rawhide thong to completely break down the tissue. Though minor variations in techniques might be employed, tanning was a tedious process that might take one woman as much as ten days [Fig. 35].

"Quilling was probably the highest attainment in the female arts. Unlike tanning, which required much brawn, quilling demanded delicate dexterity. The Sioux woman graded her quills into four sizes and stored them in bladder pouches according to size and color. By boiling roots or berries, she obtained various colors and hues. Blue Whirlwind derived red from the snakeberry root, yellow from huckleberry root, and a purplish black from the fox grape. Green dye was acquired from an unknown root, it is said, and later she got blue from a clay obtained through trade. She soaked the white quills briefly in water before immersing them in the dye. She allowed them to remain in the dye only a short time lest the core of the quill be worked out. When the color was satisfactory, she placed the quill on a piece of bark to dry in the sun.

"In quilling, the Sioux woman first softened about six quills in her mouth, with the points extending just beyond the corner of her lips. In decorating moccasins, the woman marked two guidelines on the hair side of the skin with the point of her awl. At the heel she punched two holes parallel to the surface of the skin and the guidelines. Through these holes she ran pointed sinew threads, tying a knot in the end of each to hold them fast. All sinew sewing was done through the surface of the hide so that no stitching was visible from the underside. Next she would tie a long strand of sinew to a little stick and secure the stick by stepping on it or by placing it in

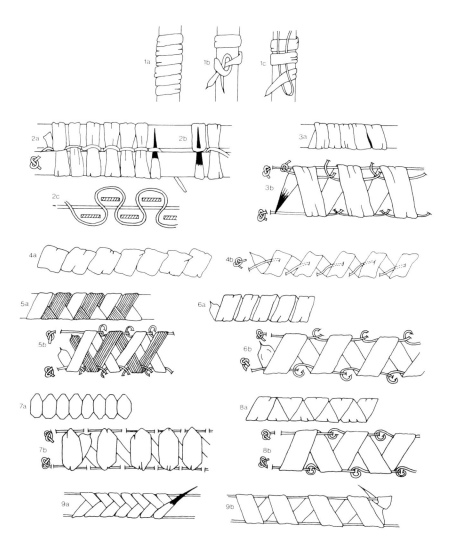

Fig. 36 Quilling techniques. *Drawing by Anne Hassrick Morales*
1. *Quilling fringe, (a) complete, (b) tying the quill, (c) sinew loop tie*
2. *Tipi "front quill," (a) complete, (b) method of starting, (c) side view*
3. *Quilling with tied sinew, (a) complete, (b) method*
4. *One-awl quilling, (a) complete (b) method*
5. *Two-quill quilling, (a) complete, (b) method*
6. *Quilling without tied sinew, (a) complete, (b) method*
7. *Stitching quilling, (a) complete, (b) method*
8. *Zigzag quilling, (a) complete, (b) method*
9. *Pipestem quilling, (a) complete, (b) method*

her moccasin. She tied the loose end of the sinew to the upper thread already stitched at the point of the knot. The thread of sinew, stretched to her foot, acted as a guide.

"After the quill was split, and the butt flattened over the side of the overgrown nails of her thumb and forefinger, it was laid under the lower sinew at the starting point and turned over tightly. Then a stitch was taken with the sinew exactly the width of the flattened quill and secured by a half hitch or loop stitch. The quill was then turned under the lower thread and a similar stitch was taken, and so on, with new quills spliced in until the desired length was reached. The quills might be used alternately from upper and lower threads. When opposing colors were used, a pleasing plaited effect was had. This stitch, the most widely used, was called 'quilling with tied sinew,' but the same effect could be had by the use of parallel rows of stitches with the tied sinew.

"At least nine different quilling techniques were employed, all having special names and many reserved for specific tasks [Fig. 36]. Thus, the quilling of the rawhide fringe of a pipe bag involved a wrapping technique; the embellishing of a pipe stem required plaiting. Fine lines for use in narrow designs, called 'one-awl quilling,' were produced with only one thread around which the quills were twisted" (Hassrick 1964:182, 191).

Fig. 37 Woman painting parfleches on stretched hide. *Photograph by John Anderson, courtesy of Jack R. Williams*

While the use of porcupine embroidery was never completely abandoned as a decorative feature, beads were increasingly employed as the principal decoration. In addition to the increased use of beads, designs themselves became more complex. Again, among the Sioux, bold simple rectangles, triangles, and bars now in the 1870s became complicated geometric designs employing interlocking figures. Fine lines of beading, extended from an element or used to connect elements, were increasingly popular. One authority suggests that this new, more complex and delicate design may have been due to the influence of Oriental rugs brought to the areas either by traders or settlers. It is true that some of the designs were strikingly similar in form to the Daghestan rugs from the Caucasus. It is doubtful, however, at this late date that the theory can ever be proved (Douglas 1953:n.p.).

While the painting of robes, tipi liners, and parfleches was an important art form in prereservation days, after the 1870s it was relegated primarily to parfleches. For this, colored earth, ground in tiny stone mortars, was stored in deerskin pouches. Red paint was made by heating a yellow rocklike substance, while black was obtained from a very dark earth or charcoal. While some women mixed their paints with a watery glue made from boiled hide scrapings, others apparently used only water. Roan Horse Woman's palette, for example, consisted of reds, ochres, yellows, dark browns, and black. Blue was a relatively modern color, and green, too, was only recently introduced. Using a creasing stick on the stretched and dampened hide, the woman stood over the hide and marked first the outline of the border. With tiny brushes made from the sharpened end of the porous rib of a buffalo, she dipped into her tortoise shell paint cups the color she desired to use on the border. When the border was completely filled in, she began to work on the central portion, creasing the outlines first and then coloring. In fresco-like technique, she kept the hide damp while painting. Sizing the painting with the cut end of a cactus leaf or glue helped to preserve it (Fig. 37).

It would seem only natural that with the strictures imposed by reservation life there would have been a loss of many traditional art forms. And indeed there was. Painted buffalo robes gave way to blankets. Red and

Fig. 38 Group of Sioux wearing chief's blankets. *Photograph by John Anderson, courtesy of Jack R. Williams*

Fig. 39 Sitting Bull wearing a Cree bandolier. *Photograph by D. F. Barry, courtesy of The National Archives*

blue stroud blankets, and, surprisingly, Navaho so-called Chief's Blankets, found much favor (Fig. 38). Bows and arrows and buffalo hide shields were no longer necessary. And yet the persistence of native art forms continued. The long, quilled strips with interspersed medallions formerly covering the seams of buffalo robes resulting from skinning the animal down the back now became colorful beaded blanket strips. Shields were made not for protection in battle, but rather for display at dances and celebrations. Among the Sioux, for example, feather bonnets were originally a protective device warn in battle to guard the wearer from harm. Now they were made to be part of the costume for festivities and parades. Among some tribes, eagle feather bonnets were a chieftain's badge of office. As a symbol of authority, they were now awarded to visiting dignitaries, often in conjunction with tribal adoption. In any case, they became an integral part of Indian costume and were worn by nearly everyone on festive occasions (Fig. 21).

While some forms of art underwent a change in function, others remained intact. This was true for many basically utilitarian articles such as painted parfleches, storage bags, baby carriers, horse trappings, and clothing. When ornamented, they exhibited the artistic expression of the maker and became, in essence, an art form in and of themselves. While most of these forms remained basically unchanged, many did undergo decorative elaboration. Others, particularly musical instruments, were more or less unaltered. Flutes underwent little or no change. Drums, however, were now made from the hoops of round flour-box lids rather than fashioned from bent wood.

The elaboration of utilitarian articles during the reservation period is no more evident than in horse trappings, particularly among the Blackfeet and Crow. The Crow women especially bedecked their horses with elegantly beaded bridles, martingales, and cruppers. More ornate yet were their saddles with the high pommels and cantles ornamented with great flannel-covered pendants bordered with shining beads. Few Plains Indian figures were more striking than a Crow woman in her red stroud dress, decorated with gleaming white elk teeth, mounted on her magnificently caparisoned horse parading around a ceremonial camp.

Despite the government's suppression of Indian religious life, particularly the Sun Dance, the Indians continued to hold dances and give feasts and gifts. These were occasions when people donned their finest attire. Now was the time to bring out one's best regalia. Some of these were cherished heirlooms. The practice of burying the deceased with all their possessions and dressed in their most handsome clothing so that they might enter the land of their ancestors looking their best, gradually waned. As this custom assumed less significance, heirlooms became not only accoutrements to one's costume as part of the showy display, but something to respectfully keep.

Summer was an auspicious time for Indians to gather. Not only did tribal members participate in the feasting, gift-giving, and dancing, but visitors from neighboring tribes, often former enemies, were welcomed to the so-called powwow. It was proper during these gala occasions that gifts should be exchanged, and as a result a kind of trade ensued. A Blackfeet might be given a tobacco bag by a Sioux, and in turn honor his guest with a pair of Blackfeet moccasins. It is to be expected that this intertribal exchange had an important influence on traditional tribal art forms so that designs and techniques were diffused from one tribe to another (Wissler 1927; Hassrick 1940). Intertribal trade was lively during the buffalo days and the practice carried on. Fig. 39 depicts Sioux warrior Sitting Bull wearing a Cree Bandolier, while Fig. 27 shows Blackfeet Wades-in-the-Water in an Assiniboine shirt and his wife, Julia, in a Sioux-style dress.

In addition to trade as an influencing factor for diffusion, there was also booty. Enemies who were killed were stripped, whenever possible, of their

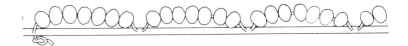

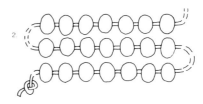

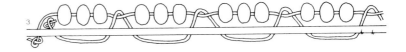

Fig. 40 Beading techniques.
Drawing by Anne Hassrick Morales

1. *Lazy stitch, side view*
2. *Lazy stitch, view from above*
3. *Overlay or spot stitch, side view*

clothing. The captors not only sported the garments around the village but undoubtedly studied the techniques of construction and design.

Counteracting this exchange of ideas, however, was the native artisan's notion that designs were property. Among several of the tribes, a craftworker or a family owned designs that others might not use, or might use only after purchasing. This concept, combined with a kind of nationalistic pride and possessiveness in what was stylishly correct, made for distinctive tribal art forms, many of which were identifiable.

Techniques as well as art forms varied from tribe to tribe, a fact that makes identification simpler, but by no means conclusive. The same methods of beading, for example, were practiced by several tribes, and when design forms were similar identification became more difficult.

Two distinct methods of beading were employed by the women; one was the so-called lazy stitch, the other, overlay or spot stitch (Fig. 40). To produce the lazy stitch, the craftswoman punched two small holes with an awl in the surface of the skin and then, tying a knot at the end of a strand of sinew, threaded it through the holes. Next she added a predetermined number of beads, usually from five to nine, to the thread, and punching two more holes in the skin, secured the sinew. Now she added the same number of beads and, placing them next to the first row, secured them in a similar fashion. Continuing, she produced a band of beads for whatever distance her design called for. The technique and finished effect resembled the earlier quillwork consisting of row upon row of decoration. In overlay beading, a large number of beads, enough to cover the entire distance of

Fig. 41 Design element. *Drawing by Anne Hassrick Morales*

a. *Crow styles*
b. *Blackfeet style*
c. *Sioux style, late*
d. *Sioux style, late*

the intended design, are strung upon the thread and spot-stitched with another thread to secure, in some instances, every other bead. Whereas the lazy stitch produced a series of ridges, the overlay stitch resulted in a smooth surface.

Three basic Plains styles have been segregated and named for the tribes who employed them: Crow, Blackfeet, and Sioux. A fourth, or Woodland type, was also popular among certain groups. While none of the styles was mutually exclusive, small tribal variations often existed.

The use of massive triangles, diamonds, and hourglasses, often bordering a background of red flannel, was popular among the Crow and to a degree the Shoshone, and possibly the Ute (Fig. 41a). The figures frequently contained small rectangles or triangles. Pale blue and lavender were favorite colors, though yellow, green, and dark blue were also used. The Crow preferred the overlay stitch.

The Blackfeet style is identifiable by the preference for large triangles, hourglasses, and diamonds, usually against a background of white (Fig. 41b). In many instances, the figures are composed of a myriad of tiny squares producing a stepped effect. Again, the overlay stitch was employed. In addition to the Blackfeet, the Sarsi, Flathead, and Plains Cree also favored both this style and technique.

Smaller designs were used by the Sioux employing triangles, hourglasses, diamonds, and rectangles, but they later added thin straight lines and forked, terraced, and crossed elements spread out against a solid background (Fig. 41c and d). Bars and stripes were also used. White and pale blue were favorite background colors, although other colors, especially red, were not uncommon. Among the Sioux, the lazy stitch was used exclusively. The Cheyenne, Arapahoe, Gros Ventres, Assiniboine, and Ute, and to some extent the Crow, each employed this style.

The Woodland type is characterized by the use of floral patterns applied with an overlay stitch on a background of either cloth or solid beading. This form was used by the Cree, Assiniboine, Crow, Nez Perce, Flathead, and to a degree the Blackfeet (Douglas 1936:91).

While the differences among the four types are distinctive enough to make the tribal identification of objects at first glance simple, the similarities among designs and techniques used by craftsmen of the different tribes employing the same style makes identification most difficult. For example, in differentiating Sioux work from that of the Cheyenne and Arapahoe, the Sioux appear to have preferred bolder elements, and their craftsmanship is, in general, less meticulous. The work of the Cheyenne, and particularly the Arapahoe, on the other hand, appears to be more delicate and the craftsmanship more meticulous. The Cheyenne seem to have favored the use of narrow bars as a design element together with dark green beads. None of these diagnostic traits are positive proofs of identity, but they do serve as hints. A tribe's partiality to a particular color may or may not have been due to an innate preference, but rather to what color beads the trader in the area had available. The Crow use of pink may have been determined by what was obtainable, whereas the Sioux rarely employed pink, perhaps because they couldn't get it.

Plains Indians materials have been collected from as early as Lewis's and Clark's first contact in 1804. George Catlin in 1833 and Maximilian a year later each gathered specimens. In the years following, material was gathered sporadically, especially by men attached to the military posts. However, not until the last decade of the nineteenth century, when the great eastern museums and collectors began combing the Plains, were large quantities of material accumulated. By the 1920s the Plains had been stripped of most of its ethnographic items, the bulk of them deposited in repositories principally in Washington and New York, and to a lesser degree in other major cities throughout the country (Feder 1965:n.p.).

Some of the people collecting this material were careful to label it, giving the date, location, and, in some rare instances, the name of the owner or maker. For a great number of pieces, however, little or no information exists, and identification becomes an educated guess. Even the conscientious collector who labeled his material was subject to making a mistaken identification. For example, items picked up on a Sioux reservation might well have included a gift from a Cheyenne or Gros Ventres and thereby mistakenly be classified as Sioux. Many museum curators and writers on the subject of Indian art seem obsessed with the need for assigning a definitive label on every object and feel compelled to give a precise date of manufacture and tribal origin. This is proper for the taxonomic character of ethnological collecting. However, the truth would be better served by suggesting a probable tribal designation or a generalized culture area term such as "Northern Plains" and by using "circa" for an approximate date.

The impression of the Plains Indians in their heyday of the 1850s, all clothed in colorful apparel astride horses bedecked in striking trappings and living in brightly painted tipis amidst dazzling baby carriers, storage bags, and such, is a somewhat erroneous picture. It is true that in the days of the buffalo, the Indians did possess handsome and colorful things, but in general, these were the property of the well-to-do and with respect to clothing were worn only on special occasions. For the average person, drab, workaday dress was standard; ordinary, unadorned dwellings were the rule. In truth, the Indian people and their villages were for the most part rather prosaic — the harshness of a nomadic, hunting existence demanded a down-to-earth approach. Photographs as early as the 1860s showing Indian villages attest to this.

The picture of Indian life is further skewed by what collectors collected. It was only natural that they should try to acquire the choice, most handsome articles as examples of native workmanship, dismissing the mundane and practical objects as uninteresting. Consequently, the vast majority of materials exhibited in museums and illustrated in books display the finest, most showy pieces of Indian arts and crafts. What practical and utilitarian items they do show are usually relegated to informative exhibits and illustrations devoted to explaining such matters as processes and techniques.

Furthermore, the amount of material collected before 1850 is relatively small. Only George Catlin's collection, made in the 1830s, was sizable. In addition, at that time very few were collecting, and there were not more than a handful of museums in which to house material. Finally, in the course of time, many objects were lost or destroyed by fire and insects so that not only is early material rare, but in its scarcity it does not impart the impression that reservation art exhibits by its sheer numbers. (Feder 1965:n.p.).

An additional incentive for the production of articles during the reservation period was the collector himself. It was not unusual for him to commission a piece. This was especially true after the turn of the century. With the opening of the national parks, tourists created still more demand. Men made bows and arrows, war clubs, pipes, and bonnets; women made tobacco bags and particularly moccasins for sale, not only directly to collectors and tourists, but also through trading posts and curio stores. While the demand for Northern Plains articles by no means ever matched the fad for collecting California baskets or southwestern pottery, basketry, rugs, and silver in the early 1900s, collectors did search the country and tourists bought souvenirs. Unlike the Fred Harvey concessionaire shops of the Santa Fe Railroad, which actively promoted the sale of Indian crafts, the Great Northern Railway was less aggressive. Nor did much of the Northern Plains material have the aesthetic appeal as art for art's sake that the southwestern and California objects possessed. These were romantic *objets d'art* that could be placed around the house as decorative conversation pieces. On the contrary, a war bonnet or club, or even a handsome beaded dress, was hardly considered a work of art. It was not much before the 1940s that the term "native art" was coined and museums displayed ethnographic specimens from an aesthetic viewpoint.

As the years passed, craftwork among the Plains Indians diminished. It was not until the mid-1930s, with the creation of the Indians Arts and Crafts Board, that a revival occurred. Combining the hope for preserving the native tradition with the real Indian need for extra income, the board encouraged the craftworkers to form cooperatives. To insure their success, the board recruited craft specialists who not only taught forgotten techniques but also encouraged the adaptation of old forms to contemporary usage. Moreover, the specialists assisted in the coordination of production and gave supervision in modern methods of marketing. As examples, the techniques for making parfleches were adapted to the production of painted rawhide wastebaskets. Possible bags were modified to become women's handbags. On the other hand, moccasins, much in demand by tourists, remained unchanged in form. Quite recently Northern Plains craftworkers have found a market in producing replicas of museum pieces, from painted buffalo robes to tobacco bags, to meet a resurgence of collectors unable to acquire old specimens. All this speaks very well for the persistence of the native craft tradition, which has been sustained for a century after the buffalo were gone.

References Cited

American Indian Art Magazine
1979   4(3): Cover Illustration.

Annual Report of the Commission of Indian Affairs
1854   Washington, D.C.

CATLIN, GEORGE
1841   *Letters and Notes on the Manners, Customs and Conditions of the North American Indians.* 2 vols. New York.
1913   *North American Indians.* 2 vols., later edition of Catlin 1841. Philadelphia: Leary, Stuart and Company.

CONNER, STUART, AND BETTY LU CONNER
1971   *Rock Art of the Montana High Plains,* Santa Barbara: The Art Galleries, University of California.

DENIG, EDWIN T.
1961   *Five Indian Tribes of the Upper Missouri: Sioux, Arikaras, Assiniboines, Crees and Crows.* John C. Ewers, ed. Norman: University of Oklahoma Press.

DOUGLAS, FREDERIC
1935   *Basketry Decoration Techniques.* (Indian Leaflet No. 68.) Denver: Denver Art Museum.
1936   *Plains Beads and Beadwork Designs.* (Indian Leaflet No. 73–74.) Denver: Denver Art Museum.
1953   *Beadwork History and Technics.* (Indian Leaflet No. 117.) Denver: Denver Art Museum.

DRESDEN, DONALD
1970   *The Marquis de Morès: Emperor of the Badlands.* Norman: University of Oklahoma Press.

DRURY, CLIFFORD M.
1958   *The Diaries and Letters of Henry M. Spalding and Asa Brown Smith Relating to the Nez Perce Mission, 1838–1842.* Glendale, California: Clarke.

Dupont Magazine
1931   March 31, p. 5.

EWERS, JOHN C.
1938   *Teton Dakota Ethnology and History.* Berkeley, California: National Park Service, Department of the Interior.
1939   *Plains Indian Painting.* Palo Alto, California: Stanford University Press.
1945   *Blackfeet Crafts.* (Indian Handcraft Series No. 9.) Lawrence, Kansas: U.S. Indian Service.
1955   "The Horse in Blackfoot Indian Culture with Comparative Material from Other Western Tribes," in Bureau of American Ethnology *Bulletin 159.* Washington, D.C.: Smithsonian Institution.
1957   "Hair Pipes in Plains Indian Adornment: A Study in Indian and White Ingenuity," in Bureau of American Ethnology *Bulletin 164,* Anthropological Papers No. 50, pp. 29–85. Washington, D.C.: Smithsonian Institution.
1958   *The Blackfeet: Raiders on the Northwestern Plains.* (Civilization of American Indian Series, No. 49.) Norman: University of Oklahoma Press.
1963   "Blackfoot Indian Pipes and Pipemaking," in Bureau of American Ethnology *Bulletin 186,* pp. 29–60. Washington, D.C.: Smithsonian Institution.
1965   *Artists of the Old West.* Garden City, New York: Doubleday.
1968   "Early White Influence upon Plains Indian Painting," in Ewers, *Indian Life on the Upper Missouri.* Norman: University of Oklahoma Press.
1983   "A Century and a Half of Blackfeet Picture-Writing," in *American Indian Art Magazine,* 8(3):52–61.

FEDER, NORMAN
1965   "American Indian Art before 1850," in *Denver Art Museum Quarterly* (Summer).

GALANTE, GARY
1980   "Crow Lance Cases or Sword Scabbards," in *American Indian Art Magazine,* 6(1):64–73.

Glacier National Park General Information for Seasons 1914, 1915, 1916
1914–16 Washington, D.C.: Department of the Interior.

Glacier National Park Rules and Regulations
1920   Washington, D.C.: National Park Service, Department of the Interior.

GLACIER PARK HOTEL COMPANY
n.d.   *Picture Writing by the Blackfeet Indians in Glacier Park Hotels.* Glacier Park, Montana (ca. 1920).
1925   "European Guide Comes to Glacier," June 1 news release, Kalispell, Montana.

GRANT, MADISON
1919   *Early History of the Glacier National Park, Montana, 1919.* Washington, D.C.: National Park Service, Department of the Interior.

GREAT NORTHERN RAILWAY COMPANY
n.d.   *Glacier National Park "See America First,"* (ca. 1913–1914).
1913   *Glacier Park Blazer,* published daily aboard Great Northern Railway's hotel train accompanying A.A.A. National Auto Tour from Minneapolis, Minnesota, to Glacier Park, Montana.
1924–70 *The Great Northern Goat:* "Blackfeet Indian Craftwork," 15(4):8–10; "United Nations Delegate Joins Blackfeet Indian in Peace Powwow," 15(8)8–10.
1958   *Glacier Park Hotels, Chalets and Cabin Camps,* St. Paul.

GRINNELL, GEORGE B.
1922   "A Note on the Blackfeet Indian Section of the Exhibition," in *Portraits of American Indians: W. Langdon Kihn.* New York: Anderson Galleries in cooperation with Art Museum of Sante Fe.

HAINES, FRANCIS
1955   *The Nez Percés: Tribesmen of Columbia Plateau.* Norman: University of Oklahoma Press.

HANNA, WARREN L.
1976   *Montana's Many Splendored Glacierland.* Seattle: Superior Publishing Company.

HANSON, JAMES A.
1982   "Trade Goods in Some L. A. Huffman Photographs," in *Museum of the Fur Trade Quarterly,* 18(1–2):1–8.

HASSRICK, PETER H.
1977   *The Way West: Art of Frontier America.* New York: Harry N. Abrams.

HASSRICK, ROYAL B.
n.d.   Field notes, in Denver Public Library Archives.
1940   Moccasins of the Dakota Indians, manuscript at Harvard University.
1964   *The Sioux.* Norman: University of Oklahoma Press.
1977   *The George Catlin Book of American Indians.* New York: Watson-Guptill.

Indian Summer
1959   Exhibit brochure.

JAMES, EDWIN
1823   *Account of an Expedition from Pittsburgh to the Rocky Mountains Performed in the Years 1819 and 1820.* 2 vols. Philadelphia: Carey.

JOHNSTON, PATRICIA CONDON
1981   "No Bull about James J. Hill's Model Farm," in *Twin Cities,* 4(12):62–68, 125–27.

KINIETZ, W. VERNON
1942   *John Mix Stanley and His Indian Paintings.* Ann Arbor: University of Michigan Press.

KITCHEL, LARRY
1921   Correspondence with Louis Hill, Sr.

KROEBER, ALFRED L.
1902   "The Arapaho," in American Museum of Natural History *Bulletin,* 18(pt. 1):36–150.

KURZ, RUDOLPH F.
1937   *Journal of Rudolph Friedrich Kurz: An Account of his Experience Among Fur Traders and American Indians on the Mississippi and Missouri Rivers During the Years 1846 to 1852.* J. N. B. Hewitt, ed. (Bulletin 115.) Washington, D.C.: Bureau of American Ethnology.

LAROCQUE, FRANCOIS
1910   *Journal of Larocque from the Assiniboine to the Yellowstone, 1805.* (Publication No. 3.) Ottawa: Canadian Archives.

LARPENTEUR, CHARLES
1898   *Forty Years a Fur Trader on the Upper Missouri: The Personal Narrative of Charles Larpenteur.* Elliot Coues, ed., 2 vols. New York: F. P. Harper.

LA VÉRENDRYE, PIERRE G. V.
1927   *Journals and Letters of Pierre Gaultier de Varennes de la Vérendrye and His Sons.* Lawrence J. Burpee, ed. Toronto: Champlain Society.

LYFORD, CARRIE
1940   *Quill and Beadwork of the Western Sioux.* Washington, D.C.: U.S. Office of Indian Affairs, Department of the Interior.

MCADAMS, CLARK
1919   "Picture Stories of the Blackfeet Indians," in *Wild Life,* 3(2):1–11.

MCGILLIS, O. J.
1942   Correspondence with J. C. Ewers, April 28.

MARTIN, ALBRO
1976   *James J. Hill and the Opening of the Northwest.* New York: Oxford University Press.

MASON, OTIS T.
1889   "Cradles of the American Aborigines," in *U.S. National Museum Annual Report for 1887,* Washington, D.C., pp. 161–235.

MAXIMILIAN, ALEXANDER PHILIP, PRINCE VON WIED-NEUWIED
1906   *Travels in the Interior of North America, 1832–1834.* Rueben Gold Thwaites, ed., *Early Western Travels,* 32 vols. Cleveland: A. H. Clark.

MORGAN, THISBA HUTSON
1958   "Reminiscences of My Days in the Land of the Ogalalla Sioux," in *Report and Historical Collections,* 29:21–62. Pierre: South Dakota Department of History.

MORROW, MABLE
1975   *Indian Rawhide: An American Folk Art.* (Civilization of the American Indian Series, vol. 132.) Norman: University of Oklahoma Press.

New York World
1921   October 9 magazine section.

NOBEL, H. A.
1920   September 23 telegram to L. W. Hill and W. P. Kenny.

ORDWAY, JOHN
1916   "The Journals of Captain Meriwether Lewis and Sergeant John Ordway, Kept on the Expedition of Eastern Exploration, 1803–1806," Milo Quaife, ed., in *Collections,* vol. 22 Madison: The State Historical Society of Wisconsin.

Progressive Men of the State of Montana
n.d.   2 vols. Chicago: A. W. Bowen and Company (190?).

REISS, HANS
1926   January 7 correspondence with Louis Hill, Sr.

REISS, T. TJARK, WITH GEORGE SCHRIEVER
1981   "Winold Reiss," in *American West,* 18(5):28–39.

Report of the Superintendent of the Glacier National Park
1911–13 Washington, D.C.: Department of the Interior.

RINEHART, MARY ROBERTS
n.d.   *The Call of the Mountains.* St. Paul: Great Northern Railway Company (ca. 1930).

St. Paul Pioneer Press
1948   "Louis Hill, Sr.," April 28, 1948, pp. 1–2.
1959   "Preview of Blackfoot Indian Arts and Crafts Exhibit," in *Sunday Pictorial Magazine,* October 18, 1959, pp. 7–9.

SCHOOLCRAFT, HENRY ROWE
1851–57 *Historical and Statistical Information Respecting the History, Condition and Prospects of the Indian Tribes of the United States.* 6 vols. Philadelphia: Lippincott, Grambo.

SCHULTZ, JAMES WILLARD
1915 *Blackfeet Tales of Glacier National Park.* New York: Forest and Stream.

SCHWARZ, TED
1982 "The Santa Fe Railroad and Early Southwest Artists," in *American West,* 19(5):32–41.

SHEIRE, JAMES W.
1970 *Glacier National Park Historic Resource Study.* (Office of History and Historic Architecture, Eastern Service Center). Washington, D.C.: National Park Service, Department of the Interior.

SMITH, HOKE
1922 "Indian Chiefs Will Make a New Tribe of Scribes." May 1 news release of Glacier Park Hotel Company, Kalispell, Montana.

STEELE, RUFUS
1915 "The Son Who Showed His Father," in *Sunset* (March).

STEPHENS, CHARLES H.
1891 Sketchbook among Blackfeet Indians, at University of Pennsylvania Museum, Philadelphia.

STEPHENS, JERE
1894 "Report on Fort Belknap Reservation," in *Eleventh Dicennial Census (1890) Report on Indians Taxed and Indians Not Taxed in the United States (except Alaska).* (Final Reports, vol. 10.)

THOMAS DAVIS, AND KARIN RONNEFELDT, EDS.
1976 *People of the First Man.* New York: E. P. Dutton.

VESTAL, STANLEY
1948 *Warpath and Council Fire.* New York: Random House.

WALTON, ANN T.
1982 *The Burlington Northern Collection.* St. Paul: Burlington Northern, Inc.

WATERS, ALVIN W.
1963 "The Last of the Glidden Tours, Minneapolis to Glacier Park, 1913," in *Minnesota History,* 38:205–15.

WILDSCHUT, WILLIAM, AND JOHN C. EVERS
1959 "Crow Indian Beadwork: A Descriptive and Historical Study," in *Contributions,* vol. 16, New York: Museum of the American Indian, Heye Foundation.

WINCHELL, NEWTON H.
1911 *The Aborigines of Minnesota.* St. Paul: Minnesota Historical Society.

WISSLER, CLARK
1904 "Decorative Art of the Sioux Indians," in American Museum of Natural History *Bulletin,* 18(pt. 3):231–75.
1910 "Material Culture of the Blackfoot Indians," in American Museum of Natural History *Anthropological Papers,* vol. 5, pt. 1.
1912 "Ceremonial Bundles of the Blackfeet Indians," in American Museum of Natural History *Anthropological Papers,* vol. 7, pt. 2.
1916 "Structural Basis to the Decoration of Costumes among the Plains Indians," in American Museum of Natural History *Anthropological Papers,* 17(pt. 1):1–23.
1927 "Distribution of Moccasin Decorations among the Plains Tribes," in American Museum of Natural History *Anthropological Papers,* 29(pt. 1):5–23.

WOOD, CHARLES, AND DOROTHY WOOD
1979 *The Great Northern Railway.* Edmonds, Washington: Pacific Fast Mail.

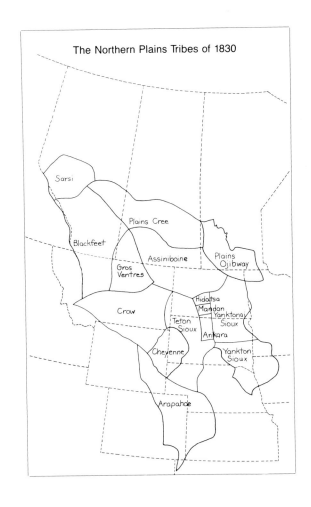

The Northern Plains Tribes of 1830

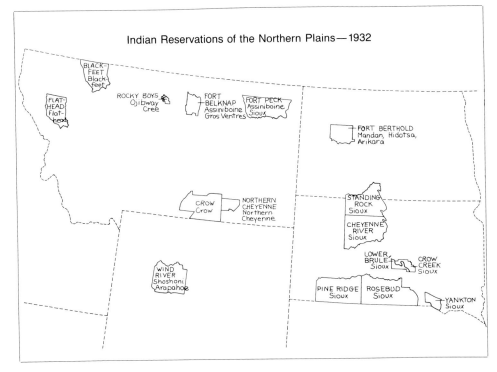

Indian Reservations of the Northern Plains—1932

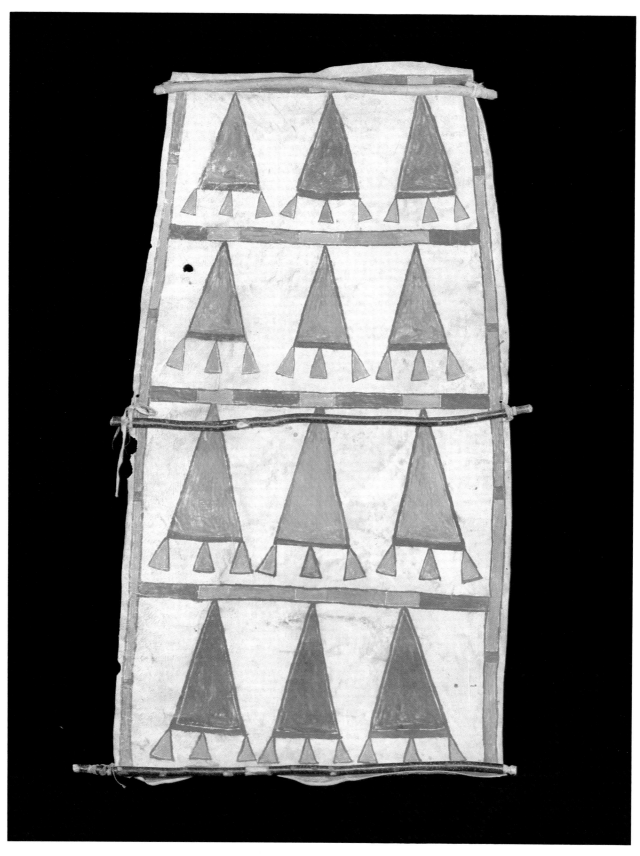

Plate 1   Tipi Door, *Cat. 204*

Plate 2   Drum Supports, *Cat. 344*

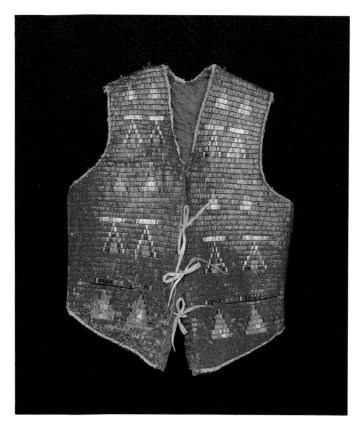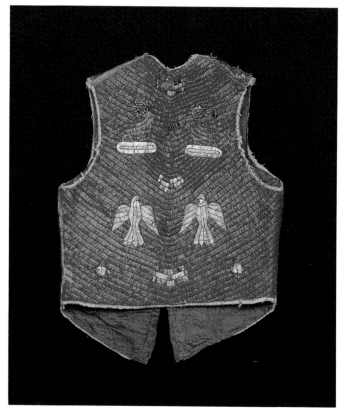

Plate 3 Vest, *Cat. 112a and b*

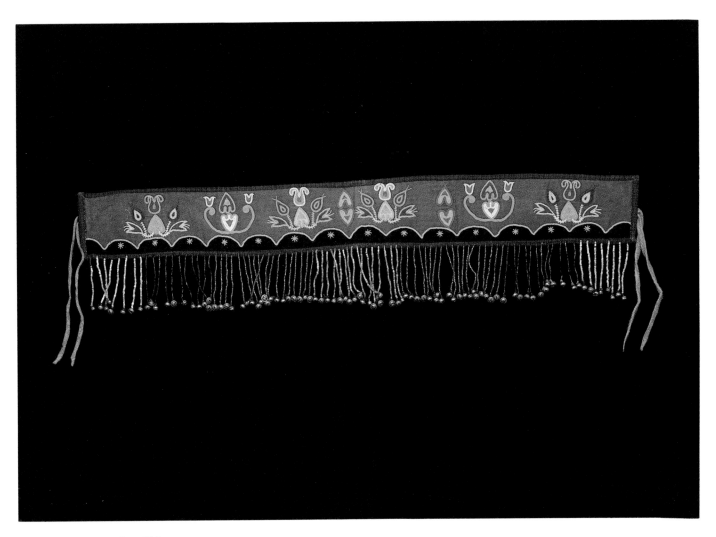

Plate 4   Martingale, *Cat. 290*

Plate 5   War Record Canvas C, *Cat. 297*

Plate 6   Horned Bonnets and Roach, *top: Cat. 38a and b; bottom: Cat. 37 and Cat. 53*

Plate 7   Dress, *Cat. 142*

Plate 8   Thunderbird Shirt, *Cat. 60a–d*

Plate 9   Ghost Dance Dress, *Cat. 353a and b*

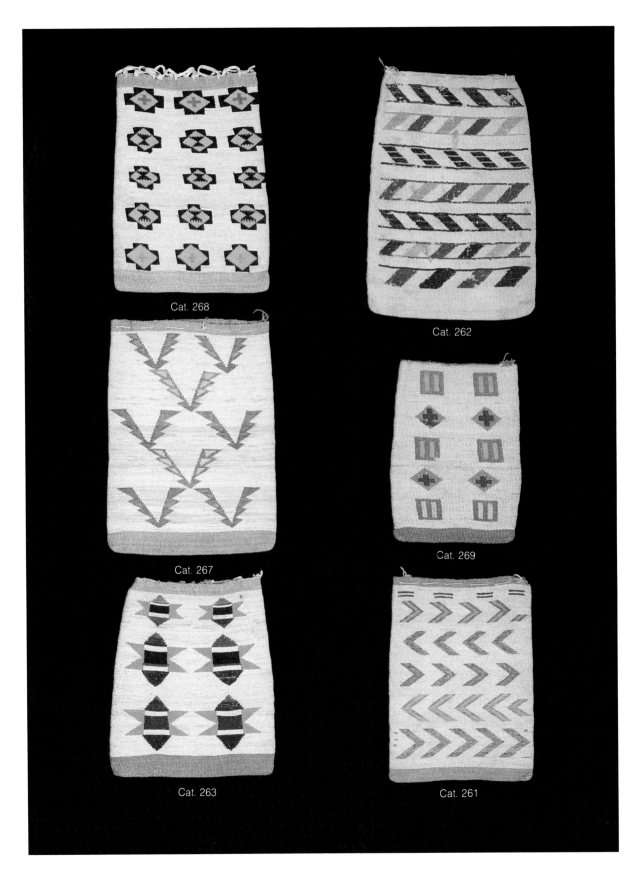

Cat. 268

Cat. 262

Cat. 267

Cat. 269

Cat. 263

Cat. 261

Plate 10 Fiber Bags, *Group I*

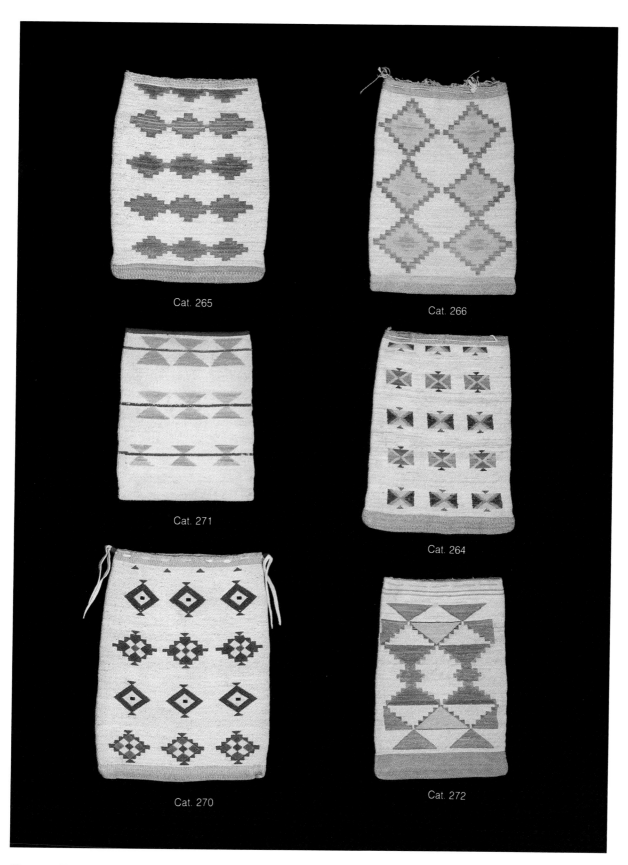

Cat. 265

Cat. 266

Cat. 271

Cat. 264

Cat. 270

Cat. 272

Plate 11 Fiber Bags, *Group II*

Plate 12 Women's Belts, *Cats. 171–177*

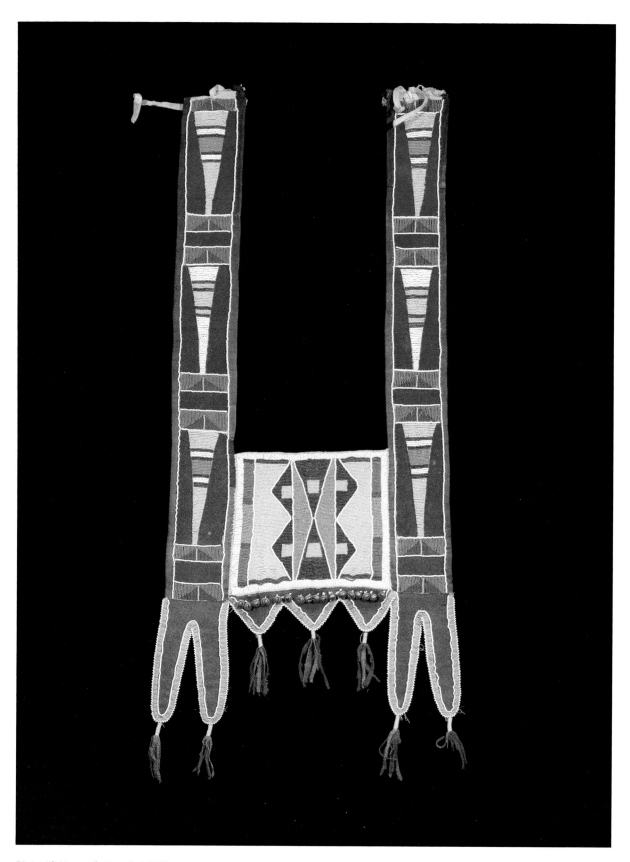

Plate 13 Horse Collar, *Cat. 276*

Plate 14 Man's Shirt, *Cat. 62*

Cat. 49

Cat. 51

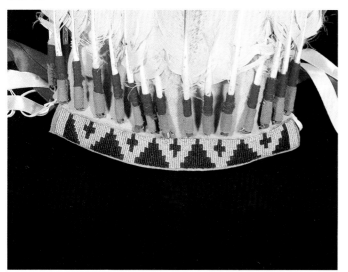

Cat. 43

Cat. 44

Plate 15 Feather Bonnet Headbands

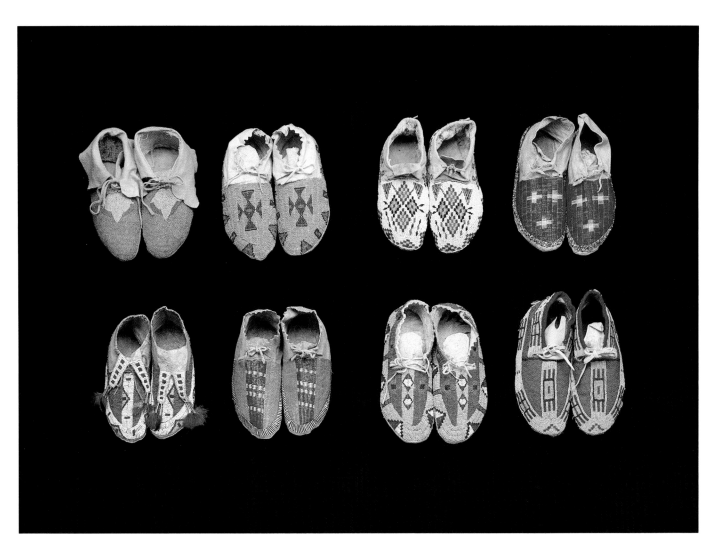

Plate 16 Moccasins, *top: Cats. 1–4; bottom: Cats. 5–8*

Plate 17 Bandolier, *Cat. 317*

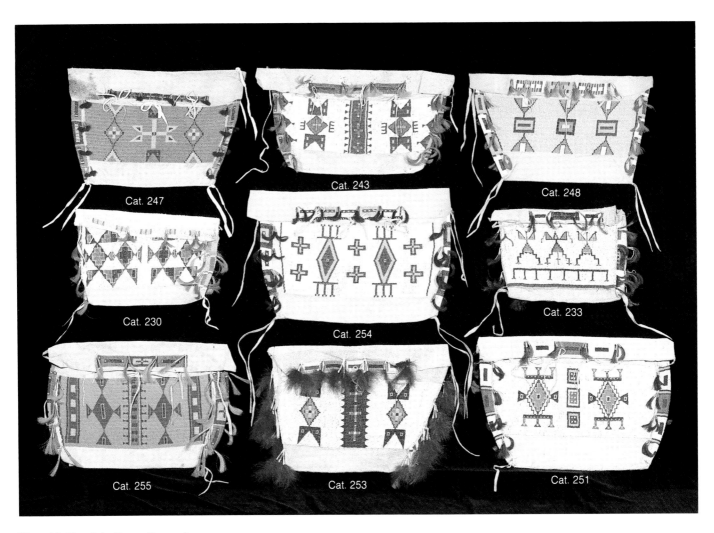

Cat. 247

Cat. 243

Cat. 248

Cat. 230

Cat. 254

Cat. 233

Cat. 255

Cat. 253

Cat. 251

Plate 18 Possible Bags, *Group I*

Cat. 247

Cat. 248

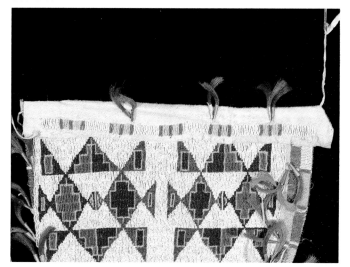

Cat. 230

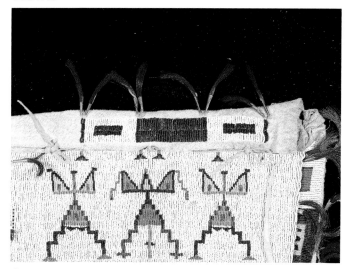

Cat. 233

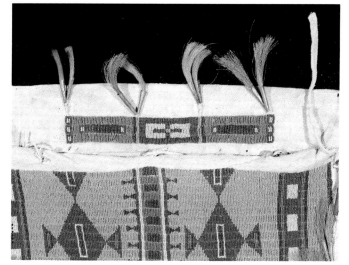

Cat. 255

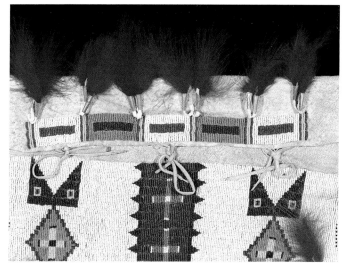

Cat. 253

Plate 19 Possible Bags, *Group I Details*

Plate 20 Lance Case, *Cat. 308*

Arts and Crafts of the Blackfeet and their Neighbors

John C. Ewers
Royal B. Hassrick
Anne E. Walton

The dates for this collection, unless otherwise noted, range approximately from 1880 to 1940.

•Indicates a color plate.

War record canvases belonging to Burlington Northern Collection are on loan to the Science Museum of Minnesota, St. Paul, Minnesota. The part of the collection belonging to the Northwest Area Foundation is on loan to the Science Museum of Minnesota, St. Paul, Minnesota. The part of the collection belonging to the Indian Arts and Crafts Board of the United States Department of the Interior is on display at the Museum of the Plains Indian in Browning, Montana. Some artifacts are on loan to the Science Museum of Minnesota.

Fig. 42 Indian school group at Blackfeet Old
Agency, 1888. *Photograph courtesy of
the Montana Historical Society*

Clothing

Moccasins

Moccasins are the most numerous and most typical articles of clothing from the Indian tribes of the Northern Plains in museum collections. Not only were moccasins worn by men, women, and children of these tribes in buffalo days, but they continued to be worn on dress occasions within the reservation period. Many older Indians have worn them daily even in recent years.

During the 1940s, members of the first generation of Blackfeet to attend school said they did not begin to wear shoes until after they started school. The group photograph of children in the school at the Old Agency on the Blackfeet Reservation in 1888 shows almost all of the youngsters wearing shoes (Fig. 42). Special Agent Jere Stephens wrote from Fort Belknap Reservation, where the Gros Ventres and part of the Assiniboine resided, in December, 1890: "The shoes that are issued to them they do not like, and will often cut the tops off to make soles for moccasins, while the bottom of sole leather they do not use at all, claiming that they cannot walk in stiff-soled shoes" (Stephens 1894:366). Apparently one good reason for the Indian's reluctance to wear the shoes received in early government issues was that little effort was made to supply shoes that fit. Thisba Morgan, a teacher at the Oglala Boarding School on Pine Ridge Reservation from 1890 to 1895, writing of her Sioux pupils, told of the "suffering their poor little feet were to endure when they were taken out of their soft-soled moccasins and put into the awful brogans furnished by the United States Government. They limped and shuffled about trying to walk in the heavy things that were blistering their feet, some leaving bleeding sores which often became badly infected" (Morgan 1958:26). Writing of the Blackfeet in 1910, Clark Wissler attributed the preservation of the art of skin dressing among those Indians to the "continued use of the moccasin instead of the white man's shoe" (Wissler 1910:63).

The younger and mixed-blood Indians adopted the white man's shoes or boots more readily than did older Indians of a high degree of Indian blood who were not actively engaged in outdoor activities. As recently as 1968, Mrs. Pauline Dempsey found that at least 100 older people among the Blood tribe of Blackfeet in southern Alberta continued to wear moccasins daily, except in winter.

For nearly two centuries Indian women of the tribes of this region have also made moccasins for gifts or sale to whites who found moccasins desirable as gifts to friends for relatives because they were novel, attractive, and useful as carpet slippers. As early as August, 1806, members of the Lewis and Clark expedition returning from their epic overland trek to the Pacific Coast, "traded for Robes and Mockasons [sic]. Some of which was handsome" during their stop at the Arikara villages on the Missouri (Ordway 1916:392). Long before tourists to Glacier National Park began to purchase Indian-made moccasins from the Blackfeet, white traders, soldiers, and Indian Agency employees were obtaining Indian moccasins for themselves or others. Many of these pieces of Indian-made footwear have found their way into museum collections.

There is evidence that, both in method of construction and surface decoration, Indian moccasins from this region have changed over the years. The most common form of moccasin among the Blackfeet and their neighbors in buffalo days was made from a single piece of soft-dressed skin, folded on the inner side of the foot and sewn together in a seam that extended around the outside of the foot and up the heel. The hard-soled moccasin, in which a sole of tough rawhide was sewn to an upper of soft-tanned skin, began to appear among the Sioux as early as the mid-nineteenth century but was rare among the Blackfeet before 1880. Glass trade beads made in Europe began to replace dyed porcupine quills for decorating moccasins before 1830. Even so, some Sioux and

Assiniboine women were quilling moccasins a fully century later. Throughout the Northern Plains, moccasin uppers fully covered with beadwork were rare before these Indians settled down upon reservations. They were never intended for daily wear, but for use on dress occasions.

There are no old-style, soft-soled moccasins in the Hill Collection. Plate 16 illustrates eight pairs of moccasins from this collection, all of which were probably made during the period 1890–1930. Although most, if not all, of these moccasins may have been collected among the Blackfeet, all are probably of Sioux or Assiniboine make. The custom of decorating moccasins with quillwork virtually disappeared among Blackfeet beadworkers before 1900, but it continued among the Sioux and Assiniboine. Notice the variety of colors in the beadwork on the three pairs of moccasins in the lower row, all of which employ the same motif prominently in their design—long, curving parallel gores, a design the Sioux sometimes referred to as "buffalo tracks."

Cat. 31 illustrates another pair of Sioux moccasins. The quillwork is applied in an old Sioux design, composed of parallel bands across the toe and instep in three-row quillwork elaborated with open rectangles. Two bands of lazy-stitched beadwork provide a border between the quilled portion and the hard sole of the moccasin.

Cat. 9 and Cat. 10 show two pairs of fully beaded moccasins that are exact duplicates of one another. This is a rare occurrence among Plains Indian moccasins and suggests that both pairs were made by the same Sioux craftswoman.

Cat. 12 pictures a pair of fully beaded Sioux moccasins with elaborately beaded, bifurcated tongue extensions. Such fancy moccasins were favored by young male dancers.

Cat. 19 shows a pair of moccasins fully beaded in the overlay stitch, in which equal-armed crosses and double feather designs are used prominently in the decorative design. This was an Assiniboine design that was also used to some extent by Blackfeet craftswomen.

Cat. 14 and Cat. 30 illustrate two pairs of the most elaborate kind of moccasins made by Indians of the Northern Plains, fully beaded on the soles as well as on the uppers. Because they recognized that these beaded-sole moccasins would have been impractical for use in walking or dancing, some writers have termed them "burial moccasins." They appear to have been most popular among the Assiniboine and Sioux during the period 1880–1910. Thisba Morgan wrote of older girls about to leave the Oglala Boarding School to get married during the period 1890–1895 making moccasins for their future husbands. "They would bead the sole of moccasins for him that told him she was willing to be trod upon under his feet and her heart crushed as he crushed the beads on the soles of his moccasins" (Morgan 1958:30). Sioux Indian women also beaded the soles of tiny baby moccasins made as gifts to new mothers. The artist Herman Haupt, who knew the Sioux during the years 1870–1890 and was aware that maidens made these beaded-sole moccasins to give to their lovers termed these moccasins simply "love moccasins" (Haupt in Winchell 1911:51–52).

Cat. 21 and Cat. 11 picture two pairs of partially beaded moccasins with geometric designs. The former bears a simple series of evenly spaced stripes across the toe and instep and a narrow beaded border around the edge of the upper, in what the Blackfeet referred to as the "cross or striped" design (Ewers 1945:41). Its prototype must have been the similar design in quillwork pictured in Cat. 31. The second, in which the front is fully beaded in a more elaborate pattern, may be of Sioux origin.

The moccasin in Cat. 20 appears to represent a variant of a pattern of moccasin design that came to be popular among the Blackfeet by the 1880s and that older Indians during the 1940s referred to as "white man sewing," "half-breed work," or "three finger beadwork." It has a U-shaped piece over the instep cut out of flannel and edged with beadwork, from which extend curvilinear lines of beadwork (Ewers 1945:41). Old photographs attest to the popularity of this design among young men during the late 1880s and 1890s.

The early reservation years also witnessed the widespread floral beadwork in the decoration of moccasins by the tribes of the Northern Plains. Two variations of these floral patterns are shown in Cat. 22 and Cat. 23. Probably of mixed-blood (Metis) origin, these floral designs appeared among all the tribes of the region, from the Cree to the Crow, and from the Sioux to the Flathead west of the Rockies. They were adopted by full-blooded craftswomen as well. One of them, Susie Red Horn, known as perhaps the best Blackfeet moccasin-maker during the 1940s, recalled that when she learned to bead moccasins during the 1890s, she used floral designs and continued to use them until the middle 1930s when the new Blackfeet Cooperative Crafts Shop ruled that only the older geometric designs could appear on moccasins sold through that market. Even so, some Blackfeet women continued to bead floral designs on moccasins they made for members of their own families or for gifts to other Indians.

Cat. 18 and Cat. 25 illustrate two pairs of high-topped women's moccasins. Blackfeet women adopted moccasins with high, soft-skin extensions at their tops after they abandoned the wearing of leggings. Three style-setters in introducing these moccasins among the Blackfeet about the year 1930 were Julia Wades-in-the-Water, Cecile Black Boy, and Mae Williamson; the latter was later president of the Blackfeet Indian Cooperative Crafts Shop. High-topped moccasins were earlier made and used by the Cree Indians. Those in Cat. 25 bear large floral units that look like Cree work, perhaps from Rocky Boy's Reservation in Montana. Cat. 18 in its use of feather designs and the lazy stitch looks more like the work of an Assiniboine beader.

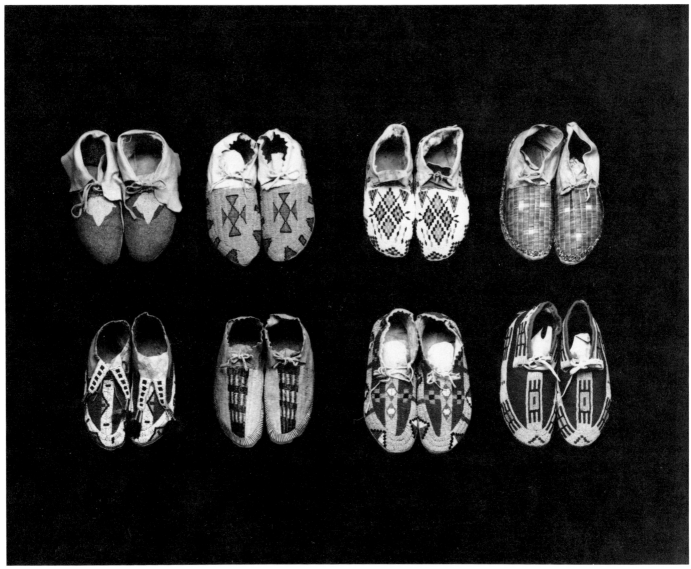

Cats. 1–8

1. **Moccasins,** *Northern Plains*
● *9½" long, 5" wide*
Museum of the Plains Indian

The striking combination of dull green, bright lavender, and gold beads signifies the extraordinary sensitivity to color harmony of the Blackfeet artist/craftsperson. A vamp is suggested by the placement of the floral ornament. (MPI 1135)

2. **Moccasins,** *Northern Plains*
● *10" long, 4¼" wide*
Museum of the Plains Indian

The uppers are completely beaded in an arresting lavender, green, and red color scheme accented by a blue outline. (MPI 1130)

3. **Moccasins,** *Northern Plains*
● *10" long, 3¾"*
Museum of the Plains Indian

These geometrically decorated beaded moccasins are of canvas with hard buckskin soles and fringe at the heels. (MPI 1142)

4. **Moccasins,** *Northern Plains*
● *10" long, 4" wide*
Museum of the Plains Indian

This pair of beaded moccasins has short cuffs with flat rims. It is made in the hard-sole style, but with soft soles. The quillwork has a cross pattern of green and yellow in a red field, and the design appears only on the toes. The beads are randomly mixed colors and run in a single row of lazy stitch around the lower border of the toes and sides. (MPI 1124)

5. **Moccasins,** *Northern Plains*
● *9¹⁄₄" long, 3¹⁄₂" wide*
   Museum of the Plains Indian

This pair of beaded moccasins is of the hard-sole variety, with a short cuff bound with plaid cotton fabric. The tongue is forked and beaded. The toe is beaded with a white stripe down the center of a green field. There is a triangle of red, yellow, and royal blue in the stripe. The same motif is repeated around the edge of the moccasin. The tongue is beaded with white and blue. The ends of the fork have two metal-cone jingles strung on thongs with purple fluffs. (MPI 1146)

6. **Moccasins,** *Northern Plains*
● *10" long, 4" wide*
   Museum of the Plains Indian

This pair of moccasins is of the hard-sole variety, with a short cuff with a sawtooth edge. The quilled element is on the upper part only. The toe is worked in orange with a large purple strip running down the center. The front of the toe is edged with red and white striped quillwork. (MPI 1126)

7. **Moccasins,** *Northern Plains,*
● *Blackfeet (?)*
   11" long, 4" wide
   Museum of the Plains Indian

This pair of beaded moccasins is of the hard-sole variety, with a short cuff with a sawtooth edge. The beaded section covers the toe as well as the heel and the cuff. The toe is decorated with a stripe of light blue in the middle of a green field. There are red diamonds inscribed with white squares inside the blue stripe. There are four orange crosses with dark blue centers in the green field. The broad blue stripe has stepped pyramids of red, white, and dark blue, and red stripes containing green squares. (MPI 1139)

Cats. 9 and 10

8. **Moccasins,** *Northern Plains,*
● *Blackfeet (?)*
   10¹⁄₂" long, 4" wide
   Museum of the Plains Indian

This pair of beaded moccasins is of the hard-sole variety, with red strouding around the top of the short cuff and a double row of fringe at the back seam. The beading covers most of the moccasin — the toe, around the sides, and the cuff. The beaded element on the toe is a dark turquoise with a pink stripe in the middle. There is a geometric pattern in the middle of the pink stripe, of burgundy, yellow, and green with three turquoise stripes at each end. This pattern is repeated on the cuff and the lower beaded section that runs around the sides. (MPI 1132)

9. **Moccasins,** *Sioux*
   9³⁄₄" long, 4" wide
   Museum of the Plains Indian

These moccasins have hard leather soles with beaded tops. The beaded design covers the top of the moccasins and continues around the backs. The buffalo track design appears on the toe. Other designs include diamonds and crosses in white, light blue, dark blue, red, and yellow-green. (MPI 1128a and b)

10. **Moccasins,** *Sioux*
   10" long, 4¹⁄₄" wide
   Museum of the Plains Indian

These moccasins have hard leather soles. The beaded tops are done in yellow-green, dark and light blue, cardinal red, yellow, and transparent grey or green beads. The design on the toe is buffalo track. (MPI 1144)

11. **Moccasins,** *Sioux*
10¼" long, 3¼" wide
Northwest Area Foundation

The decoration is beaded in lazy stitch and covers the entire vamp, extending in a narrow beaded strip around the sole seam. Red and blue inverted triangles are arranged in a white beaded field. Yellow and silver metallic beads fill the centers of some of the geometric designs. A serrated edge is the only decoration on the ankle flap of these hard-sole moccasins. (SMM 49–106)

12. **Moccasins,** *Sioux*
9½" long, 3½" wide
Northwest Area Foundation

The beading is in blue, white, and yellow, with red and green accents. The tongue is forked and contains a triangular beaded pattern in blue, light blue, and red. Two green horsehair dangles are suspended from each fork of the tongues. The heel seam is fringed and the upper rim is bordered by a dark green broadcloth strip. The beadwork is applied in lazy stitch.
(SMM 49–107a and b)

13. **Moccasins,** *Sioux*
10¼" long, 4" wide
Northwest Area Foundation

The red, white, and blue beaded decoration, consisting of two rows of geometric banding, is applied in the lazy stitch to surround and cover the seam between the upper moccasin and sole. Additional banding strips of beaded decoration are found beneath the tie, on the vamp, and on the attached two-pronged tongue. A band of indigo calico encircles the rim. Purple-dyed horsehair dangles, bound in metal bezels, are decorated with tightly wound red quills where they attach to the buckskin thongs, allowing them to hang freely and create a pleasant sound as the wearer moves. Fringe hangs from the back of the right-foot moccasin only. (SMM 49–108)

14. **Moccasins,** *Sioux*
10½" long, 3¾" wide
Northwest Area Foundation

This pair of moccasins has full beaded uppers and soles. There are geometric patterns set in a royal blue background. The stepped pyramids are red, white, dark blue, and yellow. The remaining patterns on the uppers are white and dark blue. The patterns on the soles are worked in white, yellow, and brass faceted beads. There is fringe at the heel and red cloth binding the opening at the ankle. (SMM 49–110)

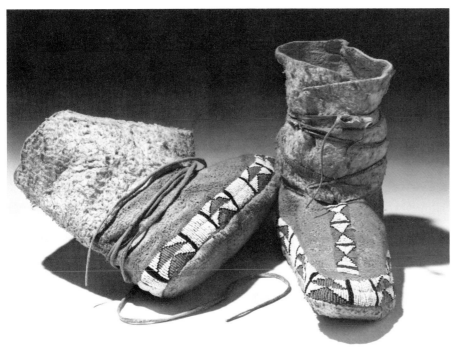

15. **Moccasins,** *Sioux or Assiniboine*
9¼" long, 7¾" high
Northwest Area Foundation

Geometric bands of decoration
beaded in the lazy stitch adorn the
center of the vamp and extend
around the entire seam of the
moccasin. (SMM 49–111)

18. **Moccasins,** *Assiniboine*
10½" long, 3¾" wide
Northwest Area Foundation

This pair of moccasins is of the
hard-sole variety. The uppers are
beaded on the toes and around the
heels. The geometric designs are
triangles, diamonds, and a stepped
figure of light blue and burgundy on
a white background. There is red
strouding at the ankle as well as
tanned hide laces and flaps.
(SMM 49–114)

16. **Moccasins,** *Sioux or Assiniboine*
10" long, 3½" wide
Northwest Area Foundation

The upper is completely covered in a
pattern of light pink mixed with white
and metallic beads. The tongue is
plain, while the rim is decorated with
green beads attached by lazy stitch.
(SMM 49–112)

17. **Moccasins,** *Northern Plains*
9½" long, 3½" wide
Northwest Area Foundation

The vamp of this moccasin is
decorated with a geometric beaded
pattern in blue, white, green, red,
and yellow. There is a beaded border
running around the upper, above the
sole seam. A diagonal checker row is
the prevailing design pattern. The
beads are attached to the buckskin
by the lazy stitch. (SMM 49–113)

19. **Moccasins,** *Blackfeet*
10⅝" long, 3½" wide
Northwest Area Foundation

The striking contrast of lavender and
apple green seed beads makes this
footwear distinctive. A strip of blue
cloth is sewn around the rim.
Buckskin fringe hangs from the back
seam. The beading is overlay stitch
in the feather design. Small triangles
adorn the border seam between the
beaded vamp and the sole.
(SMM 49–115)

Cat. 20

Cat. 21

Cat. 22

Cat. 23

Cat. 24

Cat. 25

20. Moccasins, *Blackfeet*
    10¹/₂" long, 3¹/₄" wide
    Northwest Area Foundation

    A simplified floral design grows out of the outlined U-shaped center section of green cloth. It is decorated with light blue, lavender, and dark blue bands, from which radiate red and light blue floral forms. Large dark green beads form the center of these blue flowers. The rim has a strip of the same green broadcloth. (SMM 49–116)

21. Moccasins, *Blackfeet*
    9¹/₂" long, 2³/₄" wide
    Northwest Area Foundation

    These three-piece, soft-sole moccasins have a border of green beads around the front half of the upper above the sole seam. The vamp is decorated by simple stripes across the toe and instep in blue, orange, and yellow beads. The upper rim is decorated with a thick strip of black printed calico. (SMM 49–117)

22. Moccasins, *Metis*
    10³/₄" long, 2³/₄" wide
    Northwest Area Foundation

    This pair of soft-sole moccasins has a serrated buckskin trim around the rim and a forked tongue beneath the tying thong. Beadwork covers the vamp in a floral pattern of light blue, dark blue, pink, green, and red. (SMM 121a and b)

23. Moccasins, *Metis*
    10¹/₂" long, 3³/₄" wide
    Northwest Area Foundation

    These three-piece moccasins have stiff hide soles. There is a red cloth strip with black dots around the rim. A symmetrical floral pattern is worked in turquoise, blue, white, lavender, yellow, and red. (SMM 49–123)

Cat. 26

24. Moccasins, *Blackfeet*
    10¹/₄" long, 3¹/₂" wide
    Northwest Area Foundation

    This pair of three-piece, hard-sole moccasins has a darker fringe leather strip, which surrounds the rim and is a later addition. Heel fringe extends from the stiff sole halfway up the heel seam. The vamp is beaded in a floral design that extends to the heel fringe. The side sections are worked in light and dark blue with maroon flower centers. The main design on the vamp is elaborately executed in red, green, blue, pink, yellow ochre, brown, and white, with silver metallic bead accent. (SMM 49–124)

25. Woman's Moccasins, *Plains Cree*
    10" long
    Northwest Area Foundation

    These one-piece moccasins have a side seam attaching the vent to the soft sole, extending only between the heel and toe on the outer side. The inner side, along the arch of the foot, has no seam. The seam turns upward at the heel and attaches to the cuff around the ankle sides. Beadwork is applied by lazy stitch in an elaborate floral pattern of pink, light blue, red, and yellow, accented by metallic beads. The one-piece construction, said to have been the "old" type of Blackfeet moccasin, was not limited to that tribe. (SMM 49–126a and b)

26. Moccasins, *Blackfeet or Plains Cree*
    9³/₄" long, 3" wide
    Northwest Area Foundation

    A symmetrical floral pattern covers the vamps of these moccasins. Dark blue, green, and red beads descend in a U to form blossoms. Contrasting beads edge each flower, which springs from a dark blue stalk. Dark blue broadcloth rims the upper edge. The separate tongue has a serrated edge. (SMM 49–130)

29. Moccasins, *Northern Plains*
10¼" long
Northwest Area Foundation

This pair of soft buckskin moccasins is decorated with translucent glass and china seed beads in a floral pattern encircling the entire foot. (SMM 54-31)

27. **Moccasins,** *Plains Cree*
10" long, 2¾" wide
Northwest Area Foundation

The beaded decoration on these moccasins is confined to the vamp and consists of green, pink, navy, and white stripes radiating from a central U-shaped bar to the sole. The U-shaped bar consists of three rows of colored, wrapped, horsehair strands and conceals the joining of the double-tongued section to the vamp. The ankle flap measures 2¾" and is of dark green velveteen with a red flannel inset. A soft untanned cuff enclosed the wearer's ankle and is held in place by lacing. The edge of this cuff is cut in a serrated pattern. (SMM 49-133)

28. **Moccasins,** *Sarsi or Blackfeet*
10¼" long, 3" wide
Northwest Area Foundation

This pair of two-piece moccasins has an attached, short, U-shaped tongue. The upper section is joined to a stiff sole. A black cloth decorative band is sewn around the entire rim and tongue. The beaded pattern on the vamp is a floral design of purple flowers outlined in blue, with leaves of navy blue and white. (SMM 49-134)

30. **Moccasins,** *Sioux*
10" long, 4½" wide
Museum of the Plains Indian

This pair of moccasins is of soft buckskin, beaded on both the uppers and the soles. The uppers have a green toe with small white and red triangles and brass spots. The edge is white with a red border. The repetitive pattern is a triangle of blue, yellow, red, green, and brass beads. The sole, worked in a related design of blue and yellow triangles, has a green center with red and white diagonal lines. (MPI 1123)

Cat. 35

31. **Moccasins,** *Sioux*
11¹/₂" long, 4¹/₂" wide
Museum of the Plains Indian

This pair of moccasins is of the hard-sole type, with buckskin tops and rawhide soles. The tops are decorated with quillwork strips on the toe and with beads in two rows of lazy stitch around the sides. The quillwork is in red strips with white and orange rectangles in the middle. The strip is white with a repetitive diamond pattern of red, green, blue, and brass faceted beads. (MPI 1127)

32. **Moccasins,** *Blackfeet (?)*
10¹/₂" long, 3³/₄" wide
Museum of the Plains Indian

This pair of moccasins is of the hard-sole type with partially beaded deerskin uppers and rawhide soles. The beaded elements consist of aqua stripes bisected by red triangles across the toe. (MPI 1140)
Photo: page 129.

33. **Moccasins,** *Blackfeet*
11" long, 4¹/₂" wide
Museum of the Plains Indian

This pair of hard-sole moccasins has rawhide soles and fully beaded smoke-tanned buckskin uppers. The toe is covered with turquoise-colored beads with a white stripe including an ochre and light blue buffalo track design, repeated along the white side band. (MPI 1413d)
Photo: page 126.

34. **Moccasins,** *Blackfeet (?)*
11" long, 4" wide
Museum of the Plains Indian

This pair of moccasins is of the hard-sole variety, with rawhide soles and soft uppers. The uppers are completely covered with light blue beads; the toes are decorated with red five-pointed stars. There is fringe on the heel. (MPI 1414c)
Photo: page 130.

35. **Moccasins,** *Northern Plains*
11" long, 7¹/₂" high
Northwest Area Foundation

These soft-sole buckskin moccasins are decorated with embroidered flowers on the vamp, which is circled by the three colored bindings. (SMM 54–30)

Fig. 43 Buffalo Body, Blackfeet Indian, wearing a cap decorated with strips of winter weasel skins and a pair of buffalo horns. *Portrait by Winold Reiss, photograph courtesy of Burlington Northern Railroad*

Horned Bonnets

Numerous representations of warriors carrying weapons and wearing horns on their heads, incised or painted on rock surfaces by prehistoric and early historic Indians living in or near the Rocky Mountains, attest to those people's regard for animal horns as symbols of strength. Horned bonnets with their caps covered with strips of the white skins of weasels that had been taken during the winter were worn by many outstanding warriors among the tribes of the Northern Plains in nineteenth-century buffalo days.

A century and a half ago (in 1832) George Catlin observed and pictured the Mandan second chief, Four Bears, who possessed the best war record of any man in his tribe, wearing a horned bonnet. Others of Catlin's subjects who wore these bonnets were Black Rock, a Teton Sioux chief, and Eagle Ribs, a prominent Blackfeet warrior who bragged that he had killed eight white trappers who had dared to invade the hunting grounds of his tribe. Catlin described the buffalo horns on these bonnets as "rising out of a mat of ermine skins and tails, which hang over the top of the headdress somewhat in the form that the large and profuse locks of hair hang and fall over the head of the buffalo bull" (Catlin 1841:I, 102).

During the first decade of this century, Clark Wissler found among the Blackfeet "a general belief that . . . these types of headdresses were once exclusively the regalia of members of the bull society . . . It is said that when the society ceased to exist the regalia was still transferred from person to person, the ritual and the songs of the society being used." Wissler learned that the Blackfeet regarded those bonnets as medicines capable of protecting and bringing good fortune to their owners. Ownership was transferred through rituals, and the owner was required to keep the bonnet "in a cylindrical leather case and hung on a tripod and kept out on the west side of the tipi. A smudge is made for it three times a day" (Wissler 1912:114–16).

Long after intertribal warfare ended, these bonnets continued to be highly prized status symbols among the Blackfeet. The artist Winold Reiss pictured several of them worn by some of his Blackfeet sitters during the second quarter of the present century. One of them was a tight-fitting cap covered with a mat of weasel skin strips, with a pair of full-rounded buffalo horns attached so that they stood out at the sides of the wearer's head, like the horns on the head of a buffalo. It was worn by Buffalo Body (Fig. 43). This or a very similar bonnet is preserved in the Louis W. Hill Collection (Cat. 41).

A more elaborate variant of the highly regarded horned bonnet is in the portion of the collection now in St. Paul (Cat. 38). The horns are split sections of buffalo horns only. They are wrapped in strips of red and dark blue blanket cloth, topped with strips of weasel skin. The cap is covered with a heavy mat of weasel skin strips except for a portion of the center front that reveals a band of red cloth, decorated with two rows of brass upholstering tacks. Weasel skin strips fall as pendants from each side of the bonnet at the front, and a red cloth trailer is suspended from the rear of the bonnet, which is decorated with eight pendant eagle feathers.

Still another variant of the horned bonnet appears in Cat. 40. On this bonnet the horns are longitudinally cut sections of antelope horn with dyed horsehair tips. The cap is covered with eagle and hawk feathers rather than weasel strips, and the headband in loom-woven beadwork. The tribal origin of this bonnet is not determined. It does not appear to be a Blackfeet type.

36. **Horned Bonnet,** *Blackfeet*
35" long, 10" diameter
Northwest Area Foundation

The helmet of this bonnet is covered with ermine strips. Long ermine tubes hang as drops in the back and on the sides. An 18" red flannel cloth hangs down the back of the headdress and covers the forehead in a band. Surmounting the helmet is a pair of flannel-wrapped curved horns. A row of brass hawk bells adorns the outer edge of the horns. The tips of the horns are wrapped with beads and held in position with strings of large metallic beads. Long strands of bound yellow horsehair are attached to the base of each horn. A label attached to this bonnet indicates that it may have belonged to "Charles Weasel Head." It was restored in 1982 by David Kline and Robert Kelley. (SMM 49–137)

37. **Horned Bonnet,** *Blackfeet*
● *57" long trailer, 10" diameter*
Northwest Area Foundation

This horned headdress has a cap of hide covered with strips of ermine. There is a red quilled spike in the middle of the crown. Red yarn and red stroud are wrapped around the base of the spike, with a grey fluff at the tip. The horns are plain; the tips are decorated with red and purple fluffs, pink and white quilled spikes, and orange and grey horsehair. At the base of the horns are large bundles of feathers; some are split and dyed orange and green. Blue fluffs are scattered among the ermine strips. There are long ermine skins, feathers, and gold and white silk ribbon as drops at the sides. The brow band is beaded with a light blue background, triangles of red, white, and dark blue, red crosses, and red and white squares. There is a long trailer of red stroud lined with canvas. A single row of eagle feathers is centered along the length of the trailer. The feathers are tipped with pink fluffs attached to the feathers with white plaster. (SMM 1–1102)

38. **Horned Bonnet,** *Blackfeet*
● *27" long trailer, 10" diameter*
Northwest Area Foundation

The cap is of hide covered with ermine strips. The horns are wrapped with red and blue ribbon in a crisscross pattern and supported with pink and blue beaded strands. Ermine strips accent the tips of the horns, and tanned hide strips hang from the base. Drops of ermine skins and blue and red ribbon hang from the side. The brow band is red strouding with brass buttons. The trailer of red strouding lined with canvas has feathers bound with red strouding. (SMM 1–1103)

39. **Horned Bonnet,** *Blackfeet*
41" long, 8¹/₂" diameter
Northwest Area Foundation

This horned bonnet has a cap covered in ermine strips and a pair of split bison horns. The horns are covered with green ribbon. The tips are decorated with ermine and pink fluffs. There are red-dyed, split feathers (owl?) at the base of each horn. The tangerine-colored fluffs at the crown of the helmet are attached with a brass button. Ermine tubes bound with red stroud and decorated with red feathers and blue fluffs are on the crown. The drops along the side and back are ermine skins, bound at the top with red stroud and at the bottom with pink fluffs. There is a fall of split feathers on the back. The brow band is made of glass beads, forming a pattern of stepped pyramids of light blue, lavender, and white. The lower edge of the band is bound with a green cloth, while the upper edge is decorated with red fluffs. (SMM 1–1105)

40. Horned Bonnet, *Northern Plains*
13" high, 8½" diameter
Northwest Area Foundation

This horned bonnet is covered with
eagle and hawk feathers. There are
red horsehair tips on the horns. The
brow band is covered with beaded
geometric patterns of red and blue
on a white background. Beaded
strips with small geometric patterns
dangle at the sides (yellow, blue, and
green). Two long braids of black
horsehair hang from the back.
(SMM 1–1101)

41. Horned Bonnet, *Blackfeet*
23" long, 12" wide
Museum of the Plains Indian

This headdress consists of bison
horns and ermine tails supported by
a smoke-tanned buckskin crown. The
headband is of rubberized raincoat
material. (MPI 1282)

Cat. 41

Fig. 44 Mountain Chief, Blackfeet Indian, wearing the old-style straight-up bonnet. *Photograph by Joseph K. Dickson, ca. 1910, courtesy of the National Anthropological Archives, Smithsonian Institution*

Feather Bonnets

The Blackfeet style of feather bonnet, worn by only a few outstanding warriors in buffalo days, took the form of a crown of upright feathers set in a wide band of rawhide generally covered with red cloth, in turn decorated with brass tacks. The earliest example of this style of headdress that has been preserved is said to have belonged to the famous Mandan chief, Four Bears. It was collected by the German Prince Maximilian of Wied-Neuwied in 1834 and is preserved in the Linden Museum in Stuttgart, West Germany. (A color photograph of this old piece appears on the cover of the Summer 1979 issue of *American Indian Art Magazine*.) Probably, however, Four Bears acquired this bonnet from the prominent Blood Indian chief, Seen From Afar, who is said to have visited the Mandan during the previous year.

The Blackfeet called bonnets of this type "straight-up bonnets," and they looked upon them as symbols of supernatural power, as they did their horned bonnets. Although there are no "straight-up bonnets" in the Hill Collection, we feel it important to offer a photograph of a fine example of one of those bonnets because they are known to have preceded the use of the Sioux type of flowing feather bonnet among the Blackfeet, and because a few of the old bonnets were still worn among some Blackfeet for ceremonial and parade participation until after 1930. This bonnet (Fig. 44) was worn by the veteran Blackfeet warrior, Mountain Chief (also known as Big Brave), when the photograph was taken in ca. 1910. Perhaps this is the bonnet Wissler stated was transferred to Big Brave in the days before the end of intertribal warfare. Big Brave "paid a horse for it. Not long after he received it, he wore the bonnet in a battle and through its power escaped many bullets and arrows and was unharmed" (Wissler 1912:116).

The Sioux type of flowing feather bonnet was not adopted by the Blackfeet until the middle 1890s, a full decade after the intertribal wars ended on the Northern Plains. Probably this bonnet came to the Blackfeet through exchanges of gifts with their former enemies, the Assiniboine, farther east. The new-style bonnet quickly gained favor among the Blackfeet, in part because they did not look upon it as a sacred headdress — anyone could wear one. Some Blackfeet men soon became skilled makers of these Sioux-style bonnets.

One of the earliest illustrations of a feather bonnet appears on a Mandan pictographic robe collected by Lewis and Clark in 1804, now at the Peabody Museum at Harvard University. There is probably no way of determining the tribal identity of the wearer. It may be that the mounted warrior represented is a Mandan, but it could portray any one of a number of enemy tribesmen including Cheyenne, Assiniboine, and Sioux.

Seventeen years later, in 1821, Charles Bird King painted Petalesharo, the Pawnee chief, wearing a typical feather bonnet (Hassrick 1977:29). Mato Tope's robe collected in 1833 by Maximilian among the Mandan and now in the collection of the Bern Museum, Switzerland, shows warriors and horses wearing feather bonnets. Karl Bodmer's copy of Mato Tope's robe also indicates warriors with bonnets (Plate 25 in Ewers 1939). In a self-portrait of a hand-to-hand fight with a Cheyenne chief, Mato Tope wears a feather bonnet (Thomas and Ronnefeldt 1976:22), while Catlin in his facsimile of Mato Tope's exploits shows him and his horse both wearing bonnets (Catlin 1841:1, 68). Catlin's portrait of Wolf Chief shows the Mandan chieftain wearing a bonnet (1841:1, 104).

Other Catlin (1841) portraits showing individuals wearing bonnets include the Sioux "Brother of Dog" (Fig. 274 in II), the Oto "Loose Pipe Stem" (Fig. 143 in II), and the Crow chief, "He Who Jumps Over Everyone," (I, 216). Catlin also pictures the "Sioux Chiefs War Dances" (I, 267), stating that the men wore "headdresses of war-eagle quills." He also refers to "headdresses of war-eagle quills" being worn by participants in the "Last

Race" of the Mandan Okeepa ceremony. Bodmer's paintings of Northern Plains Indians show no figures wearing feather bonnets, but he did make a drawing of an individual bonnet, which Maximilian referred to as a "feathered cap" (Thomas and Ronnefeldt 1976:116). Rudolph Kurz depicts an Omaha Indian wearing a feather bonnet and pictographic robe in his sketch dated May 5, 1851 (Plate 37 in Kurz 1937).

One of the earliest feather bonnets extant is that collected by Colonel Sword at Fort Leavenworth in 1838, now in the collection of the American Museum of Natural History, New York City. (See cover, *Denver Art Museum Summer Quarterly* 1965.) No tribal identification is given for this bonnet, but Fort Leavenworth, Kansas, was located in the territory of such tribes as the Omaha, Otoe, Missouri, Iowa, Kansa, and Pawnee.

The typical feather bonnet, a crown of black-tipped eagle feathers, appears to have been popular among many of the Missouri River tribes from the Pawnee and Omaha in the south to the Mandan and Crow to the north. While popularly referred to as "the Sioux-style bonnet" and certainly worn by them as well as the Cheyenne and Arapahoe, the widespread use of the style does not warrant the implication that it originated among the Sioux any more than with any other tribe.

Informants among the Sioux explained that any man might wear a bonnet. Some were purchased from medicine men at the price of a horse and themselves became "medicine." Certain rules might be prescribed for their care. They served as protective devices against bullets and arrows in battle. One the other hand, anyone might make and wear an effective bonnet; the magic power of the eagle features in themselves was believed to ward off harm. Catlin's reference to bonnets as "headdresses of war-eagle quills" implies the relationship of the headdress to war, but he is not explicit.

Among the Cheyenne, not only was the eagle feather bonnet a protective device, but with it often went specific rules and obligations. The renowned chief, Roman Nose, wore a bonnet made for him by Ice, which included two taboos: one, that the wearer must never shake hands with anyone; the other, that he might not eat food taken from a dish with a metal implement (Grinnell 1922:II, 120). Roman Nose wore the bonnet in many battles, riding back and forth within 25 yards of the enemy, whose shots had no effect. But in the Battle at Beecher Island, though realizing he had inadvertently eaten some bread with a metal fork a few days before, he nonetheless wore his bonnet to battle and was killed.

Not all men believed in the efficacy of the war bonnet as a protection against harm in battle. Pejuta Sapa or Black Medicine (Coffee) was a Brulé Sioux participant in the Battle of the Rosebud against General Cook's forces in June, 1876. In this fight he counted four coups. In 1942 he reported that he never wore a bonnet, but preferred to carry other medicines for protection. He recalled that his friend, Little Hawk, depended on a bonnet, but in battle a bullet severed the thong laced through the feathers around the crown, with the result that the feathers fell over his face, seriously endangering his life. Coffee's remark was, "Only a fool would fight with a face full of feather" (Hassrick n.d.).

Among some tribes the eagle feather bonnet may have been a badge of office worn only by distinguished officers or head men. Catlin points out that only dignitaries might wear the split horn headdress with the cap of ermine tails and trail of eagle feathers, but they were not the exclusive property or badge of chieftainship. Furthermore, they were worn in battle as a symbol of the leader's power. Catlin makes no comment upon what if any protective qualities the horned headdresses might posses, but he does state that Mato Tope, the Second Chief, was alone among the Mandan entitled to wear the horns having "the power to lead all others in time of war" (Catlin 1841:II, 117 seq.). Catlin shows "The Black Rock" chief of the

Nee-caw-wee-gee band of the Sioux wearing a split horn bonnet with a trail of eagle feathers and describes him as "head leader or war chief of his band" (Plate 91 in II). According to Ewers, the upright eagle feather bonnet was "worn by a few Blackfeet leaders" and as such may have been a badge of office (Ewers 1958:118).

In general, 24 to 36 feathers were required for a bonnet consisting of the tail feathers from two to three eagles. Formerly, rather elaborate ceremonies were associated with capturing the eagles. Men purified themselves with sweat baths and made offerings. They dug pits along promontories over which eagles were observed to fly. Camouflaging the pits with sticks, sod, and grasses and baiting them (usually with a rabbit), the hunter climbed in and lay in wait. When the eagle approached that bait, the man grabbed its legs, pulled it into the pit, and wrung its neck. More recently, eagles were shot with rifles. The value of the tail feathers and, in consequence, the cost of a war bonnet varied from one to three horses. Depending upon the scarcity of eagle feathers and the demands of the barterers, values varied from time to time. Among the Sioux, the price of a bonnet was one horse (Hassrick 1964:160). Prince Maximilian gave their value as equal to "one good horse" and mentions the Crow's gift to the Blackfeet of many valuable items including "costly feathered caps." Later, when the Crow visited the Blackfeet, the latter failed to reciprocate, much to the disgust of the Crow (Thomas and Ronnefeldt 1976:117).

Cat. 50, identified as Blackfeet, is a typical feather bonnet of the early twentieth century. The design motif on the beaded brow band and the use of light-colored beads encircling the red stroud bindings at the base of the quills was favored by the Blackfeet. Cat. 46 is a classic Sioux golden eagle feather bonnet. The red-dyed horsehair and white eagle down fluffs attached to the tips of the feathers with lime plaster are features common to most bonnets. Hawk feathers and ermine skins, as pendants attached to the rosettes at the sides of the brow band, supplement the power of the eagle feathers in protecting the wearer from harm.

Cat. 45 is a Sioux bonnet made from the feathers of the mature golden eagle. Referred to by the Sioux as "black bonnet," such a bonnet was considered equally effective as a protective device. Cat 51, a trailing black bonnet, has been identified as either Cheyenne or Sioux. Trailing bonnets were designed for warriors on horseback.

42. **Feather Bonnet,** *Blackfeet*
16" high, 12" wide
Museum of the Plains Indian

The bonnet is of eagle feathers
tipped with white fluffs and white
horsehair on a felt cap. The quills are
wrapped with red strouding and
bound with hide thongs. The brow
band, made from a woman's belt, is
framed with red strouding. The band
pattern is an hourglass figure with
two triangles. This pattern is repeated
three times; repeats 1 and 3 are red
with dark blue in the center and light
blue triangles; repeat 2 is green with
a dark blue outline for the center and
light blue triangles. These are set in a
white field. Ribbon side drops are
grey, orange, and white. (MPI 974)
Photo: page 126.

44. **Feather Bonnet,** *Northern Plains*
● *16" high, 12" wide*
Museum of the Plains Indian

This eagle-feather bonnet is
decorated with bells and dangles.
The beaded brow band is a
progression of double triangles of
light blue, with navy blue borders
and red centers on a white ground.
The quills of the eagle feathers are
decorated with red, wrapped, woolen
fabric, tied with white thread and
decorated with small bells. On either
side of the headband are quilled
rosettes with green and red circles of
quillwork around a plain leather
center. This is ringed overall with a
band of blue beads. From the
rosettes are suspended two bunches
of hawk feathers. Next to the rosettes
is a mirror. (MPI 978)

45. **Feather Bonnet,** *Sioux*
15" high, 8" diameter
Northwest Area Foundation

The feathers are dyed crimson with
tips of yellow-dyed horsehair attached
with plaster. The quills of the feathers
are bound with red stroud and grey
fluffs. The ermine drops are full pelts
with some green ribbon and a brass
bell. The brow band is predominantly
white with three stepped pyramids
interspersed with crosses of red, dark
blue, and silver faceted beads.
(SMM 1–1106)

46. **Feather Bonnet,** *Sioux*
19" high, 7" diameter
Northwest Area Foundation

This bonnet is made with eagle
feathers. Red horsehair and white
fluffs are attached to the tips of the
feathers with plaster. The base of the
feathers is wrapped with red
strouding and attached grey fluffs.
Feathers and ermine skins serve as
drops at the sides. The brow band is
beaded in a stepped pyramid pattern
of blue, green, and yellow in a white
background. (SMM 1–1109)

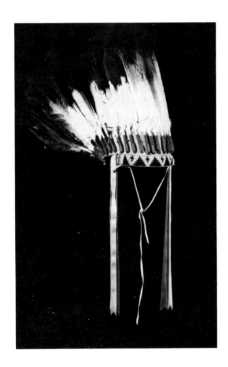

43. **Feather Bonnet,** *Northern Plains*
● *15½" high, 14" wide*
Museum of the Plains Indian

This bonnet has green and red
strouding at the base of the eagle
feathers. The headband is beaded in
a stepped pyramid of navy blue with
red outline and red and blue maltese
crosses on light blue. Ribbon side
drops are red and pink. (MPI 977)

Cat. 46

47. **Feather Bonnet,** *Crow*
17" high, 8" diameter
Northwest Area Foundation

This eagle-feather bonnet is made of undyed feathers bound at the base with light blue fluffs, red stroud, and strips of hide. The brow band is decorated with stepped pyramids of white and blue, set in a pink background. On each end of the band is a disc of yellow beads, with a design of light blue and red crosses, edged with white beads. Three tanned-hide strips hang from the center on each disc. These are bound with strips of red, and some have red fluffs at the ends. There are ribbon drops of blue, green, red, yellow, pink, and white. (SMM 1–1110)

48. **Feather Bonnet,** *Northern Plains*
16" high, 13¹/₂" wide
Museum of the Plains Indian

This eagle-feather bonnet is decorated with a quill-wrapped rawhide strip of orange and yellow. At the base of each feather is a red woolen fabric strip wrapping the feather and tying it to the felt cap. Small red feathers rise from the red cloth at the base. At the top of each feather is a small tassel of weasel fur and orange horsehair. The brow band is beaded with a design of orange inverted triangles, with a navy blue outline on a light blue background. There are weasel-fur side drops. The beaded band is further decorated with a band of printed cotton fabric. (MPI 1264)

49. **Feather Bonnet,** *Blackfeet*
● *15" high, 12" wide*
Museum of the Plains Indian

This bonnet is of spotted eagle feathers, wrapped at the base with red felt and tied with narrow strips of white, unsmoked leather. The tips of the feathers are decorated with red fluff feathers of indeterminate origin, glued to the eagle feathers with a white circular piece of fabric. The beaded brow band has a series of red triangles, with narrow blue bases on a white ground, pointing across the band. There are trailers of green, white, and blue ribbon. (MPI 1265)

52. **Feather Bonnet,** *Blackfeet*
16" high, 11" wide
Museum of the Plains Indian

The bonnet is of eagle feathers
tipped with red horsehair. The quills
are bound with red strouding and
buckskin. The brow band is beaded
with a stepped pyramid design of
blue and red, with red crosses
between them on a white
background. The band is bound with
red stroud. There are side drops of
ermine, brass, beaded chain, and
red and blue ribbons. (MPI 1413c)
Photo: page 130.

50. **Feather Bonnet,** *Blackfeet*
16¹/₂" high, 13" wide
Museum of the Plains Indian

This bonnet is fashioned from the tail
feathers of a golden eagle. There are
white fluffs at the tip of each feather
and around the base. The quills are
bound with red strouding and tanned
hide. The beaded brow band is a
row of triangles; the bottom ones are
red, while the top one is light blue
with a dark blue diving line. There
are discs at either end of the brow
band — a pink whorl with a dark blue
background. Tinsel borders the brow
band on the top. Eagle feathers and
fluffs with green, pink, and red
ribbons form the side drops.
(MPI 1266)
Additional photo: page 129.

51. **Feather Bonnet,** *Cheyenne or Sioux*
● *16¹/₂" high, 13" wide*
53" long trailer
Museum of the Plains Indian

Eagle feathers are placed on the
buffalo hide cap, which is lined with
a maroon, polka-dot, calico print. The
label indicates it was worn by the
"noted Chief Lonesome." The
streamers of buffalo hide are
interspersed periodically with
reddish-orange feathers. The beaded
brow band has green stepped
pyramids, with yellow and red or blue
centers, on a white background.
(MPI 1273)

Fig. 45 White Grass wearing roach.
Photograph courtesy of Burlington Northern Railroad

Roaches

Headdresses (Cat. 53) of deer and porcupine hair, referred to as roaches, were common throughout much of the Great Plains and Eastern Woodlands. Among the Sioux, for example, members of certain warrior societies, such as the Kit Foxes, were entitled to shave the sides of their heads. By cutting the central area short so the hairs stood erect and leaving the scalp lock intact, they in effect roached their hair (Hassrick 1964:18). It may be that originally these headdresses were signs of membership in particular clubs, but in reservation days, when warrior societies had lost their meaning, roaches became part of the costume of men engaged in social dancing, especially in the so-called Grass Dance.

Most roaches were equipped with a flat, carved bone, often engraved. Placed on the upper surface, it served to spread the hairs. To this spreader was attached a cylindrical bone into which an eagle feather was inserted in such a manner that it spun in response to the dancer's antics. Some roach spreaders were made with two cylinders so that two feathers could be worn. This example, rather than having a conventional spreader, has five trade mirrors sewn to the top.

Hair Extensions

Among the tribes of the Northern Plains, the Crow Indians were especially known for the fondness of their men for long hair. Some allowed their hair to grow to remarkable lengths. One of their leading chiefs in the mid-nineteenth century was known by the name of Long Hair. As a young man, he had a dream that he would become great in proportion to the length of his hair. By the age of fifty he was said to have had hair 36 feet long, although the trader Denig, who knew him well, reported that "no single stalk was longer than usual among females of our own color." This remarkable length was achieved by adding lengths of hair "stuck together with the gum of the pine tree" (Denig 1961:193–94).

As early as 1805, the first trader known to have traveled with, and left an account of, the Crow tribe reported: "Those whose hair is not long enough lengthen it with horsehair which they gum to their own and divide in the same manner as the others" (Larocque 1910:66–67).

Older Blackfeet Indians recalled that after they had settled on reservations, some of their men had their hair cut short. This was in response to pressure from the agents, who wanted them to become more like white men. However, the newly shorn Indians obtained from the Crow pendants of long hair that they could wear under their feather bonnets on "dress occasions" and thus create the illusion that they still possessed long hair.

One of these hair extensions in the Hill Collection appears to be of human hair and is 35 inches long (Cat. 55). The hair is suspended from a narrow transverse band with tie strings at each end. In the beaded design on the band are three swastikas separated by small diamonds on a white background. It is further decorated with five rows of small, red-painted discs of buckskin gummed to the hair. Whether or not this pendant was of Crow make, the hair pendant is certainly a Crow-style man's ornament.

Quilled Headdresses

Porcupine quilled headdresses, worn at the back of the head and possibly attached to the scalp lock, were worn by the men. Karl Bodmer's painting in 1834 of Fort Union shows a figure on horseback wearing such a headdress (Thomas and Ronnefeldt 1976:49). Cat. 56 is from the Sioux, with whom this type of ornament was popular. The quill-wrapped rawhide strips are attached to a piece of smoke-tanned hide, and from the bottom is suspended a white horse tail. Quilled strings dangle from the top, ending in red and green feathers and tin-can cones. It was not unusual for the wearer to insert one or two eagle feathers at the top.

53. **Roach Headdress,** *Northern*
● *Plains*
   13″ long, 2½″ wide
   Museum of the Plains Indian

   This roach headdress is of dyed
   porcupine and red deer hair. Five
   trade mirrors sewn to the top serve
   as a spreader. Braided horsehair is
   attached to the base. (MPI 1274)

54. **Hair Extension,** *Northern Plains*
   28″ long, 8″ wide
   Museum of the Plains Indian

   This hair attachment is of human hair,
   with a beaded band at the top. The
   beads are light royal blue and
   cardinal red, and are arranged in
   diagonal stripes. The hair hangs in
   locks wrapped in two rows with dyed
   cotton thread. The upper row of
   thread is yellow, while the lower
   fastenings are red. (MPI 1283)

55. **Hair Extension,** *Northern Plains*
   35″ long, 9″ wide
   Museum of the Plains Indian

   The hair hangs from a beaded band
   decorated with three swastikas
   separated by small diamonds on a
   white field. Rows of red-painted
   leather spots decorate the hair.
   (MPI 1284)

56. **Quilled Headdress,** *Sioux*
   39″ long, 2¼″ wide
   Museum of the Plains Indians

   The headdress is of quill-wrapped,
   rawhide strips attached to a piece of
   smoke-tanned hide, with a white
   horse tail at the base. The quills are
   dyed red, orange, yellow, aqua, and
   purple. Blue and white beads edge
   the hide backing. Quill-wrapped hide
   strips terminate with metal cones and
   green and red feathers. Two bone
   hairpipes are attached at the top of
   the headdress. (MPI 1324)

Men's Shirts and Leggings

Destruction of the buffalo did not deprive the Indians of Northern Plains of the basic materials they had been accustomed to using for ceremonial garment construction. Since aboriginal times, these Indians had made men's and boys' shirts and leggings from the skins of smaller mammals, such as the deer and bighorn sheep. Indians of wealth and position had preferred the lighter and still more finely textured skin of the antelope for summer wear. Even before these Indians settled on reservations, some of them wore clothing made of woolen blanketing or lighter fabrics furnished by traders. In early reservation days, Indian agents, whose duty was to bring civilized ways to the Indians, encouraged them to adopt "citizen dress" — which for men meant wearing of cloth shirts, coats, and trousers.

Yet Indians who actively participated in ceremonies persisted in wearing traditional styles of garments on such occasions. It made no difference whether these items were made by women of their own or neighboring tribes.

Men's skin shirts and leggings were originally made to match, employing the same designs in the long, quilled or beaded panels applied over the shoulders and over the long seams of sleeves and leggings. However, over the years, shirts and less highly valued leggings tended to become separated as their ownership was transferred from one Indian to another, or from an Indian to a non-Indian collector. Some Indians who wore beaded leggings could never afford a handsomely decorated skin shirt made to match.

Assiniboine and Sioux-Style Shirts

At the beginning of this century, Clark Wissler ventured the opinion that the porcupine-quilled men's shirts of the Blackfeet were of "an intrusive type since the decorations are almost identical with some observed among the Assiniboine" (Wissler 1910:122). Most likely those Assiniboine-like shirts owned by the Blackfeet at that time actually were made by Assiniboine craftswomen. During the 1940s and 1950s, elderly Blackfeet and Assiniboine men and women recalled that after the intertribals wars ended, these formerly hostile tribes exchanged visits and gifts. One of the articles the Blackfeet most desired at that time was the quilled shirt, but by then (the 1880s) Blackfeet women were doing very little quillwork.

Cat. 60 shows a very handsome shirt with quilled strips over the shoulders and down the arms, and a quilled neck flap in the form of an elongated U-shape. The neck opening is bound with strouding, and long skin fringes fall from the seams and bottom of the shirt. Underneath each of the neck flaps (at front and back), a thunderbird is painted in solid blue-green, suggesting that the shirt may have had a sacred value to its original owner (Plate 8). Both the cut and decoration of this shirt suggest that it is of Assiniboine origin about the turn of the century.

Cat. 59 pictures front and back views of another fine quilled shirt. The shirt is large and the over-shoulder strips are much longer than usual. The quills are applied in a six-row pattern providing a colorful design made up of small blocks of color, which is repeated in the decoration of the neck flap. This also appears to be in the Assiniboine style of about the 1900 period.

There are several beaded men's shirts in the Hill Collection that offer beaded designs of Siouan origin but that were also copied by Blackfeet beadworkers since ca. 1920. Since both Blackfeet and Assiniboine beaders employed the overlay stitch, the tribal origin of the shirts that show that method of applying the beads is doubtful.

Cat. 68, Cat. 70, and Cat. 81 bear Assiniboine designs but may have been made by a Blackfeet woman seeking to imitate Assiniboine beadwork. On the other hand, the shirt pictured in Cat. 67 employs the cross and pointed designs favored by western Sioux women. They are in lazy-stitch beading, so this piece probably is of Teton origin.

Blackfeet-Style Shirts

At the beginning of this century, Clark Wissler was told that the Blackfeet skin shirts decorated with weasel-tail pendants of hair locks were war shirts. Formerly considered sacred, these shirts were transferred from one owner to another in very definite ritual procedures as were horned bonnets and "straight-up" bonnets. That was the traditional way. But Wissler found that by his time, these shirts, "are now given and sold quite freely" (Wissler 1912:111–13). Informants considered the weasel-tail shirts to be an older type than was the shirt decorated only with hair locks, which they said was of Sioux origin.

The oldest Blackfeet shirt, and probably the oldest man's shirt, from any of the Northern Plains tribes in the Hill Collection appears in Cat. 62 and Plate 14. It exhibits several characteristics of shirts made and used by the Blackfeet before they settled down to reservation life in the 1880s, although that does not mean this shirt *could not* have been made at a later date. Its front and back are made of two deerskins with the leg extensions trailing at the sides. These skins are tied, not sewn together, at the sides. The bands applied over the shoulders and down the sleeves are relatively narrow and are decorated with the older "big beads" (also known as "pony beads") used by Blackfeet women before they began to employ the smaller "seed beads" not long before the buffalo days ended. The use of only two colors of these larger beads — blue and white — followed a precedent illustrated in Karl Bodmer's portraits of prominent Blackfeet leaders wearing decorated shirts in the summer of 1833 (Thomas and Ronnefeldt 1976:121, 134, 136). The neck flaps (at front and back) are of red strouding decorated with brass tacks, which contrast sharply with the color of the skin shirt, as do the spots painted on the upper portions of the body and sleeves. Pendants from the sleeves are both white weasel tails and locks of black hair. There is every indication that this handsome shirt is of a type that prevailed before 1875.

Two other weasel-tail shirts, cut in the older style with pendants of deer legs at the sides, are shown in Cat. 77 and Cat. 78. Both of these shirts are decorated with large beaded rosettes in the center of the front and back. These beaded rosettes replaced porcupine-quilled rosettes used earlier for these designs. In the summer of 1833, Prince Maximilian learned that the quilled rosettes appearing on Blackfeet men's shirts were a foreign fashion, recently borrowed from the Assiniboine to the east (Maximilian 1906:XXIII, 99). During the 1940s older Blackfeet Indians recognized shirts decorated with "water bugs" (tadpoles) and "file markings" (the parallel stripes) such as the one in Cat. 78 as old-style war shirts. These two shirts probably were made within the reservation period, but in cut and decoration, they hark back to earlier prototypes.

Karl Bodmer pictured the head chief of the Blood tribe, Bull's Back Fat, in 1833 wearing a red cloth shirt with skin sleeves, decorated with narrow bands of blue and white beads and "file markings" (Thomas and Ronnefeldt 1976:136). Dress shirts entirely of trade cloth were not uncommon among the Blackfeet in the reservation period. A handsome one of dark blue blanket cloth in the Hill Collection appears in Cat. 76. The use of light-colored beads as background in the chest rosette and the strips over the shoulders and down the sleeves caused these features to stand out sharply from the dark cloth garment. The neck opening is bound with red cloth, and the shoulder and arm seams, as well as the bottom of the shirt, are decorated with long, cut-skin fringes. A note on a tag attached to this shirt states that it was purchased from Eagle Tail Feathers, who was a Piegan. This shirt probably dates from the turn of the century.

The most unique and also the best-documented man's shirt in the Hill Collection may also be the most recent one. It appears in Cat. 82 and Fig. 30. This shirt was made by the wife of the prominent Piegan leader, Wades-in-the-Water, in partial fulfillment of a dream in which the white man's God appeared to him, and took pity on him, and gave him the power of this shirt. It is not a typical Blackfeet shirt at all. The triangular neck flap is a style favored by the Sioux. The 22 round red spots beaded on each of the sleeve panels are not forms commonly used in Blackfeet bead embroidery. The shirt lacks beaded over-shoulder panels. This shirt should remind us that the creation of articles resembling ones seen in dreams sometimes led to the making of novel items that were tribally atypical. In this dream, Wades-in-the-Water also was given a distinctive pattern of face painting consisting of lines of white dots on his cheeks and forehead. A portrait of Wades-in-the-Water wearing this shirt by the artist Langdon Kihn was exhibited at the Anderson Gallery in New York City in a show that opened March 20, 1922. The portrait was pictured in the catalogue of that exhibition.

Possibly Wades-in-the-Water's dream itself might have been influenced by his knowledge that one of the most famous war shirts among the Blackfeet during the second half of the nineteenth century was said to have been given to its first Indian owner by the white man's God in a dream. It had become known as "the Lord's shirt." Given to the warrior, Big Plume, on a war expedition, it was later worn as war medicine by the dreamer and his brother, Bear Chief, on several successful raids. Not one but several versions of this shirt survive in the present century (Ewers 1958:192–93).

Wades-in-the-Water's shirt was dreamed and created more than three decades after the intertribal wars ended. Even so, Wades-in-the-Water was himself a veteran of that warfare. As a teenager, he had taken the scalp of an Assiniboine, and he may have been the last Piegan to have taken an enemy scalp.

Cat. 57

Cat. 58

Cat. 59a

Cat. 59b

57. **Shirt,** *Sioux*
18" long, 18" wide shoulders
Northwest Area Foundation

This shirt is cut in modern fashion after a European prototype. Two skins are sewn at the shoulder and side seams leaving a circular neck opening. A front center opening with two brass buttons leads to a high collar. The placket is edged with a narrow line of pink-red quillwork. There are two breast pockets edged with fringe. The pockets have a quillwork cross and quarter moon in red, white, and orange. Above each pocket is a floral design in pink and orange. The shoulder, side, and arm seams are completely fringed. There is a yoke quill design in pink, scarlet, and orange, also fringed, on the back of the shirt. (SMM 49–88)

58. **Shirt,** *Unspecified tribe*
27" long, 20" wide shoulders
Northwest Area Foundation

This man's shirt, cut in poncho fashion, is decorated with quilled bands on the sleeves and body. The bands have a red background and a dark blue triangular design, with yellow squares in the center of each sequence. The bands are edged on one side with long fringe. The bottom of the shirt and edges of the sleeves are cut in a fringe-like pattern rimmed with a single line of ochre color. The neck is rimmed with a strip of fabric. (SMM 49–90)

59. **Shirt,** *Assiniboine*
33" long, 21" wide shoulders
Northwest Area Foundation

The body is two separate skins, joined at the shoulder seam, with a neck opening. The sleeves are semi-attached with the underseam tied by thongs. A sewn seam begins at elbow length. The sides are joined by thongs and decorated with quill bands, two on the body running from the front, over the shoulder seam, and down the back, and one on each arm. The colors are purple, yellow, scarlet, and green on a pink background. Long fringe runs down one side of each band. Quill triangular medallions adorn the front and back of the neck. The front medallion is slit and edged with fringe. (SMM 49–91)

Cat. 60a

Cat. 60b

Cat. 60c

60. **Shirt,** *Assiniboine*
● *25" long, 25" wide shoulders*
Northwest Area Foundation

This old-style man's shirt is of a single, unsmoked, soft hide, slit to form the neck opening, then folded to hang over the shoulders. The sides are open and held together with thongs. Sleeves are open from the shoulder seam to the elbow, then closed in a seam from elbow to cuff. The sleeves are fringed the full length and adorned by quillwork bands. A triangle pendant, fringed and covered with quillwork, hangs from the neck at front and back. The pendants each cover a painted bird. Attached to one pendant is a short lock of human hair bound in beadwork and adorned by an ivory button and a pony bead. (SMM 49–92)

Cat. 64a

Cat. 64b

61. **Shirt,** *Blackfeet (?)*
30" long, 24" wide shoulders
Northwest Area Foundation

This shirt in poncho fashion has deer leg ornamentation on the lower portion. The sides are closed by ties; the sleeve is sewn shut. The sleeve seams are fringed, as are the shoulder bands. Fringed pendants adorn the front and back. Bands of quillwork extend over both shoulders and down each sleeve. The design is orange, pink, and red. The area surrounding the front pendant is painted red. (SMM 49–93)

62. **Shirt,** *Blackfeet*
● *32" long, 24" wide shoulders*
Northwest Area Foundation

This shirt is of naturally shaped deerhides. The sleeves hang loose, ending in fringe. The yoke on both front and back is of red stroud cloth, decorated with brass buttons. Grey scalp locks dangle on the front yoke; dyed, yellow horsehair locks, on the back. The locks are bound with sinew and red fluffs. Four geometrically beaded strips descend from the shoulders, down each sleeve, in a pattern of green on white. The fringe on the sleeves is of ermine skins with red and green yarn and red fluffs and scalp locks, bound at the top with embroidery floss, quills, yarn, and large beads. The bodice is covered with brown painted spots. Fringed buckskin hangs from the shoulders and hem. (SMM 1–1040)

63. **Shirt,** *Northern Plains*
23" long, 25" wide shoulders
Northwest Area Foundation

This shirt is of deerskin with bead and quill decoration. It is cut poncho fashion, folded over, with a hole for the head. The sleeves are tubular, with the seam completely stitched to the wrist. The bottom is heavily fringed. Red blanket cloth covers the neck opening in a narrow band. The opening is decorated with a rectangular rawhide strip. (SMM 1–1043)

64. **Shirt,** *Assiniboine*
32" long, 16" wide shoulders
Museum of the Plains Indian

This skin shirt is decorated with quilled shoulder and sleeve strips and painted a yellow ochre color. Fringe hangs from the strips on the sleeve. The quillwork pattern is a series of diamonds — four abreast on each strip. Each of the two groups of diamond shapes is divided into a panel by a stripe of white, pink, and green quills. The diamonds are half purple and half white in a pink field. (MPI 1398)

Cat. 65a

Cat. 65b

Cat. 66a

Cat. 66b

65. **Shirt,** *Assiniboine*
26" long, 17" wide shoulders
Museum of the Plains Indian

This skin shirt is decorated with fringed, quilled shoulder strips, sleeve strips, and neck pieces. The primary decorations are purple triangles in a yellow background. There is a green stripe at the base, a set of three triangles with pink and purple zigzag design, and another green stripe. On the shoulder the triangles point to the center of a yellow field. On the arm the bases of triangles are together at the elbow. There are purple lines at the cuff end of the strip. The neck pieces have a geometric pattern in a strip in the center of a yellow field bordered in purple. The strip on the front is red, green, and yellow with a purple border; the strip on the back is a series of purple triangles tacked in a pink stripe. (MPI 1399)

66. **Shirt,** *Assiniboine*
22" long, 17" wide shoulders
Museum of the Plains Indian

This yellow-ochre painted skin shirt has quilled strips on the shoulders and sleeves. Long fringe hangs from the sleeves, shoulder strips, bottom hem, and throat pieces. Clipped crow feathers are attached to green felt on the shoulders. The quilled strips are pink with a row of long purple triangles on the bottom and top. Each strip is edged by three stripes of white, purple, and white. The throat pieces have a purple cross in the center of a pink field, bordered with purple. (MPI 1400)

67. **Shirt,** *Sioux*
33" long, 22" wide shoulders
Northwest Area Foundation

This shirt is of the old style — sewn with the skins of at least two animals, joined by a seam at the shoulders, with an opening for the head. At the front and back neck opening is a triangular, separate piece of skin, decorated by a beaded border. On the front, the pendant acts as a closing piece. Beaded bands pass over the shoulders and arms, with decoration in blue, yellow, silver metallic, and green beads on white. The sleeve and shoulder seams are fringed. Along the fringes and beaded bands are locks of hair, bound with strips of green flannel. The lower portion of the shirt is painted yellow-ochre. (SMM 49–89)

68. **Shirt,** *Northern Plains*
26" long, 20" wide shoulders
Northwest Area Foundation

This man's shirt is of modern cut with closed sleeves and side seams. One neck side is cut in a V, and two triangular pendants close the neck opening. The pendants are bordered by beaded bands with fringed edges. Beaded bands run over both sleeves and over the front and back of the shirt. Beading is in blue, light blue, green, orange, and white, in the overlay stitch. (SMM 49–96)

Cat. 69

69. **Shirt,** *Sioux or Assiniboine (?)*
31" long, 24" wide shoulders
Northwest Area Foundation

This shirt is in the modern style. It is cut from white, unsmoked skin, joined at the shoulder seams. A U-shaped neck opening replaces the slit triangular pendant. The sides are tied by leather thongs. The sleeves are closed, with small, fringed cuffs. Along the seam of each sleeve is long fringe. The bottom of the shirt is also fringed. Beaded bands run over each shoulder and sleeve, with a beaded decoration in dark blue, green, red, light blue, and yellow on white. The neck is bordered by several rows of beadwork. In the center of both front and back is a beaded circle with a cross-shaped emblem. All beading is lazy stitch. (SMM 49–97)

Cat. 70

70. **Shirt,** *Northern Plains*
25" long, 19" wide shoulders
Northwest Area Foundation

This man's shirt is of unsmoked skins sewn at the shoulders. Each side is open and tied with three leather thongs. The long sleeve seams are entirely edged in fringe, hanging 30" at its longest. The sleeves are attached to the body by a fringed seam across the top half of the sleeve. The neck opening is decorated by a triangular, beaded pendant at the front and back, also edged by fringe. The collar was once bordered with a strip of red cloth. The front neck pendant has red, light and dark blue, and yellow beads. The two beaded bands on the body contain a pattern of elongated isosceles triangles in dark blue against light blue. The border of the band is beaded in alternating yellow and orange. The bands on the sleeves are similar. (SMM 49–99)

71. **Shirt,** *Assiniboine*
25" long, 32" wide chest
Museum of the Plains Indian

The buckskin shirt has beaded panels at the throat and the back, two beaded shoulder strips, and a strip on each sleeve. There is short fringe on the front and back closing panels and long fringe on the sleeve. Most of the beadwork is white with geometric patterns in pink outlined with green. (MPI 1408)

72. **Shirt,** *Crow*
22" long, 21" wide shoulders
Museum of the Plains Indian

This hide shirt has twisted fringe along the back of the sleeve, and fringe over the shoulder seam. The sleeves are tailored, but the hide outlines are retained on the body. Red strouding surrounds the neck. There are geometric beaded shoulder strips, arm strips, and small panels in front and back. The primary colors are dusty pink, dark green, yellow, light blue, dark blue, and white. (MPI 1402)

Cat. 71a

Cat. 71b

Cat. 72a

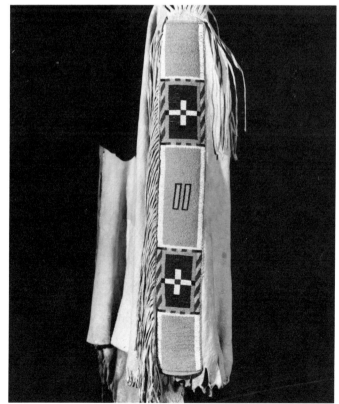

Cat. 72b

Cat. 73a

Cat. 73b

Cat. 74a

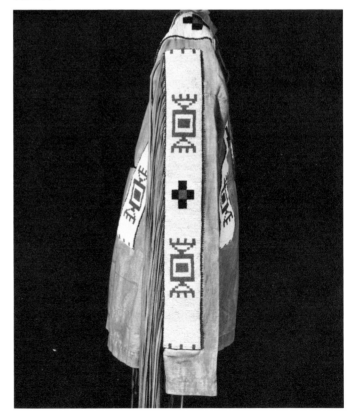

Cat. 74b

73. **Shirt,** *Blackfeet*
31" long, 23" wide shoulders
Museum of the Plains Indian

This buckskin shirt has decorated
throat pieces, shoulder strips, and
sleeve strips. Fringe of moderate
length hangs from the sleeves,
shoulder seams, throat pieces, sides,
and hem. The sleeves are lined with
cotton muslin. The throat pieces have
stylized floral motifs in red, blue,
green, and yellow, bordered in pink
and green. The back piece has a
different floral motif around a disc.
This panel is in several shades of
blue, red, and green. The shoulder
seams repeat the stylized floral motif
in red and blue with a border of pink
and blue. The sleeve strips are
geometric patterns on a solid white
field; one pyramid is in yellow and
dark blue with a pink and blue
border and the other is in yellow and
dark blue with diagonally placed
turquoise and yellow rectangles,
forming a double stripe. (MPI 962)

74. **Shirt,** *Blackfeet*
27" long, 20" wide shoulders
Museum of the Plains Indian

This canvas shirt has been painted in
imitation of tanned hides (buckskin). It
has beaded strips with a buckskin
backing over the shoulders and on
the arms, and triangular neck pieces
on front and back. Long buckskin
fringe hangs from the arm strips. The
bead patterns on the shoulder strips
and the arm strips are in orange and
blue on white. The neck piece
repeats one of the designs on the
strips in orange bordered by small
orange rectangles, a single line of
blue, and loops of orange. (MPI 963)

75. **Shirt,** *Blackfeet (?)*
33" long, 20" wide shoulders
Northwest Area Foundation

This shirt is decorated with beaded
bands running from front to back and
over the sleeves. The design is the
same for each strip and is in navy
blue, green, yellow, and red against a
light blue background. The fringe
attached to the outer edges of each
band is ornamented with ermine
pelts. The neck opening is bound
with red trade cloth. Matches Cat.
109. (SMM 1–1112)

Cat. 76a

Cat. 76b

76. **Shirt,** *Blackfeet*
30" long, 32" wide
Northwest Area Foundation

This woolen shirt is made from
strouding. It is decorated with white
fringe along the bottom, as well as
across the back of the shoulder
seam, and along the length of each
sleeve. The neck opening is banded
with red cloth. Bands beaded in spot
stitch pass over each shoulder and
down each arm. The sewn-in
shoulder and sleeve fringes are of
buckskin, wrapped intermittently with
quills. White weasel skins and silk
ribbons hang from each shoulder.
(SMM 1–1044)

Cat. 77a

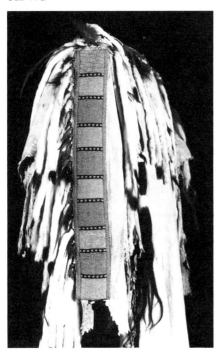

Cat. 77b

77. Shirt, *Blackfeet*
37" long, 20" wide shoulders
Museum of the Plains Indian

This buckskin shirt is cut in the old style, with the original lines of the animal skin present. Ermine skins fall in profusion from the beaded strips on the sleeve and the beaded panel on the front. The ermine skins are decorated with brightly dyed feathers of green, yellow, blue, orange, purple, red, and pink with round brass beads and bells. Scalp locks, tied with sinew and porcupine quills, brass and glass beads, feathers, and cloth, are attached to the red strouding at the neck opening. The scalp locks include a pair of black braids and two bunches of reddish hair bound with ermine strips. Beaded strips on the sleeve have light blue, and pink squares divided by a stripe of blue and yellow. Beaded panels across the shoulders are white with a dark blue geometric pattern repeated four times. The beaded disc at center front has a centered four-pointed star of dark blue, light blue, and pink, in a field of white with circles of dark blue green, and pink. Pink ribbon is attached to the ermine. (MPI 1401)

Cat. 78

78. Shirt, *Blackfeet*
32" long, 22" wide shoulders
Museum of the Plains Indian

This buckskin shirt is of more recent cut and painted an ochre color with tadpole designs; the sleeves are tailored. Stripes go around the arms. There is red strouding at the neck with bunches of human hair bound at the top with buckskin and orange fluffs, alternating with ermine skins as fringe. The ermine is bound with red strouding and thongs with the same fluffs. Beaded strips on the sleeve have royal blue background with stepped, half yellow and half red pyramids outlined in dark blue. Shoulder strips are beaded with a stepped, right triangle motif in pink, yellow, and dark blue. The discs have three beaded geometric figures in orange, red, and blue against royal blue. A tassel is in the center of the disc. Hair and ermine tassels form fringe on the arms. (MPI 1403)

Cat. 79a

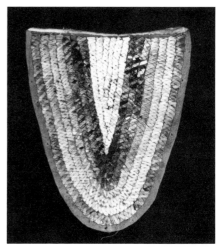

Cat. 79b

79. **Shirt,** *Blackfeet*
26" long, 19" wide shoulders
Museum of the Plains Indian

This tailored shirt has beaded strips over the shoulders and on the sleeves, with geometric motifs of triple diamonds and stars on a green field. Each design has a yellow square in the center, with diamonds or stars in red. The triangular neck pieces are decorated with plaited quillwork in a pattern following the contour of the triangle. The colors, from outside to inside, are red, yellow, purple, and white. Ermine tails, capped with red strouding, fall from the neck pieces and the beaded strips on the arms. The ermine tails on the sleeves have colored feathers attached to the tips — fuschia on the left sleeve and blue on the right. Red stripes are painted across the chest, the back, and around the sleeves. (MPI 1404)

Cat. 80a

Cat. 80b

80. **Shirt,** *Blackfeeet*
30" long, 15" wide shoulders
Museum of the Plains Indian

This skin shirt has long fringe on the back of the sleeve and around the front of the neck panels. The shoulder and sleeve panels have rose-red stars in a light blue field. The front and back neck panels are triangular in shape with a striped geometric pattern of beadwork in aqua, turquoise, orange, and green. The edge of the triangle has a string of openwork beads in royal blue. The long fringes on the sleeves are strung with green and pink tubular beads. (MPI 1405)

Cat. 81a

Cat. 81b

81. **Shirt,** *Northern Plains*
30" long, 20" wide shoulders
Museum of the Plains Indian

This buckskin shirt has beaded strips on the sleeves and over the shoulders. Neck pieces appear on the front and back. Long fringe hangs from the beaded panels. The beaded patterns are crosses of brass faceted beads bordered with red and white, a triple diamond with the top half in dark blue and bottom in white, and a white inverted U — all on royal blue. The neck pieces are triangular with a V-shaped design alternating in white, yellow, and red. (MPI 1406)

Cat. 82a

Cat. 82b

Cat. 82c, Cat. 33, Cat. 42, Cat. 106

82. **Shirt,** *Blackfeet*
31" long, 19" wide shoulders
Museum of the Plains Indian

This beaded buckskin shirt was
made by Julia Wades-in-the-Water for
her husband, Wades-in-the-Water. The
shirt is made in the modern style. It
has beaded sleeve strips and throat
pieces. The pattern on the sleeves
consists of two rows of red circles on
white, ending in a triple diamond in
the same colors. The throat pieces
are triangular with stripes of turquoise
interrupted by red triangles. There is
fringe around the throat pieces and
on the sleeves. (MPI 1407)

83. **Shirt,** *Blackfeet (?)*
33" long, 19" wide shoulders
Northwest Area Foundation

Quilled bands adorn this shirt along
the sleeves and over each shoulder.
Long fringe hangs from the sleeves.
A triangular quillwork pendant
featuring a five-pointed star hangs at
the neck. The pendant is also
decorated with fringe. (SMM 49–95)

Cat. 83

Indian-made Shirt of Non-Indian Style

The handsome buckskin shirt shown in Cat. 85 is Indian-made but follows a non-Indian pattern that includes turned-down collar, turned-up cuffs, patch pockets, and a long vertical panel covering the buttons on the upper front. These are combined with cut-skin fringes pendant from the sleeves and beaded decoration on collar, cuffs, pockets, and panel. The elaborate cartouche on the pocket suggests this shirt was made as a gift for, or on the order from, a particular individual. The floral beadwork is in the Metis style, but this shirt could have been made by an Indian woman of one of the tribes on the Northern Plains about the turn of the century.

Boy's Suit

Cat. 85 pictures an Indian-made suit for a small boy comprised of a buckskin jacket and trousers to match. Both garments appear to be adapted from wearing apparel of white manufacture. The shirt is long-sleeved, with a four-button front opening, four patch pockets, and a low collar. To give it something of an Indian character, cut-buckskin fringes are inserted at the shoulder seams, and the pockets are decorated with quillwork. The trousers have a fly, but they are decorated with cut fringes along the vertical seams and bands of floral quillwork.

The floral designs in the quillwork appear to be of Metis origin. It is less likely that this suit was made for an Indian boy than that it was made with great care by an Indian woman of one of the tribes of the Northern Plains as a gift to the child of a non-Indian friend. It is tempting to think that it might have been intended for a young relative of Louis W. Hill, Sr., but there is no documentation to prove that.

Matching Leggings and Shirts

Cats. 86 and 87 form a set of matching shirt and leggings. The beaded strips on the shirt match the beaded strips on the outside of the leggings. Headdresses and moccasins could be added in the dominant pattern to complete the handsome ensemble.

84. **Shirt,** *Northern Plains*
31" long, 20" wide shoulders
Northwest Area Foundation

This Indian-made, non-Indian style shirt has floral beadwork decorations. (SMM 1–1042)

85. **Boy's Suit,** *Cree*
37" long, 12¹/₂" wide
Museum of the Plains Indian

This two-piece boy's suit is patterned after the white man's clothing. There is fringe along the shoulders and across the back and quillwork in a floral pattern on the four pockets, the back shoulder yoke, and on the trousers. The quills are dyed pink, green, purple, yellow, red, and white. (MPI 959)

Cat. 86, Cat. 87, Cat. 32, Cat. 50

86. **Shirt,** *Blackfeet*
32" long, 22" wide shoulders
Museum of the Plains Indian

This skin shirt has beaded strips on the sleeve and shoulder and at the neck. The pattern on the strips is a large double buffalo track in yellow and red with a black cross in the center, in an aqua field. This pattern is repeated three times. Each design is separated from the others by a triple diamond with a yellow center and dark blue outline. The neck piece has a four-pointed star of red and yellow, alternating with four white teardrops in a black field, above a white cross, in a field of aqua. There are ermine skins wrapped with red stroud, intermixed in the fringe at the sleeve. There is buckskin fringe off the shoulder strips and around the neck pieces. Three small ermine tails are attached to the bottom of the triangular neck piece with a brass button. There are red fluffs on the ermine fringe. Matches Cat. 87. (MPI 1413a)

87. **Leggings,** *Blackfeet*
31" long, 16" wide
Museum of the Plains Indian

This pair of buckskin leggings has cuffs laced with red stroud. The beaded strips are yellow and red in an aqua field. A red Maltese cross is on the inside of the leg. The beaded strips have a double buffalo track design, in yellow and red in an aqua field. Matches Cat. 86. (MPI 1413b)

129

88. Shirt, *Blackfeet*
36" long, 21" wide shoulders
Museum of the Plains Indian

This skin shirt is cut in the modern style. There is skin fringe at the shoulders, beaded arms, and shoulder strips, and a medallion at the neck. The beaded panels are decorated with geometric patterns in black, yellow, and red on royal blue. The discs have jagged lines in the same colors, radiating from a central red circle, and an ermine skin at the center. (MPI 1414a)

89. Man's Leggings, *Blackfeet*
35" long, 15½" wide
Museum of the Plains Indian

This pair of skin leggings is decorated with beaded strips, with a triangular spot on the inside. The strips are light blue with a dark blue border and red stepped pyramids outlined in dark blue. The triangular spot is beaded in the same colors. There is fringe along the side. (MPI 1414b)

Cat. 88, Cat 89, Cat. 34, Cat. 52

Fig. 46 Sumner W. Matteson's photograph of Assiniboine young man at Sun Dance encampment on Fort Belknap Reservation, 1906, wearing trousers, vest, gauntlets, and cowboy hat. *Photograph courtesy of the National Anthropological Archives, Smithsonian Institution*

Men's Leggings

A fine pair of buckskin leggings in the Hill Collection, pictured in Cat. 109, matches the shirt in Cat. 75. The shape of the neck flap and the variant of the feather design in the beaded panels indicate that these garments are of Assiniboine style, even though they might have been made by a Blackfeet woman in imitation of Assiniboine work during the early years of the century. The leggings are of an older and closer-fitting pattern than the pair in Cat. 107, which has a broad, trailing flap decorated in floral beadwork. In addition, they have a vertical strip beaded with a row of pyramid-like forms composed of small rectangles, which the Blackfeet referred to as "mountain designs." Although the Assiniboine used these designs, it is most likely that these leggings were made by the Blackfeet during the early decades of this century.

The designs appearing on the broad, beaded strips of another paid of skin leggings are of Sioux type (Cat. 93). Even so, the beads are embroidered in the overlay stitch suggesting that the work was done by an Assiniboine or possibly a Blackfeet woman after the turn of the century.

The leggings in Cat. 103 are fashioned of blanket cloth with muslin strings for attaching them to the wearer's belt. They are decorated with vertical strips on the outside of the leg and beaded in the "mountain design" so popular with the Blackfeet.

The leggings in Cat. 94 show the outside of one and the inner side of the other. They are of blue blanket cloth with green cotton trim, rendered still more colorful by use of floral designs in the beadwork on the vertical panels. The beadwork is in the Metis style, but the tribe of origin has not been determined.

In the Hill Collection are several pairs of leggings made of blanket cloth on which the decoration is confined largely to a rectangular area at the bottom of the front of each legging. A fine example appears in Cat. 97. These leggings are of red Hudson's Bay blanket cloth, and the beaded rectangles and the elaborated U-shapes above them are applied to green trade cloth. These leggings probably are of Crow origin.

There is historical justification for referring to leggings decorated with such rectangular panels at their bottoms as "Crow-style leggings." They were worn by Crow chiefs who were members of the first delegation from their tribe to visit Washington, where they were photographed in 1873. That was a decade before the disappearance of the buffalo in Crow country. The leggings were also worn by Crow chiefs, led by Plenty Coups who visited Washington in 1880, and they are found in well-documented collections from the Crow Indians (Wildschut and Ewers 1959:9 –10, Figs. 2, 10). Even so, Blackfeet and Flathead men were photographed wearing leggings of this type only a few years after the buffalo were gone. Among the young Piegan warriors who posed for the group photograph at Old Agency on the Blackfeet Reservation in 1888 (Fig. 24) are several men known to have been members of the last generation of Blackfeet to have participated in intertribal horse raiding. Observe that they wore this style of leggings made of blanket cloth with cloth shirts obtained ready-made from white traders.

An example of the Crow-style leggings made of skin appears in Cat. 104. It is not necessarily any older than the blanket cloth leggings. The leggings pictured in Cat. 100 are of green blanket cloth, and the base material of the rectangular patch is of red cloth. The simplified floral units in the beadwork indicate Metis influence. Leggings decorated with floral beadwork appeared among the Crow Indians at least as early as the 1890s and were popular among them during the early decades of this century. Some of the leggings of this Crow style appear to have been decorated by applying beaded women's leggings to the blanketing material to form the bottom rectangular decoration. Possibly this borrowing of the form of the women's leggings to provide decoration for a man's leggings explains the origin of the Crow-style leggings among the tribes of the Northern Plains.

Beaded Buckskin Trousers

Cat. 111 shows front and back views of a pair of Indian-made buckskin trousers, beaded on the front with six pairs of crossed United States flags and on the back with the same number of rectangular cross-hatched designs. In addition, narrow bands of beadwork were applied about the waist and bottoms of each leg, with other beaded lines around the legs above the banded beadwork and in vertical lines on the outside of the garment extending from bottom to top bands. Most probably these trousers were intended for Indian wear in Fourth of July parades rather than as a present for a white man. One of Sumner Matteson's photographs (Fig. 46) taken on the Fort Belknap Reservation pictures a young Assiniboine or Gros Ventres man wearing a combination of garments, which included a pair of fringed buckskin trousers, beaded gauntlet gloves, a dark cloth vest, striped cloth shirt, and a cowboy hat! The trousers in the Hill Collection may be of about the same period as that photo — 1906.

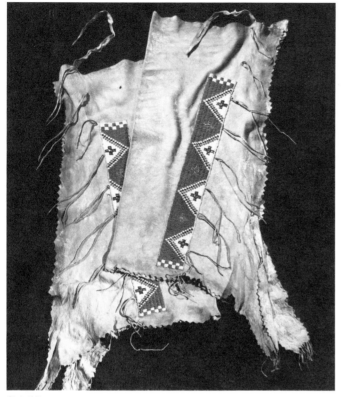

Cat. 90

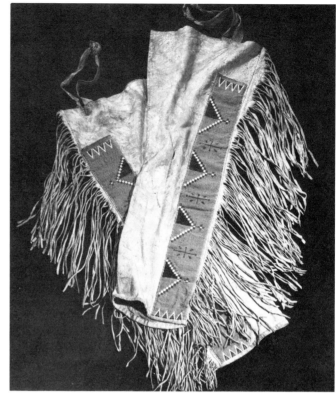

Cat. 91

Cat. 92

Cat. 93

90. **Man's Leggings,** *Arapahoe,*
Cheyenne, Sioux (?)
30½" long, 15" wide
Northwest Area Foundation

This pair of man's leggings is made
of unsmoked skin — one hide for
each legging. The beaded strip
attached to the side seam of each
legging has a triangular motif in
white, red, gold, orange, and light
blue against a darker blue
background. This strip was sewn
separately with lazy stitch onto a
piece of skin and attached to the
legging. A narrow stripe of red-ochre
paint appears along the bottom and
side edges of each legging.
(SMM 49–63)

91. **Man's Leggings,** *Shoshone (?)*
31" long, 13½" wide
Northwest Area Foundation

This pair of man's leggings is made
of single, unsmoked skins. A
separate fringed piece has been
added, along a beaded band with a
design in silver, white, red, and yellow
on a green background. The bottom
rim of the legging is hemmed and
has no fringe. The beaded band
is woven and attached to a separate
piece of skin that is sewn to the
legging. (SMM 49–64)

92. **Man's Leggings,** *Sioux*
Arapahoe, Cheyenne group
30" long, 16" wide
Northwest Area Foundation

This pair of man's leggings is made
of single unsmoked skins. The thong
forms a decorative fringe along the
stitching. The bottoms of the leggings
are full and trailing. The beaded
decoration has a vertical strip running
the length of each legging, with a
triangular motif in blue, red, gold,
white, and yellow against a white
beaded background. The base of
each strip consists of three narrow
bands of red, white, and blue.
(SMM 49–66)

93. **Man's Legging,** *Northern Plains*
29" long, 12" wide
Northwest Area Foundation

This pair of leggings has a beaded
strip running the length of the side.
Four narrow blue beaded bands are
attached to each design, running
across the bottom half at regularly
spaced intervals. The long vertical
beaded strip contains designs in
black, mustard, red, blue, and lighter
blue beads in a feather design, on a
white beaded background. The
leggings are fringed vertically down
the outer sides. Shorter fringe rings
the bottoms. The tops have a thong
for attachment to a belt.
(SMM 49–67)

94. **Man's Leggings,** *Northern Plains*
30" long, 13½" wide
Northwest Area Foundation

This pair of man's leggings is of navy
blue blanket material, with the lower
and outer edges in green fringed
cloth. The side seams have leather
thongs and bells descending the
length of each leg. There is an
asymmetrical floral design on each
legging of pink, blue, white, light and
dark green, and brick-red beads.
(SMM 49–68)

95. **Leggings,** *Northern Plains*
30" long, 12½" wide top
Northwest Area Foundation

These red felt leggings are decorated
with geometrically beaded strips. The
fringes are of the same cloth, cut
slightly on the bias to flare at the
bottom. The fringe is enhanced by
selvege decoration. (SMM 49–69)

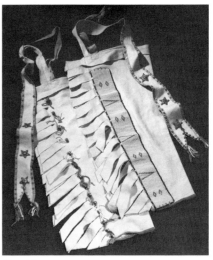

Cat. 96

96. **Man's Leggings,** *Assiniboine (?)*
28" long, 10¹/₂" wide
Northwest Area Foundation

This pair of man's leggings is of orange blanketing folded on a slight bias and fringed. There is a thin strip of red velvet-like material rimming the bottoms. Spaced along the outer edge of each legging are thongs of red, white, and blue yarn with metal stars attached. Along the outer seam edge of each legging is a beaded band set on canvas, with a design of triangles and alternating diamonds sewn to the canvas by the overlay stitch. The whole piece is attached to the orange cloth legging material. (SMM 49–70)

97. **Man's Leggings,** *Crow*
30" long, 13" wide
Northwest Area Foundation

The leggings are of blue blanket cloth. A cloth thong at the hip attaches the leggings to a belt. Decoration consists of spaced skin thongs and a beaded, rectangular red woolen cloth. (SMM 49–71)

98. **Man's Leggings,** *Blackfeet (?)*
38¹/₂" long, 15" wide
Northwest Area Foundation

This pair of leggings is made from purple blanket cloth. There is a rectangular panel on the bottom of the legging. A narrow strip of red cloth borders the lower and outside edges. The panel is rimmed in white beads and contains a beaded floral design in yellow, red, light and dark blue, light green, and pink. Above the panel on the outside edge is a parabola-shaped medallion of the same fabric, edged with beads. (SMM 49–72)

Cat. 99

99. **Man's Leggings,** *Blackfeet (?)*
29¹/₂" long, 13" wide
Northwest Area Foundation

These leggings are of blue strouding with a white selvege at the outside edge. A thin strip of yellow fabric runs along the bottom rim. Attached to the bottom of the strip is a white cloth fringe running up the outer side flap. A lengthwise rectangular panel, bordered with a thin strip of print cloth surrounding a thicker border of white beads, is at the base. The interior of the rectangle is composed of red fabric set in four vertical rectangular panels, interspersed with three strips of beadwork in blue, red, yellow, pink, and green. (SMM 49–73)

100. **Man's Leggings,** *Northern Plains*
31" long, 14¹/₂" wide
Northwest Area Foundation

These Crow-style leggings are of dark green blanket material, trimmed on the outer and bottom edges with strips of lavender and red cloth. A rectangular patch of red felt cloth at the lower part is trimmed by light blue beads. The design is in green, yellow, light and dark blue, and gold metallic beads. A four-petaled, red beaded flower outlined in blue is sewn onto green fabric above the red cloth. (SMM 49–74)

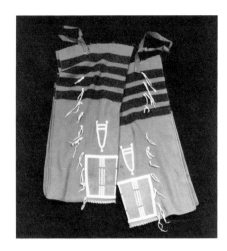

101. **Man's Leggings,** *Crow*
33¹/₂" long, 15" wide
Northwest Area Foundation

This pair of leggings is made of
a red Hudson's Bay blanket. The
bottom is bound with green wool. A
green wool panel near the bottom
has a beaded decoration with a white
border and light blue, yellow, red,
and dark blue stripes. Another green
wool figure above this has a border
of white beads. Tanned hide laces
are used to form the seam.
(SMM 49–288)

102. **Man's Leggings,** *Blackfeet*
31" long, 13" wide
Northwest Area Foundation

These leggings are identified as
having belonged to Fish Wolf Robe.
They are made of a single piece of
skin that has been folded and
fringed. The beadwork band, applied
as a strip to the hide, consists of red,
yellow, and blue beads against a
white beaded background. A
distinctive red beaded insignia
resembling an inverted A is sewn
directly on the inside of the legging
by the lazy stitch. Small leather
thongs strung with brass beads are
attached to the lower half of the
legging. The lower edge has been
cut in a tooth pattern. (SMM 54–19a)

104. Man's Leggings, *Crow*
26" long, 10" wide
Museum of the Plains Indian

These leggings are heavily fringed at
the side seams, while the thongs
are only slightly fringed. A red strouding
square at the bottom of each legging
is decorated with beadwork and red
strouding strips. The beadwork is
executed in light blue, black, and
red, with a diagonal chain weave on
the two central strips. (MPI 1340)

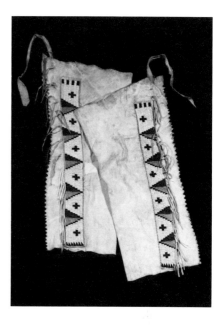

105. Man's Leggings, *Assiniboine*
28" long, 11" wide
Museum of the Plains Indian

These beaded buckskin leggings
have serrated edges. A series of
thongs runs down the outer edge of
the beaded strip. The colors of the
strip are blue, yellow, and red against
a white background ornamented with
pyramids and crosses. The pyramids
are outlined in blue and split into red
and yellow halves. The crosses have
blue arms and a red center square.
(MPI 1341)

103. Man's Leggings, *Northern Plains*
31½" long, 13" wide
Museum of the Plains Indian

These leggings are of blue strouding,
rimmed with yellow-orange fabric. A
beaded strip of buckskin decorates
each legging in a stepped pattern on
a white background. The colors are
red, yellow, blue, and green. The
thongs are of muslin. (MPI 1078)

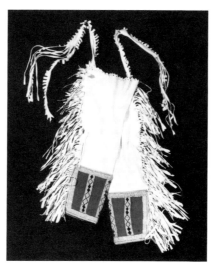

Cat. 104

106. Man's Leggings, *Blackfeet*
35" long, 10" wide
Museum of the Plains Indian

This pair of buckskin leggings is decorated with a beaded strip and a triangular spot. There is fringe along the outside seam and around the triangle. The pattern on the strip is of white, stacked hourglass figures. Two of these figures appear side by side in a dark red field. The pattern is repeated three times. (MPI 1342)
Photo: page 126.

107. Man's Leggings, *Blackfeet*
32" long, 15" wide
Museum of the Plains Indian

These leggings of white unsmoked leather have a beaded strip with a white, lilac, teal blue, and red checkerboard design on a light blue background. A strip of reddish leather in a scalloped pattern appears along the outer edge of the beaded strip. A floral design decorates the lower half of the legging. (MPI 1344)

108. Man's Leggings, *Gros Ventres (?)*
32" long, 14" wide
Northwest Area Foundation

This pair of smoke-tanned leggings is decorated with green twined fringe. The beadwork consists of circle and feather designs next to a beaded border strip and amber-colored pony beads knotted into the fringe. (SMM 1–1056)

Cat. 109

109. Man's Leggings, *Northern Plains*
33" long, 14" wide
Northwest Area Foundation

This pair of skin leggings has fringe along the outer side seams. Brown and red spots are painted on the body. A beaded band worked in geometric patterns on an orange background runs the outer length of each legging. Matches Cat. 75. (SMM 1–1111)

110. Chaps, *Sioux*
36" long, 10" wide bottom
Northwest Area Foundation

These Western-style cowboy chaps are joined in the front and are open at the back. They are made of unsmoked hide lined with white cotton cloth. Geometric beaded strip decoration and regularly placed thongs adorn the sides of the chaps. (SMM 49–65)

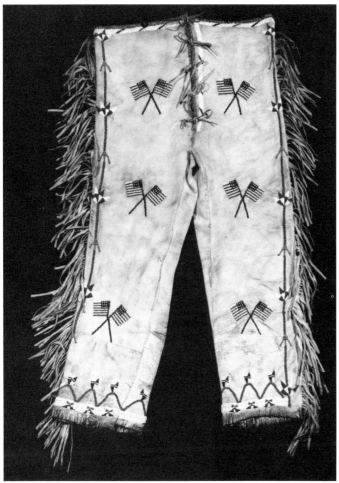

Cat. 111a

Cat. 111b

111. **Man's Trousers,** *Northern Plains*
35½" long, 17" wide
Museum of the Plains Indian

These leather trousers have
beadwork on both sides and fringe
on the edges. The front is decorated
with American flags in red, white,
and green, strategically placed up
and down the length of each leg. The
front and back fringed side seams
are beaded in a linear design of
green, white, red, and blue. The
back has small checkered squares in
green and white (resembling
semaphore flags), interspersed with
red and white beaded crosses. A
yellow cloth ties across the small of
the back. The top is rimmed with a
red calico strip and the bottom is
fringed. (MPI 960)

Vests

Indian men of the Northern Plains adopted the custom of wearing vests from the whites. Some young men among the Western Sioux were wearing vests more than a century ago — a year or more before Sioux and Cheyenne warriors decisively defeated Custer's cavalry on the Little Bighorn in 1876. In 1879 L. A. Huffman photographed a Sioux man clad in an elaborately beaded vest that included beaded representations of an elk and American flags (Hanson 1982:4). Although the Sioux were probably the first Indians of this region to wear beaded vests, photographs taken around the turn of this century on many reservations of the Northern Plains and the adjacent plateau west of the Rockies show men wearing decorated vests. The Sioux liked to dress small boys in miniature versions of men's beaded vests.

Although Indians made some vests of buckskin following patterns of white men's vests, the great majority of Indian vests were fashioned of commercial cloth to which the Indians added decoration to the front and back or to the front surface alone. A fine example from the Hill Collection is a Sioux vest completely covered with colorful quillwork (Cat. 112). While only geometric designs appear on the front of this garment, two elk and two eagles appear on the back. The Sioux regarded elk power as a very potent love medicine. Probably this vest was made to be worn by a young Sioux dandy during the early years of this century.

The vest in Cat. 115 is more typical of Sioux work during the early twentieth century. Two large and typically Sioux geometric designs stand out from a solid background of light-colored beads.

Many vests beaded in large floral designs were worn by young men from the Cree tribe westward; the Flathead, and their neighbors west of the Rockies, wore floral-design vests during the early years of this century. This testifies to the widespread acceptance of Metis-style symbols among these tribes, by that time. Cat 119 offers a well-documented example from the Blackfeet. The name "Philip B. H." executed in beads at the upper right may indicate that this garment was originally intended for a person of that name. But photographs taken in the mid-1920s show this vest worn by Fish Wolf Robe, a well-known Piegan dancer, who was a member of a large party of Blackfeet recruited by Louis Hill, Sr., to participate in the celebration of the centennial of railroading in America at Baltimore, Maryland, in 1927.

Vests made of dark cloth served as background for floral designs in bead embroidery as in Cat. 121. Photographs of prominent Blackfeet and Flathead Indians show that such vests were worn by men of some prominence among these tribes before 1910.

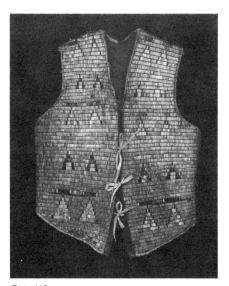

Cat. 112a

Cat. 113a

114. **Vest,** *Blackfeet (?)*
15½″ long, 13″ wide
Museum of the Plains Indian

The front of this vest is beaded in a diamond pattern. The diamonds have green centers and are bordered with a single row of red and a double row of royal blue beads. They are set in a field of grey translucent beads. The field is bordered by a double row of green beads and purple fabric. The back of the vest is of black cotton. (MPI 952)

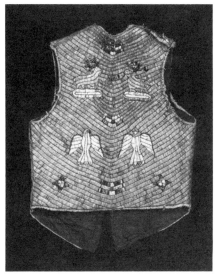

Cat. 112b

112. **Boy's Vest,** *Sioux*
● *14″ long, 14″ wide*
Museum of the Plains Indian

This vest is decorated with quillwork. The front has a stepped pyramid motif repeated in pairs ten times, two pockets, and hide ties. The colors are orange, green, blue, yellow, and purple on red. The inside is lined with a dark cotton cloth. The neck, arm openings, and bottom are bound with green thread. The back shows a pair of birds, a pair of elk, two four-pointed stars, and geometric patterns in the same colors. (MPI 1409)

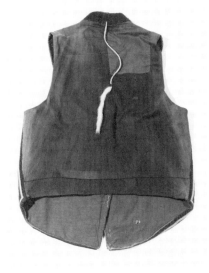

Cat. 113b

113. **Vest,** *Blackfeet*
25½″ long, 19″ wide
Museum of the Plains Indian

This vest has a beaded front and a red and green cloth back. There is an ermine-tipped thong at the base of the neck. The beading is solid throughout the front of the vest. The background is red with yellow borders, blue stars, and moons, outlined in yellow. (MPI 946)

Cat. 115, Cat. 129, Cat. 135, Cat. 7

115. Vest, *Sioux*
22" long, 18" wide
Museum of the Plains Indian

This beaded buckskin vest has a lining of muslin. The vest is bound in black velvet around the front opening, neck, armholes, and hem, with skin fringe along the hem. The front ties are pink ribbon. The beaded pattern on the front is a large, stepped diamond with triangles at the top and bottom and arrows at the side points. The diamonds and triangles are blue, yellow, and red. There is a yellow, light blue, and brass cross in the center of the diamond. The arrows are blue, and an E appears on the bases of the blue triangles. This motif is repeated on a white field on each half of the front and enlarged on the back. Blue beads and brass spots border the sides, armholes, and front opening. (MPI 1411)

Cat. 116a

Cat. 116b

116. **Vest,** *Assiniboine*
15" long, 17" wide
Museum of the Plains Indian

This fully beaded best has a light blue background with patterns in blue, red, yellow, green, black, pink, white, and dark blue. An eight-pointed star encloses a red square with a border of black and white accents. The points are dark blue with pink accents. A geometric figure is yellow, red, green, and black. The bottom border is a red and white sawtooth pattern. The vest is edged with purple cloth, and the front is closed with pearl buttons. (MPI 1412)

117. **Vest.** *Northern Plains*
19½" long, 15" side
Northwest Area Foundation

The outside of this three-piece skin vest is completely covered with beadwork, while the inside is lined in a black figured cloth. Geometric patterns decorate the front of the vest, and four thong ties are attached to the front closing. (SMM 49–85)

118. **Vest,** *Blackfeet (?)*
19" long, 14" wide
Northwest Area Foundation

The beaded floral decoration on this vest is applied only to the front which is made of canvas covered with red flannel and lined with cotton sateen. The back of the vest is made of soft skin and also is lined in sateen. (SMM 49–86)

119. **Vest,** *Blackfeet*
23" long, 20" wide
Museum of the Plains Indian

This vest has a beaded front and upholstery fringe at the armholes and bottom. A symmetrical floral design has a light blue background. The flowers and leaves are stylized in green, dark red, orange, mauve, light green, and yellow. Red cloth edges the beadwork. (MPI 945)

120. **Vest,** *Northern Plains*
29" long, 19" wide
Museum of the Plains Indian

This beaded vest has a white background with a twining floral design in three shades of green. The flowers are beaded in red, white, blue, yellow, dark blue, orange, grey, grey-brown, and lilac. (MPI 948)

121. **Vest,** *Blackfeet*
22½" long, 18" wide shoulders
Museum of the Plains Indian

This vest has a beaded floral pattern on a black wool background. The floral pattern includes white stems, two shades of green leaves, with flowers and buds in pink, mauve, light blue, dark blue, and yellow. There are metal buttons around the arm, neck, and front openings. A purple binding runs around the neck, arms, front, and bottom. The back of the vest is black cotton. (MPI 951)

Cat. 122a

Cat. 122b

122. **Man's Vest,** *Northern Plains*
21" long, 18½" wide
Museum of the Plains Indian

This vest has a solid beaded front, and a beaded back on a background of blue strouding. An artichoke-like floral design at the base of the vest is beaded in blue, pink, and red, with a flower rising above it in the same colors, plus green beads and sequins. An American flag blooms from the top leaf of each plant. The back consists of floral beading in yellow, orange, pink, light and dark blue, red, brown, and sequins. (MPI 957)

Cat. 123a

Cat. 123b

123. **Vest,** *Blackfeet*
21" long, 18½" wide
Museum of the Plains Indian

This vest is of blue strouding with designs in white dentalia. It is unlined and rimmed with red patterned calico. (MPI 949)

Hairpipe Breastplate

Plains Indians and white traders knew the long, light-colored, tubular beads, such as are strung on rawhide cords in the decorative breastplate shown in Cat. 124, as "hairpipes." Shortly after the Revolutionary War, white wampum-makers in Bergen County, New Jersey, began to make hairpipes of several lengths from the lips of large conch shells brought to the port of New York as ballast in ships from the Bahamas. As early as the opening years of the nineteenth century, some Plains Indians were using hairpipes as hair ornaments. By the middle of that century, the Comanche and their neighbors on the southern plains were making breastplates in large numbers of these pieces strung horizontally in a number of rows, one over another. After the Civil War, the use of hairpipe breastplates spread northward over the plains to other tribes. The Sioux were using them by 1870, the Assiniboine by 1882, and the Blackfeet by the early 1890s. By that time, traders were offering them to Indians in another material — bone from the legs of cattle furnished to white hairpipe-makers by Armour and Company of Chicago. The new bone hairpipes were stronger and much less apt to break than the earlier shell ones.

Hairpipe breastplates were never intended for protection in war. Rather, they were decorative ornaments that became very popular among young Grass Dancers of many tribes by the turn of the century. Cat. 124 is made of very long hairpipes in the style preferred by tribes of the Northern Plains. The cords on which the pipes are strung are attached at each end to tough vertical strips of commercial leather. Blue and red beads are strung on cords in the center. There are long hide fringes at the sides. The breastplate was suspended from the wearer's neck by the rawhide cord. (A detailed history of the white manufacture and Plains Indian use of hairpipes appears in Ewers 1957.)

Loop Necklaces

A type of necklace favored by many Indian men among the tribes of the Northern Plains for wear on dress occasions during the early years of this century was made of several parallel strands of shell, glass, or metal beads that fell in broad U-shaped bands over the chests of their wearers. This style of necklace is sometimes referred to as a "Crow necklace," which may indicate its tribe of origin. The type certainly was popular among Crow leaders as early as 1880. A majority of the Crow chiefs who accompanied Head Chief Plenty Coups to Washington in 1880 wore loop necklaces when their official photograph was taken in the nation's capital (Fig. 2 in Wildschut and Ewers 1959).

In 1910, N. A. Forsyth pictured the Piegan Blackfeet chief, Little Dog, in his tipi wearing a loop necklace that was further elaborated with round shell ornaments known to the trade as "moons." They were made from large Bahaman conch shells by the same Bergen County, New Jersey, wampum-makers who had made the shell hairpipes. Little Dog's necklace was much like one in the Hill Collection, pictured in Cat. 128. It combines three shell moons with ten beaded strands fastened at each end to vertical strips of tough harness leather to form a loop necklace. Cat. 127 illustrates a much simpler loop necklace composed of 11 strands of disc beads.

Fig. 47 Members of the bar association after adoption into tribe. Indian at left is wearing armband, *Cat. 131.*
Photograph courtesy of the National Anthropological Archives, Smithsonian Institution

Armbands

Armbands have long been a fashionable item of men's attire. Karl Bodmer's painting of the leader of the Buffalo Bull Society (Thomas and Ronnefeldt 1976:217) portrays the figure wearing what may be a metal band around his biceps. The beaded armbands of reservation days are of Blackfeet make (Cat. 130 and Cat. 131). The use of five-pointed stars as decorative elements was most probably drawn from the American flag.

Breechclouts

It is probable that men among the tribes of the Northern Plains wore no breechclouts before the arrival of white traders in their country. Yet by 1833–1834 when the German scientist Prince Maximilian met them, the men of all the tribes wore breechclouts. When Governor Isaac I. Stevens, traveling westward in search of a route for a railway from St. Paul to the Pacific Coast, met Blackfeet leaders in council in 1853, he observed that each of them wore "a breach-cloth of coarse blue cloth" (*Annual Report of the Commissioner of Indian Affairs for 1854*:203). Elderly Blackfeet Indians in the early 1940s testified that in their youth men's breechclouts were of cloth, but they understood that in earlier times breechclouts were sometimes made of the soft and pliable skin from the tops of old tipis. Cloth continued in favor for breechclouts worn by men on those occasions when they donned shirts and leggings of skin or blanket cloth during the early decades of this century. A black velveteen breechclout in the Hill Collection has colorful floral designs beaded on both front and back in Metis style (Cat. 132).

During the early decades of this century some Blackfeet men wore breechclouts of colored cloth, to which emblems and beaded figures of birds or animals were applied. Two examples from the Hill Collection are decorated with beaded eagles. One offers a front view of this great bird with its wings spread, head turned, and grasping arrows in its claws, much as it appears on the reverse of United States coins (Cat. 134). The other has a realistic eagle in side view, holding a flower in its claws, surmounted by three large stars, all within a shield-like form. (Cat. 133). It was worn so that the eagle emblem was visible below the wearer's back; the breechclout passed between the wearer's legs, and the other end hung down at the front, showing the crossed arrows and stars.

Theodore Last Star (whose Indian name was Weasel Feather), a prominent member of the group of Blackfeet Indians who greeted the Great Northern's Empire Builder and entertained tourists in the large hotel at Glacier Park Station during the 1940s, wore a buckskin breechclout decorated on both front and back with a large conventional steerhead in beadwork, worn facing the observer. (See Winold Reiss portrait in Walton 1982:45.)

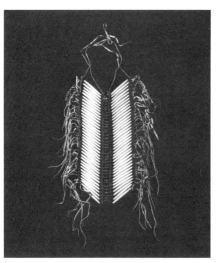

125. Necklace, *Blackfeet*
15" long
Museum of the Plains Indian

This necklace of porcelain disc beads, with French brass beads interspersed, is strung on a buckskin thong. A medicine pouch with light blue and white beads is attached. (MPI 1290)

124. Hairpipe Breastplate, *Northern Plains*
19" long, 10" wide
Northwest Area Foundation

This breastplate consists of two sections of bone hairpipes, interspersed with varicolored beads. (SMM 54 – 37)

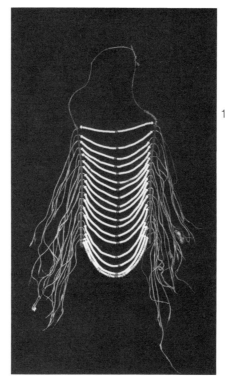

127. Necklace, *Crow (?)*
16" long, 12" wide
Museum of the Plains Indian

This necklace is composed of 11 strands of bone discs, each with a turquoise bead at the center. Graduated in length, the strands are supported between two rawhide strips. (MPI 1174)

Cat. 125

126. Necklace, *Crow*
18" long, 12" wide
Museum of the Plains Indian

This necklace has 18 strands of bone discs. A red bead is placed in the center of each strand with a large white bead at each end. Eight beads are strung on the twisted rawhide fringe at the sides. (MPI 1173)

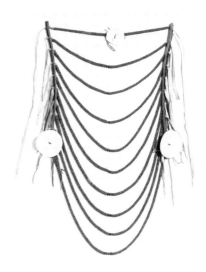

128. Necklace, *Northern Plains*
20" long, 15" wide
Museum of the Plains Indian

This necklace of turquoise glass beads is strung on ten rawhide thongs. At the center of each strand is a brass bead. Three conch shells are attached, and tanned-hide fringe hangs from the sides. (MPI 1413e)

129. **Armbands,** *Ojibway or Cree (?)*
12½" long, 2⅝" wide
Museum of the Plains Indian

This pair of beaded armbands is
made on canvas. The pattern on the
bands is a symmetrical floral design.
The flowers are red and yellow; the
buds are red, orange, white, and
blue; the stem is black. The
background is aqua. The armbands
are bordered in white and red. There
are green ribbon ties at the ends.
(MPI 1073) *Photo: page 142.*

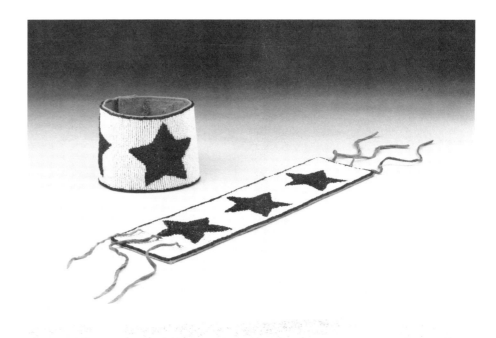

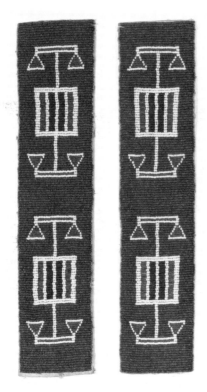

131. **Armbands,** *Blackfeet*
11¾" long, 3" wide
Museum of the Plains Indian

This pair of armbands is beaded on
heavy canvas. The pattern consists of
three five-pointed stars on a white
field, with a green border. The stars
are dark purplish-blue faceted beads.
(MPI 1069) *See also page 146.*

132. **Breechclout,** *Northern Plains*
42½" long, 19½" wide
Museum of the Plains Indian

This breechclout was converted from
two aprons by joining the two pieces
with fabric. They are lined with black
patterned calico and rimmed with
green silk ribbon. The floral bead
design is executed on black
velveteen in green, light blue, white,
red, violet, purple, yellow, pink, dark
green, dark blue, and mauve.
(MPI 1096)

Cat. 132a

Cat. 132b

130. **Armbands,** *Blackfeet*
14½" long, 3⅛" wide
Museum of the Plains Indian

These armbands are beaded in
identical patterns. The design is
outlined in white on a light blue field.
A rectangle has outer stripes of red
and two inner stripes of green,
separated by two rows of white
beads. The center white stripe
continues outside of the rectangle on
either side, to a wide red-beaded bar.
At either end of each bar are red,
inverted triangles. (MPI 1325)

134. **Breechclout,** *Blackfeet*
54" long, 15½" wide
Museum of the Plains Indian

This breechclout is made of
olive-colored blanket material, with a
piece of lighter green material laced
through slots across the front. It is
ornamented with a beaded heart
containing the American eagle in red,
white, and blue on a light blue
background. This is bordered with
red, yellow, and blue. The entire
heart is fringed with a white material.
(MPI 1288)

133. **Breechclout,** *Blackfeet*
54" long, 16" wide
Museum of the Plains Indian

This breechclout is of red strouding
with applique. The front shows a pair
of crossed arrows in white cotton
fabric with details embroidered in
gold floss. Two black velveteen
five-pointed stars are appliqued on
the front. The design is set into a red
panel with a black velveteen border.
The back has a beaded shield
design of eagle and stars. (MPI 1287)

Gauntlet Gloves

Indian men of the Northern Plains tribes adopted the custom of wearing skin gloves with long, flaring cuffs extending well up the lower part of the arm from army officers who were stationed at military posts in the Indian country during the last quarter of the nineteenth century. Some Indian women made these gloves for army officers and decorated them with fancy beadwork on the outside of the cuffs. Prominent Indians also began to wear these gloves on dress occasions, and they continued to be in some demand among Indians for parade wear even after the market for gauntlet gloves among whites had virtually disappeared by the early 1940s.

Floral designs were favored by Indian women in the decoration of gauntlet gloves. They were applied to the skin surfaces of the cuffs with or without a contrasting colored, beaded background. A pair of the former kind appears in Cat. 135. The floral designs are in the Metis style.

Gauntlets

Young Indian dancers preferred to wear long cuffs bearing colorful quilled or beaded designs, instead of the more confining gauntlet gloves. Cat. 139 shows a handsome pair of gauntlets, probably of Northern Plains origin, beaded entirely in geometric designs. The gauntlets in Cat. 140 bear the Metis floral designs popular among Indians of most Northern Plains tribes. The porcupine-quilled gauntlets in Cat. 136 may be of Assiniboine make.

135. **Gauntlet Gloves,** *Cree or Crow*
16" long, 7" wide
Museum of the Plains Indian

This pair of gloves is made of buckskin. There is long fringe on one side of the cuff and embroidered decoration on the back of the hand. The decoration on the cuff consists of a plant with three flowers. The stem is green. The flowers are red with interiors of blue, orange, dark green, and brass on a white field, lined with red material. (MPI 1028)

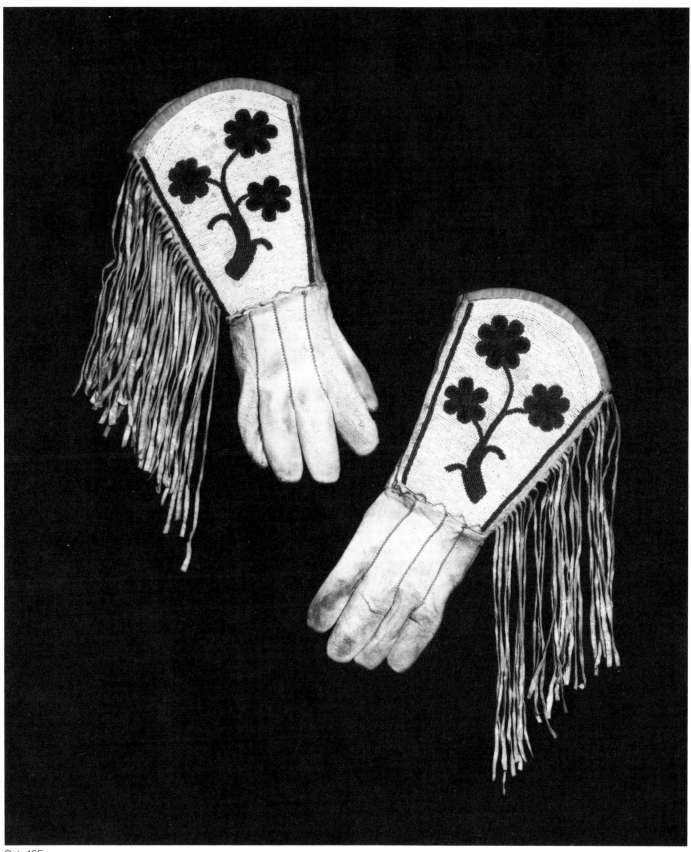

Cat. 135

Cat. 136

Cat. 137

136. **Gauntlets,** *Assiniboine*
5½" long, 4¾" wide
Museum of the Plains Indian

This pair of quilled cuffs is decorated in geometric patterns with a stepped diamond of yellow, aqua, and purple on a pink field. At the base is a beaded strip, consisting of a green rectangle with a triangle of blue and orange. There is long fringe along the side, and black cotton cloth edges the entire circumference of the cuff. (MPI 1155)

137. **Gauntlets,** *Blackfeet*
8¼" long, 6¾" wide
Museum of the Plains Indian

The gauntlets are completely beaded with a different pattern on each. The beads are light blue, royal blue, red, yellow, and green — placed in geometric patterns. There are accents of transparent lavender beads. The fringe along the side is strung with larger green beads. (MPI 1157)

138. **Gauntlets,** *Blackfeet*
9½" long, 6½" wide
Museum of the Plains Indian

This pair of beaded cuffs is decorated in a series of blue and orange rectangles forming a double stepped diamond on a white background. The cuff is edged with green strouding and fringed at the side. (MPI 1160)

Cat. 139

Cat. 138

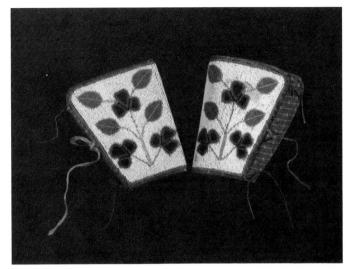

Cat. 140

Cat. 141

139. **Gauntlets,** *Northern Plains*
7³/₄" long, 6¹/₄" wide
Museum of the Plains Indian

These beaded gauntlets are
decorated with round, faceted, and
tubular glass beads. The gauntlet is
covered with a field of light blue
beads with a red, white, and grey
border. Red beads and grey tube
beads form a repetitive diamond
pattern. There is a box-and-bar
pattern in red and grey. A triple row
of black beads is arranged in a
diagonal pattern along the edge,
further decorated with a lacy pattern
of yellow transparent tube beads
and dark blue faceted beads.
(MPI 1031)

140. **Gauntlets,** *Northern Plains*
6³/₄" long, 5³/₄" wide
Museum of the Plains Indian

These beaded gauntlets are
decorated with a floral design in
light blue, mauve, purple, orange,
green, and dark blue on a white
background. They have a rolled
calico rim of violet, and they tie with
buckskin thongs. The three
flowers — resembling three-leaf
clovers — are outlined in mauve and
orange and have green and purple
centers. The light blue leaves are
also outlined in mauve.
(MPI 1039a and b)

141. **Gauntlets,** *Kutenai*
7" long, 5¹/₂" wide
Museum of the Plains Indian

These cuffs are decorated in a
beaded floral design on a white
background. The colors are green,
red, mauve, and yellow. (MPI 1035)

Women's Attire

Attire for a Northern Plains woman consisted of an elkskin dress, leggings, moccasins, a belt, and robe. Early dresses varied in style. Among the Plains Cree, Plains Ojibway, and Blackfeet, a sheath, supported by shoulder straps with detachable sleeves was in vogue (Plate 245 in Catlin 1913:II) while the Mandan woman wore only a wraparound skirt (LaVérendrye 1927:341). By the 1830s, dresses fashioned from two elkskins were in general use. These were sewn together at the hind quarters forming the shoulders and sleeves, the tail being folded over at the opening for the neck, becoming a decorative element. The shoulder seams were embellished with a narrow band of quill or beadwork as were the necks and hemlines (Plates 13, 17, 25, 29, 31, 52, 53, 81, 94, 95 in Catlin 1913:I; see also Wissler 1910). Fringe extended from the underside of the sleeves, the side seams of the dress, and around the bottom. As time passed, the amount of decoration was increased so that among the Blackfeet and Sioux, the entire yoke might be ornamented. The Blackfeet preferred undulating bands of beads usually in alternating colors of blue and white. The Sioux yokes most commonly were composed of a solid background of light blue interspersed with geometric figures. What had been a tail now became a vestigal U-shaped design and was referred to as a turtle (Fig. 19 in Lyford 1940). The Crow, Cheyenne, and Arapahoe retained the bands of beadwork along the shoulder seams and around the neck and hemline while often ornamenting the yoke with rows of elk teeth or cowrie shells. Yokes decorated with floral patterns were popular among the Crow and Cree.

Cat. 142 shows a fringed, elkskin dress ornamented with blue and white "pony" beads in the typical undulating pattern favored by the Blackfeet. The dress is further decorated with imitation elk's teeth carved from bone and pink and green "basket beads" terminating in brass bells. The skirt is further embellished with a triangle of red and blue stroud with a blue and white "seed bead" border. Seed beads of the same color form a border above the hem. Two ermine skins hang from the shoulders to complete the costume.

Cat. 150 and Cat. 148 show Crow dresses of the late reservation period. In Cat. 150 red velveteen replaced red stroud as a background for displaying a wealth of cowrie shells. The sleeves and hemline are decorated with blue ribbon. The model wearing the dress with the beaded bodice in floral designs in Cat. 148 is wearing Sioux leggings, but Crow moccasins. Such decorative dresses as this were popular among both the Plateau people as well as northeasterners such as the Plains Cree and Plains Ojibway.

Cat. 151 is a Cheyenne girl's dress decorated with cowrie shells and narrow bands of beading. The triangles formed by the beading at the hem are painted with red ochre. Mescal beans and ribbons complete the decoration. The Cheyenne were especially partial to long fringe.

Cat. 145 is a classic Sioux dress of the early reservation period showing a solid light blue beaded yoke with simple triangles in dark blue and the "turtle" element at the center. Cat 146 shows a Sioux dress of a later date, exhibiting the complexity of design not found in the earlier Sioux beadwork.

Women's leggings were short, tubular garments tied at the outside and secured below the knee with a leather thong. Since the dresses were long (reaching quite below the knees), only the exposed lower third of the leggings was decorated. The Sioux, Cheyenne, and Arapahoe leggings overlapped and possessed a band of beading along the sides somewhat covering the ties. The Cheyenne and Arapahoe often decorated this band with metal studs (Wissler 1910).

Cat. 155, Cat. 156, and Cat. 157 show three pairs of Blackfeet leggings. Each is made of canvas to which beading is applied by overlaid stitching.

Red flannel forms the top. Each exhibits the stepped motif in the diamonds and triangles so popular among Blackfeet beadworkers. Cat. 159 illustrates a pair of Crow leggings with red flannel or stroud tops while Cat. 162 shows the Crow craftswoman's fondness for calico as a lining. Cat. 160 shows the Cheyenne use of an overlapping flap ornamented with brass studs. Cat. 161 is a pair of Sioux leggings fashioned similarly to Cheyenne leggings. The flaps are decorated with stylized thunderbirds, a design not commonly found in Sioux beadwork. Cat. 152 is probably an Assiniboine pair of leggings, dating sometime after 1900.

Belts were an essential part of female attire, serving as a support for knife and sheath, awl and case. Frequently, pouches and bags for such things as lighting equipment, ration cards, and sewing materials also hung from the belt. Dress belts were highly ornamented with beads, brass carpet tacks, or both. Long leather pendants reaching to the ankles and decorated with metal studs were often worn. Belts, formerly made of rawhide, later became popular in commercial leather.

Men's belts were seldom decorated, for they were utilitarian in supporting leggings, breechclout, and scabbard, and they were obscured by the front and rear flaps of the breechclout. However, some men wore decorated belts over their shirts. The belts featured here, however, are assumed to be women's.

Cat. 179 is a Blackfeet belt decorated with spot-stitched beadwork on commercially tanned harness leather while Cat. 177, also Blackfeet, is a canvas belt embellished with beads.

Cat. 175 displays a clear and simple pattern of playing-card symbols with hearts and diamonds in red, clubs and spades in black, all against a pale blue background. The use of cherries and strawberries, Cat. 173, is equally non-Indian in character but nonetheless attractive. Cat. 174 is a Crow belt with beaded border and rectangular beaded sections interspersed with areas of exposed commercial leather.

Long pendants called "dangles" ornamented with brass tacks (see Cat. 170) were a common accoutrement to women's belts. This example is part of what may be an Assiniboine belt. German silver discs or "conchos" (Cat. 180) attached to harness leather were fashionably decorated with metal discs diminishing in size from top to bottom. Cat. 168 and Cat. 169 show unusually wide beaded belts or girdles in a floral design. They may be of Flathead origin.

Complementing the women's costumes were long necklaces called breastplates made of bone and glass beads. Referred to as "hairpipes," the tubular bone beads were originally made from conch shells and worn suspended from the hair on either side of men's foreheads (Plate 30 in Catlin 1913:I). Later, the hairpipes were mass-produced in the east and became a popular item of trade.

Cat. 165 and Cat. 163 show two typical examples of Northern Plains breastplates. Cat. 164 is a simpler form in that it lacks the beaded sections.

While formerly the buffalo robe was the principal outer garment, elk hide was also used, especially among women for summer wear. Deer hides were not uncommon for children's wear. Robes were often ornamented with quilled, and later beaded, strips applied lengthwise from head to tail. During butchering, the hide was often cut down the back and peeled off from side to side. To make a robe necessitated sewing the two halves together again. The beaded strips covered the seam.

Dress robes were decorated in a variety of ways. Some men wore robes pictographically displaying their war records; others preferred painted geometric designs. One such design was the "black bonnet" or "sunburst," consisting of a series of concentric circles composed of lozenges or "feather" elements. The Sioux, in particular, favored this style. Women also wore painted robes but only those bearing geometric designs. The "border and box" design was believed by some to represent a stylized buffalo carcass, with sausage-like elements representing the good things to eat. In addition to being painted, the robes might be decorated with quills or beads. One especially popular decoration was a series of transverse lines running parallel with the length of the robe (Ewers 1939).

With the loss of the buffalo, robes were displaced by blankets. The few robes that were painted on reservations at the turn of the century were generally done as collectors' pieces by old warriors. These were primarily for display and not for wearing. Some beaded elkskin robes were made by women for their use or as costumes for their daughters. Now stroud blankets in red, blue, and green found favor. Often the colors were combined, red and blue being particularly popular. Though sometimes referred to as "courting blankets" when it was customary for a young man to wrap himself and his sweetheart completely in a blanket as he sought her favor, these blankets might be worn by anyone.

No matter whether the stroud blanket was of one or two colors, the blanket strip was attached so that it appeared horizontally when worn. Unlike the buffalo robes where the strip covered the seam, when red and blue blankets were sewn together, the strips ran transversely to the seam. Blanket strips varied in length and width, averaging 60 inches long and 5 inches wide. The Blackfeet seemed to prefer wider strips; the Sioux and Cheyenne, narrow ones. The strips themselves were bands of beadwork generally interspersed with three or four medallions. Occasionally the medallion appeared at one end, and in such instances the other end terminated in a bar (Wissler 1910).

The Crow painted child's robe (Cat. 187) may have been worn as a badge of having undergone a special ceremony. The beaded blanket strip was formerly decorated with three ermine skins.

The painted buffalo robe in Cat. 301, possibly of Cheyenne origin, shows a bison hunt at the top, and wolves hunting elk and antelope toward the center. Below this is a village scene with two men smoking pipes, a woman with an ax, horsemen, men with feathered bonnets and shields, a dog, and several horses. From the subject matter, this would appear to have been a commissioned piece painted by an Indian artist to show a panorama of Indian life. Prereservation wearing robes (seen in pictographics) were painted by men to display their exploits in battle and on horse-stealing forays. Village scenes and buffalo hunts were not portrayed.

The model in Cat. 186 wears a beaded elkskin robe. Row upon row of beaded lines was a popular decorative feature of Crow art.

Cat 181 shows a beaded Sioux blanket strip sewn on a red and blue stroud blanket while Cat. 185 illustrates a Crow example applied to a green Hudson's Bay blanket.

142. **Dress,** *Blackfeet*
   ● *47" long, 16" wide shoulders*
   Museum of the Plains Indian

   This skin dress has a yoke of
   pony beads in bands of blue and
   white. The neck edge is pink, blue,
   and white beads. The bodice is
   ornamented with imitation elk teeth.
   Ermine tails hang from the
   shoulders. Pink and green beads
   and brass bells are on the fringe.
   The skirt has fringe and a red and
   blue stroud triangle, with a white
   and blue beaded border, also along
   the hem. (MPI 1390)

143. **Dress,** *Sioux*
   46" long, 19" wide shoulders
   Museum of the Plains Indian

   This skin dress has a beaded yoke
   done in lazy stitch, with short fringe
   at the sleeve, side seams, and hem.
   There is a double row of beading
   around the hem with tin-cone
   dangles at each side. Green, red,
   yellow, and dark blue geometric
   designs are placed on a field of
   light blue. Faceted brass beads are
   incorporated into a central cross,
   flanked by diamonds containing
   small crosses. (MPI 1394)

Cat. 144

Cat. 145

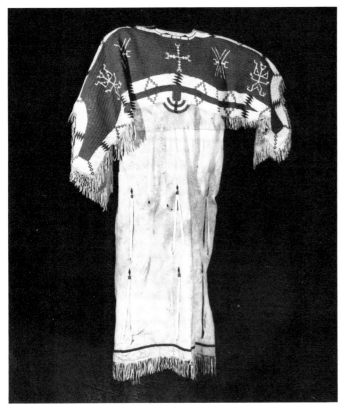

Cat. 146

Cat. 147

144. **Dress,** *Sioux*
43" long, 46" across sleeves
Northwest Area Foundation

The beaded yoke is decorated with
geometric patterns in white, yellow,
red, dark green, and dark blue on
a light blue background. Beaded
spots of the same colors are on the
lower part of the dress and border.
Fringe hangs from the hemline and
beaded spots. The beadwork is in
lazy stitch. (SMM 49 – 103)

145. **Dress,** *Sioux*
66" long, 66" across sleeves
Northwest Area Foundation

This dress is fashioned of two elk
hides with the side seams sewn
shut and the sleeves left open. The
beaded yoke has a background of
light blue with geometric patterns in
dark blue, white, yellow, red, and
brass faceted beads. The strip of
beads at the hem is white, red, and
aqua. The beads are applied with
sinew in lazy stitch. Evenly placed
thongs are fastened to the lower
part of the skirt. (SMM 1 – 1113)

146. **Dress,** *Sioux*
51" long, 22" wide shoulders
Museum of the Plains Indian

This skin dress has a beaded yoke,
worked in lazy stitch, of geometric
designs and figures in red, white,
and royal blue on turquoise. A
border of white beads, interspersed
with pyramids (composed of
squares and trapezoids in red,
yellow, and royal blue) surrounds
the yoke. The primary design is a
large cross in red, blue, green, and
white, centered in the yoke, with an
X and figure placed symmetrically
on either side. There are small
patches of turquoise beadwork on
the skirt and a turquoise border at
the hem. The sleeves and hem are
fringed and hide fringe hangs from
the skirt. (MPI 1389)

147. **Dress,** *Northern Plains*
40½" long, 23" wide shoulders
Museum of the Plains Indian

This skin dress has brightly colored
translucent tubular glass beads in
floral designs on the front, back,
and cuffs. The flowers and leaves
are in various shades of red, pink,
blue, yellow, and green. The hem
has a double row of tinsel and
rhinestones. (MPI 964)

148. **Dress,** *Crow*
41½" long, 20" wide shoulders
Museum of the Plains Indian

This dress of purple velveteen has
beaded floral designs in orange,
pink, light and dark green, ochre,
light blue, and white on the front,
back, and sleeves. The neck has an
inset panel of red strouding
bordered by green ribbon. The
sleeves and hems are edged with
pink ribbon. (MPI 966)

Cat. 149a

Cat. 149b

149. **Dress,** *Crow*
50" long, 21" wide shoulders
Museum of the Plains Indian

This green velveteen dress is
beaded with floral designs in glass
and metal. The colors are light blue,
orange, royal blue, yellow, green,
red, burgundy, and white. Brass
and steel faceted beads add
highlights. The cuff, the seam
beneath the arm, and the hem are
bordered with red silk ribbon. There
is a fringe of woven metal wire at
the cuff and hem. Metal sequins are
sewn to the ribbon. (MPI 967)

150. Girl's Dress, *Crow*
39″ long, 18″ wide shoulders
Museum of the Plains Indian

This girl's dress is of burgundy-red velveteen, with the neck of blue edged with black. The bodice is decorated with rows of cowrie shells. The sleeves and the arms are decorated with light blue ribbon. (MPI 969)

151. Girl's Dress, *Cheyenne*
30″ long, 13″ wide shoulders
Museum of the Plains Indian

This girl's dress is of tanned hide with twisted fringe on the ends of the sleeves, along the sides, and at the hem. There is beadwork on the shoulders, the neck, the skirt, and the hem. The patterns are linear, worked primarily in white, red, and blue, with some aqua and green on the shoulders. Cowrie shells are strung in rows on both the front and back bodice of the dress. A row of mescal beads is attached to the hide fringe along the breast, back, and to three clusters of ribbons. The ribbons are red and purple, and a single gold; they hang from red rosettes, also of ribbon. The beads along the hem are worked in a zigzag pattern. Small transparent tubular beads are attached to some of the fringe. (MPI 968)

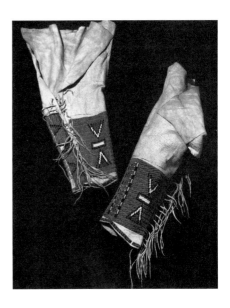

152. Woman's Skin Leggings,
Assiniboine
18¹/₂″ long, 10″ wide top
Northwest Area Foundation

The leggings are closed by a drawstring series of thongs, which form a decorative fringe on the outer side. The decoration on the lower part of the leggings is beaded in geometric designs. (SMM 49–75)

153. Child's Leggings, *Northern Plains*
10″ long, 5¹/₂″ wide
Northwest Area Foundation

These small boy's leggings are made of red flannel. (SMM 49–76)

154. Woman's Leggings, *Blackfeet*
13½" long, 15" wide top
Northwest Area Foundation

These red flannel leggings are brilliantly decorated with geometric beadwork on a canvas backing. After the beadwork was done, the backing was applied to the flannel. (SMM 49–77)

155. Woman's Leggings, *Blackfeet*
12" long, 13" wide
Northwest Area Foundation

This pair of woman's leggings is beaded with two shades of blue and red on a white field. The center is sewn in overlay stitch; the white border strips, in lazy stitch. White seed beads decorate the bottom of the legging. Red wool flannel strips enclose the four edges. Buckskin thongs are threaded through the flannel for a closing. (SMM 49–290)

156. Woman's Leggings, *Blackfeet*
12" long, 15" wide
Northwest Area Foundation

This pair of woman's leggings is beaded in overlay stitch with red, green, and yellow diamonds and triangles, on a white field. Alternating green and white strips of lazy stitch enclose the top and bottom of the design. A red flannel strip completes the composition. (SMM 54–36)

Cat. 157

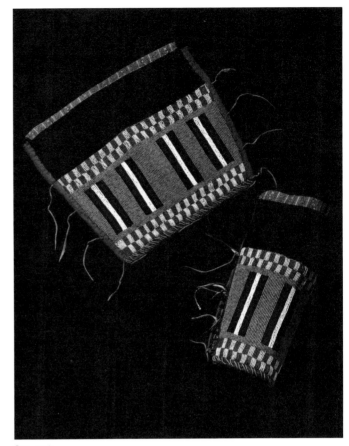

Cat. 158

157. **Woman's Leggings,** *Blackfeet*
12¹/₂" long, 13" wide
Northwest Area Foundation

This pair of leggings is beaded on
canvas. Red flannel strips are sewn
on the four sides of the legging.
Buckskin and thongs are attached
to the sides for fastening. The white
background on the upper and
lower beaded borders is in lazy
stitch. The border is decorated with
a pyramid against a beaded field.
Blue and gold beads are worked in
overlay stitch. (SMM 54–41)

158. **Woman's Leggings,** *Blackfeet*
12" long, 13¹/₂" wide
Northwest Area Foundation

These red, white, and blue striped
woman's leggings are bordered with
light blue and pink checkerboard
strips, which flank a center filled
with metallic rose beads. A broad
navy flannel band and red flannel
strips at the sides and bottom
enhance the color scheme. Red
and white cotton fabric backs the
work. The translucent seed beads
are applied to the hide in both the
lazy and overlay stitch.
(SMM 54–42)

159. **Woman's Leggings,** *Crow*
16¹/₄" long, 11" wide
Museum of the Plains Indian

These leggings are of red strouding
with a muslin flour sack extending
the top. They are lined at the sides
and bottom with green strouding.
The white-striped beadwork is
confined to the red base of the
leggings. (MPI 1068)

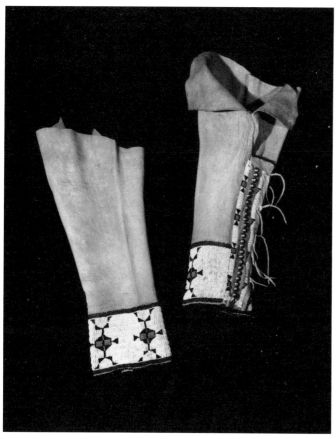

Cat. 160

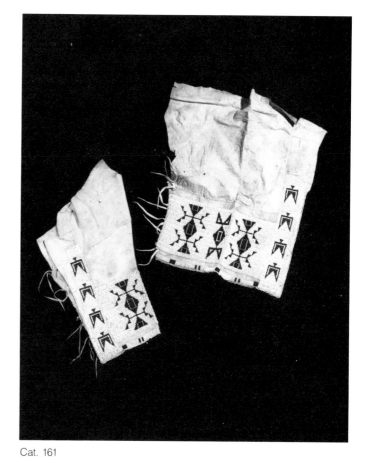

Cat. 161

160. **Woman's Leggings,** *Cheyenne*
17" long, 12" wide
Museum of the Plains Indian

These leggings are decorated with a strip of beaded material approximately 5" wide. The closing flap has a square of beaded material encircling a row of 24 brass studs. The flap is edged with metallic beads extending to the bottom of the legging. The main beaded design is a series of pinwheel forms in pink, black, red, and blue on a white background. A green beaded strip rims both bottom edges. The flaps are decorated with thongs. (MPI 1334)

161. **Woman's Leggings,** *Sioux*
19" long, 13½" wide
Museum of the Plains Indian

These beaded leggings are decorated with a thunderbird design of blue, red, green, and yellow beads on a white background. A beaded strip at the bottom of the leggings is separated from the main beaded panel by a thin strip of buckskin. (MPI 1335)

162. **Woman's Leggings,** *Blackfeet*
12½" long, 13" wide
Museum of the Plains Indian

This pair of woman's leggings consists of a beaded panel with red calico uppers, backed with red, printed, floral-patterned cloth. The beaded panels are worked in alternating strips of light blue and red, and yellow and blue checkers. The beaded sections are bordered by serrated buckskin. (MPI 1355)

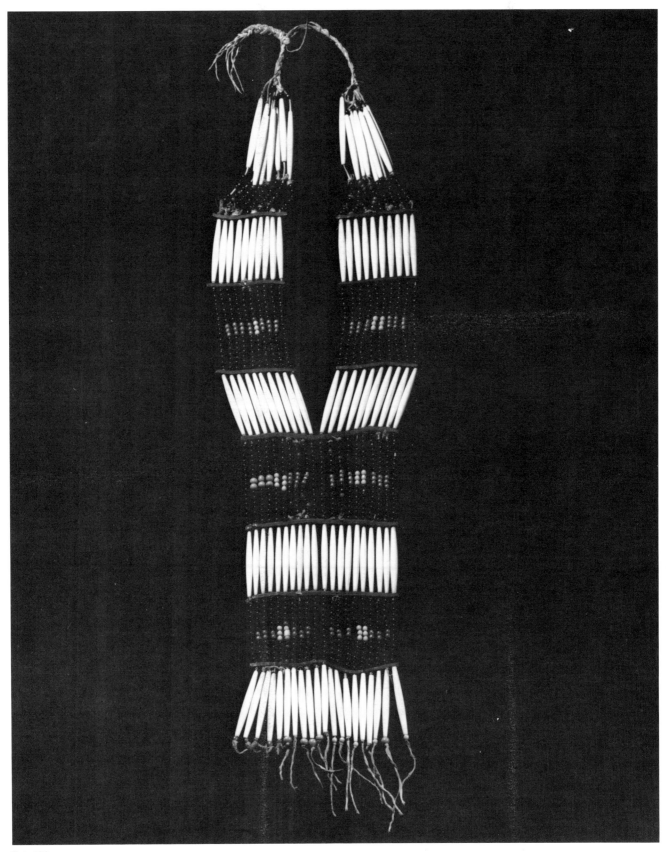

Cat. 163

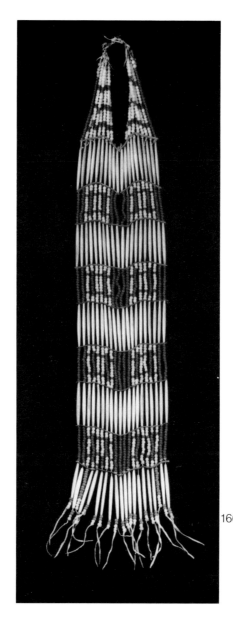

Cat. 166a

Cat. 166b

Cat. 164

163. **Breastplate,** *Northern Plains*
36" long, 7" wide
Northwest Area Foundation

Tubular hollow bones are placed
vertically in rows separated by
alternating rows of large beads to
form this handsome ornament.
(SMM 1–701)

164. **Breastplate,** *Northern Plains*
36" long, 8½" wide
Museum of the Plains Indian

This breastplate is composed of
rows of hairpipes of varying lengths;
each is separated by a strip of hide,
bordered by either brass or blue
glass beads. Strands of yellow and
white glass beads form the neck
piece. (MPI 1298)

165. **Breastplate,** *Northern Plains*
48" long, 9" wide
Museum of the Plains Indian

This necklace of hairpipes is
interspersed with white and blue
beads of various shades forming
rectangular designs. (MPI 1300)

166. **Cape,** *Northern Plains*
14" long, 15" wide
Museum of the Plains Indian

This beaded cape has a lining of
white cotton fabric with blue dots.
The geometric floral design on the
front is set on a white background.
The pattern on the back is similar.
The colors on one side are royal
blue, light blue, ochre, red, yellow,
and pink. At the shoulder and
around the neck is a geometric
border of stripes and squares in
light blue, pink, and red. The
bottom of the cape has a fringe of
black and white bugle beads, light
blue and white glass beads, and
Turkish coins. The other side is
beaded in light blue, pink, ochre,
aqua, yellow, and red. (MPI 1030)

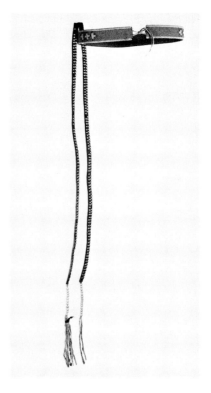

167. **Cowrie Shell Cape,** *Sioux*
      18¾" long, 33" wide
      Museum of the Plains Indian

      This woman's blue wool cape is
      decorated with 11 rows of cowrie
      shells. A red silk ribbon binds the
      neck opening. (MPI 958)

170. **Woman's Belt with Dangle,**
      Northern Plains
      32" long, 1½" wide
      Northwest Area Foundation

      This beaded belt is made of
      harness leather decorated with
      glass beads. The pattern consists of
      stepped pyramids of yellow and
      red, on a royal blue background
      with a pink border. Two rows of
      beads are attached longitudinally by
      lazy stitch to one side. A dangle,
      made of harness leather covered
      with brass nails, hangs in two strips
      from the belt. The two ends are
      decorated with a tassel of orange
      cloth strips encased by a string of
      light blue bands. (SMM 49–247
      and 49–248)

169. **Woman's Girdle,** *Flathead*
      33" long, 8" wide
      Museum of the Plains Indian

      This beaded woman's girdle is lined
      with blue patterned calico. The
      center flower is silver and light blue
      with an interior rosette of light pink
      and red. The motif, outlined in navy
      beads, becomes stems leading to
      four red and yellow flowers, with
      four green leaves, on a white
      background. (MPI 1086)

168. **Woman's Girdle,** *Flathead*
      31" long, 7¼" wide
      Museum of the Plains Indian

      The centerpiece of this beaded
      girdle is a geometric flower of
      lavender, white, red, blue, yellow,
      and pink. The flowers on either side
      have stylized dark blue stems and
      green leaves. The blossoms are
      blue, brown, yellow, and pink,
      outlined in red. One line of metal
      beads and a thin strip of beading
      that alternates the light blue of the
      background with colors from the
      flowers forms the edge. (MPI 1085)

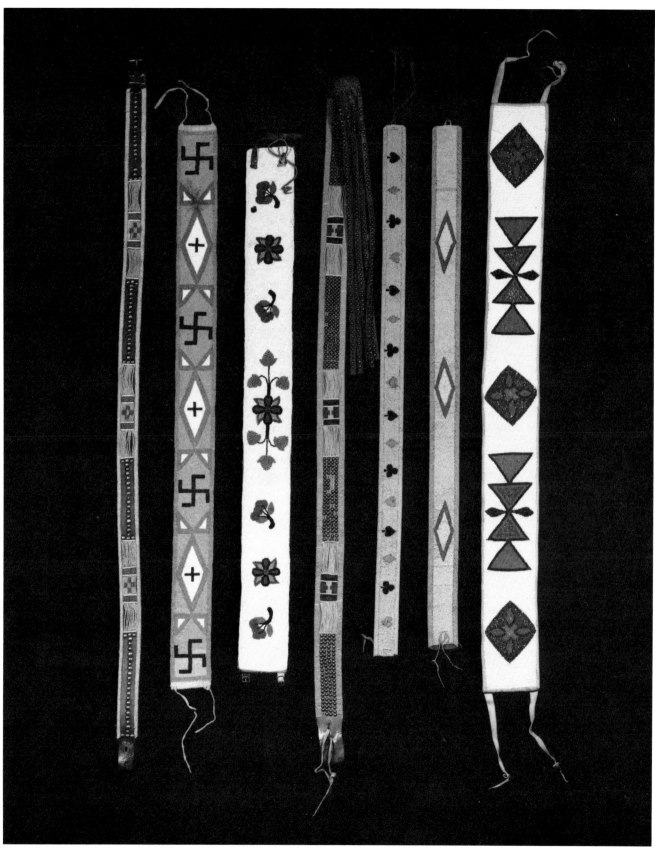

Cats. 171–177

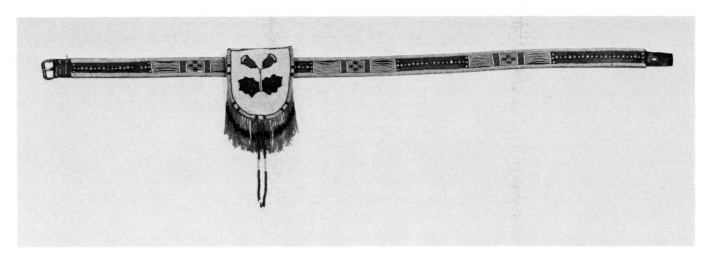

171. **Belt with Pouch,** *Crow*
● *47³⁄₄" long, 1¹⁄₂" wide*
Museum of the Plains Indian

The pouch of tanned hide is stiffened with rawhide. The front flap is beaded with a double oakleaf and double acorn motif in green, red, yellow, and dark blue, in a light blue field bordered in dark blue with pink, green, and white stripes applied in a rolled fashion. The sides are decorated with small rectangles of dark blue and orange on light blue. Beaded fringe of light green, red, and dark blue hangs from the flap. The belt has alternating rectangles of tacks and beadwork, and a harness buckle. (MPI 1040a and b)

172. **Woman's Belt,** *Northern Plains*
● *38" long, 2³⁄₄" wide*
Museum of the Plains Indian

Geometric patterns and a repeated cross motif form the beaded decoration of this canvas belt. The beaded background is light blue. White diamonds outlined in red and dark blue swastikas make this a handsome belt. (MPI 1189)

173. **Woman's Belt,** *Northern Plains*
● *35" long, 3¹⁄₄" wide*
Museum of the Plains Indian

This belt is patterned with cherries and strawberries, interspersed with geometric floral patterns. The beaded design is in red, light and dark green, yellow, pink, and mauve on a white background. (MPI 1048)

174. **Woman's Belt,** *Crow*
● *65¹⁄₂" long, 2" wide*
Museum of the Plains Indian

This combination of tacks and beadwork against a lavender background makes this woman's belt unique. (MPI 1056)

175. **Woman's Belt,** *Blackfeet*
● *35¹⁄₂" long, 1³⁄₄" wide*
Museum of the Plains Indian

This belt is ornamented with playing card symbols arranged on a light blue background in a red/black sequence. (MPI 1055)

176. **Woman's Belt,** *Blackfeet*
● *35¹⁄₂" long, 1³⁄₄" wide*
Museum of the Plains Indian

This belt is of heavy harness leather with thong fastenings. The beadwork is in a geometric pattern of lavender and blue beads accented by yellow and red diamond shapes. (MPI 1058)

177. **Woman's Belt,** *Blackfeet*
● *39" long, 3³⁄₄" wide*
Museum of the Plains Indian

This beaded canvas belt, with buckskin edging and cloth backing, is sewn in the overlaid stitch. The pattern is a repetition of two geometric designs; one is a square with a slightly floral interior; the other is a sequence of four triangles. The square design is purple, green, and red, outlined in navy blue. The triangular element is red and silver, outlined by blue. The background is white. (MPI 1185)

178. **Woman's Belt,** *Blackfeet*
37¹⁄₂" long, 3" wide
Museum of the Plains Indian

This woman's belt is completely beaded on heavy harness leather. The pattern, repeated three times, consists of an eight-pointed sun in dark blue with a green center, flanked by a dark blue pointed cross. The design is worked in a light blue field with pink border. (MPI 1043)

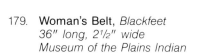
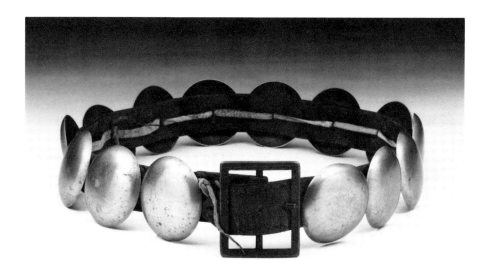

180. **Woman's Belt;** *Northern Plains*
32" long, 2¼" wide, 2½" discs
Museum of the Plains Indian

This heavy harness leather belt is fashionably ornamented with 14 German silver discs, or "conchos." (MPI 1049)

181. **Blanket and Strip,** *Sioux*
85" long, 64" wide
Museum of the Plains Indian

This large beaded strip is sewn on a red and blue stroud blanket. The strip has three discs decorated with stepped triangles alternating with small crosses, radiating from the center. The stepped triangles are red, yellow, and dark blue; the crosses are red with yellow centers. The bars dividing the discs have stepped triangles stacked in pairs on either side of hourglass figures. These have yellow and red centers with a light blue border. Originally, brass hawk bells were attached at the center of each disc. Only one remains. (MPI 1259)

179. **Woman's Belt,** *Blackfeet*
36" long, 2½" wide
Museum of the Plains Indian

This woman's belt is beaded on heavy harness leather. The decoration consists of a repetitive pattern composed of a cross, striped rectangle, diamond, striped rectangle, and a cross. The cross is red; the rectangle alternates red and blue stripes; and the diamond is red, yellow, and blue on a light blue field. The edge is rolled. (MPI 1190)

Cat. 181

Cats. 182–184

182. **Blanket Strip,** *Blackfeet*
80" long, 7" wide
Museum of the Plains Indian

This beaded blanket strip has a
base of canvas. Three discs are
evenly spaced on a white
background. Interspersed are red
hourglass figures outlined in blue.
The red and white discs are
bordered by evenly spaced red and
blue rectangles. (MPI 1368)

183. **Blanket Strip,** *Sioux*
38" long, 1³/4" wide
3¹/2" medallions
Museum of the Plains Indian

This beaded buckskin blanket strip
is sewn with sinew in the lazy stitch.
Four discs at evenly spaced
intervals have two crosses with arms
in red, and two in white. A white
spot tips each arm. The strip has a
green center bordered on each
edge by red, yellow, and blue, on a
white field. (MPI 1373)

184. **Blanket Strip,** *Crow*
53" long, 4¹/4" wide
Museum of the Plains Indian

This beaded blanket strip has three
evenly spaced discs with series of
concentric circles dividing into
sections with large dark blue Xs.
The circles are dark blue, aqua,
red, green, yellow, pink, and white.
The X has a white border. The
entire disc is surrounded by red
strouding. Yarn-wrapped leather
fringe wrapped in aqua and
orange wool thread is attached to
the center of the discs. The strips
between the discs each have a
cross centered between two panels
of triple diamonds that are half red
and half white, set in a light blue
field with an orange border. The
cross is dark blue with a yellow
cross inside, on a white field
bordered in dark blue. (MPI 1370)

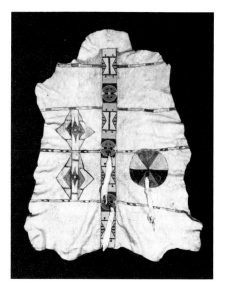

187. **Child's Robe,** *Crow*
60" long, 52" wide
Northwest Area Foundation

This skin robe is decorated with evenly spaced painted bands intersected by a beaded strip containing three discs. A white weasel skin hangs from the center of each disc. Three geometric designs pained in red, yellow, and green to the right and left of the beaded strip fill the space between the traverse lines. The strip is light blue with triangles of red, yellow, blue, and white. The discs are beaded in pink, light blue, green, dark blue, red, and white beads, on a field of red stroud cloth. (SMM 1–1125)

185. **Blanket Strip,** *Crow*
65" long, 4³/₄" wide,
6¹/₄" medallions
Museum of the Plains Indian

This beaded strip has four discs decorated with dark blue diamonds radiating from a red center, with a red border against a twisted rectangle shape in pink and dark blue, on a light blue field. Ermine skins hang from the center of each disc. One disc is decorated with colored feathers and ribbons. The panels between the discs are composed of a red diamond with a yellow inscribed triangle and two grey-blue triangles at either end. There is a border of green triangles within a pink stripe. The end rectangle has a red geometric shape with a yellow and green interior. The strip is sewn on a green Hudson's Bay blanket. (MPI 1371)

186. **Robe,** *Crow*
66" long, 44" wide
Museum of the Plains Indian

This elkskin robe is beaded in rectangular rows of orange, light blue, and dark green with insets of light green, light blue, red, yellow and orange, separated by dark blue squares and white or yellow insets. Fringe with red beads and bells hangs from the bottom row. (MPI 1262)

Children's Life

Dolls

Although a number of Indian women living on the reservation of the Northern Plains made costumed dolls for sale to non-Indian collectors during the second quarter of this century, the pair of dolls in Cat. 188 is especially noteworthy on two counts. The dolls were intended to represent well-known members of a tribe other than the maker's, and the maker was recognized as one of the most gifted craftworkers of the region at the time these dolls were made.

These dolls were created by Juanita Tucker, a member of the Assiniboine tribe living on Fort Belknap Reservation in Montana. She intended them to represent Two Guns White Calf, one of the sons of White Calf, the last head chief of the Blackfeet in Montana, and the wife of Two Guns. Two Guns was a favorite model for artists because of his strikingly handsome profile. This couple were members of Blackfeet Indian groups that traveled to major cities in the United States under the sponsorship of the Great Northern Railway and Louis W. Hill, Sr., its president, to publicize Glacier National Park. This pair of dolls was sold through the Northern Plains Indian Arts and Crafts Association Shop in the newly established Museum of the Plains Indian on the Blackfeet Reservation in 1941. It was purchased by Louis W. Hill, Jr., and added to his father's Indian collection.

In developing her miniature representations of this couple Juanita Tucker must have worked from photographs, for Two Guns White Calf had been dead for a number of years. The dolls stand one foot high. Their heads are of tough, dark brown hide; their bodies, of cloth. Both wear white buckskin garments. Mrs. Tucker took pains to show Mrs. White Calf in a dress of traditional Blackfeet style decorated with parallel, meandering bands of beadwork across the top. Two Guns wears a fur bandeau around his head and a cloth breechclout decorated with transverse bands of ribbonwork. The narrow bands of beadwork on his shirt and leggings are made to match. In his left hand he carries a tobacco pouch beaded with an equal-armed cross on a light background. It is noteworthy that the beads are applied in the lazy stitch much used by Assiniboine beaders but rarely employed by the Blackfeet save for the decoration of women's dresses.

Baby Carriers

Designed as an easily transportable protection for infants, baby carriers were often highly ornamented to honor their occupants. The Cheyenne, Arapahoe, and Sioux carriers were in reality bundles tied at the front with openings at the top forming hoods for the infants' heads. On the simpler bundles, only the hoods were decorated, with either quills or beads. More elaborate carriers were fully beaded, and these generally were lashed to frames of thin slates, two of which extended well above the top. These were commonly decorated with brass carpet tacks and ribbons. The Blackfeet, and such plateau people as the Kutenai, Flathead, and Shoshone, sewed their skin bundles to tapering, elongated boards rounded at the top, which extended above the hood and opening for the baby's head. It was this area that was commonly decorated with beadwork. Most Crow bundles were further secured by several decorated flaps tied in the front. These, like the Cheyenne carriers with frames, could be suspended from the mother's back, propped against a tipi, or hung from a saddle pommel (Mason 1889).

Cat. 200 shows what more properly might be called a baby bundle. The upper half of deerskin is decorated with quill embroidery; the lower half is of commercial cloth. It has been identified as being either Cheyenne or Arapahoe. Cat. 201 is a Cheyenne baby bundle with only the hood decorated with beads. Cat. 202 shows a fully beaded baby carrier ornamented with upholstery tacks and ribbons. Save for the diagnostic differences in design elements, Sioux carriers were very similar to Cheyenne carriers.

Cat. 199 is a Crow carrier showing the bundle secured to a board with four flaps sewn to the bundle. What appears to be a beaded butterfly at the base is unusual and not in the tradition of Crow design. Cat. 198 shows a Blackfeet carrier. A bib of deerskin covers the bundle, which is laced to secure the baby. Cat. 195 is a Kutenai carrier, showing hood and lacing. Cat. 196, also Kutenai, shows a bib similar to the Blackfeet example.

Baby's Bonnet

The stiff and heavy baby's bonnet in Cat. 203 is an example of cultural adaptation at its worst. The Cheyenne infant must have endured sheer discomfort for the sake of its mother's misguided sense of elegance.

Cat. 188

188. **Dolls,** *Assiniboine-made*
12" high
Northwest Area Foundation

The female doll, made by Juanita Tucker around 1941, wears an example of the traditional dress of a Blackfeet woman: a leather dress, leggings, moccasins, and a beaded headband around her braids. Her fringed dress has long, closed sleeves and a beaded and fringed yoke. The leggings are bound by thongs, and the beaded belt has a bag attached. All the beadwork is lazy stitched in red, blue, black, and light blue. The male doll is said to represent Two Guns White Calf, one of the sons of White Calf, the last head chief of the Blackfeet in Montana, and the female doll represents his wife.
(SMM 52–5a and b)

189. **Male Doll,** *Cheyenne (?)*
21" high
Museum of the Plains Indian

This doll is of buckskin with beads defining the face and hair ornament. The hair is part of a human scalp, bound with fur. The beads on the hair are light blue, red, and green with red and green dangles. The clothes consist of a fringed buckskin shirt and leggings with a beaded strip in white and green with geometric ornaments of light and dark blue, pink, and red. The shirt is belted with quill-wrapped rawhide in red, white, purple, and orange. There is a breastplate of light blue, yellow, and red, and a beaded flower of red and yellow with a blue, red, and yellow stem attached to the shoulder. Mescal beans are laced to the sides and shoulders. Three rows of beads adorn the neck (amber, green, pink, and red). A beaded necklace of white, blue, and red has orange feathers. The moccasins have fully beaded uppers and soles of green, light blue, yellow, and red.
(MPI 1179)

190. **Female Doll,** *Cheyenne*
15½" high
Museum of the Plains Indian

This doll of smoke-tanned buckskin has features of white and blue beads with hair ornaments of white and pink. The hair is a human scalp. The dress is decorated with white, blue, yellow, pink, and green beads in strips and geometric patterns. The sleeves are fringed, and the hem has a fringe of blue, white, green, yellow, and pink beads and tin-cone dangles. The leggings are white with a red and blue pattern. The moccasins are beaded in white in a striped pattern. (MPI 1180)

191. **Toy Baby Carrier,** *Kutenai*
13¼" long, 6" wide
Museum of the Plains Indian

This toy baby carrier laces up the front and is beaded at the base, around the hood, and at the top of the cradleboard. Green, white, clear red, navy blue, clear white, brown, and yellow beads are used.
(MPI 1110)

Cat. 189

Cat. 190

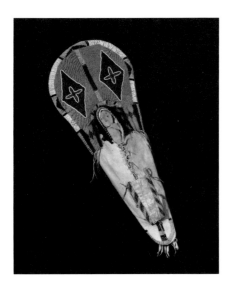

192. **Toy Baby Carrier,** *Crow*
24" long, 9½" wide
Museum of the Plains Indian

This toy baby carrier is of buckskin stretched over wood. Beaded decorations are at the top, at the foot, and on the rawhide flap. The beadwork at the top forms a field of pink for two diamonds outlined in white with translucent blue interiors. A red cross with a blue center appears in the middle of the diamonds. There is a border of white with blue, yellow, and green insets with green triangles. Yellow, green, light blue, and red beads encircle the opening, which contains a doll with black bead eyes. The opening is partially bordered by black and red strouding. The baby is of wood covered with hide and cloth. The rawhide flap has light blue and red beads in alternating diagonal strips. The pattern at the foot is yellow with red and blue beads. (MPI 1234)

193. **Baby Carrier,** *Kutenai*
30" long, 11" wide
Museum of the Plains Indian

This beaded smoke-tanned baby carrier has a floral design in red, green, brown, mauve-pink, and silver on white. There is an interrupted-stitch, beaded design on the apron of the cradleboard, in a floral pattern. A strip of orange borders the top edge of the carrier. (MPI 1103)

194. **Baby Carrier,** *Kutenai*
29" long, 12" wide
Museum of the Plains Indian

This baby carrier is decorated in a floral design elaborated by an orange and black supplementary pattern on either side of the hood and repeated on the apron. The main design is orange, black, pink, green, and silver, with a black outline. The edge of the apron is serrated and lined with green cloth. The edge of the cradleboard is also rimmed with green cloth. (MPI 1104)

195. **Baby Carrier,** *Kutenai*
36" long, 15" wide
Museum of the Plains Indian

This baby carrier is decorated in a checkerboard-like progression of colors. The upper area contains white, red, and green squares; the second row and the two vertical rows on either side are worked in orange, white, and green; the lower pyramid is red, green, and white. There are pencil marks throughout, indicating the original intent of the maker. (MPI 1115)

196. **Baby Carrier,** *Kutenai*
39" long, 14" wide
Museum of the Plains Indian

This baby carrier is decorated in a beaded floral design of purple, green, light green, red, brown, and navy blue, outlined in black. A line of fringe crosses the back. (MPI 1118)

197. **Baby Carrier,** *Kutenai*
39" long, 13¼" wide
Museum of the Plains Indian

This baby carrier of white unsmoked leather is decorated with beading at the top in blue, green, red, yellow, and black, executed in triangles and circles. The apron is serrated at the outer edge. The pattern consists of three circles worked in blue with a red inner design and interrupted-stitch lines radiating from the circles. (MPI 1121)

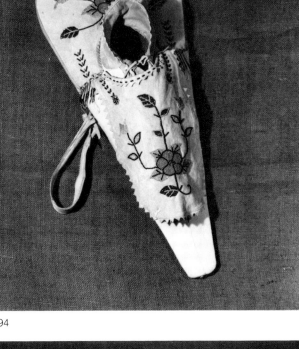

Cat. 194

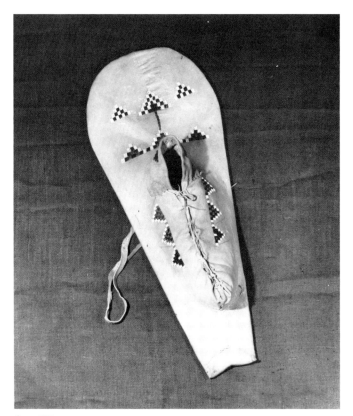

Cat. 195

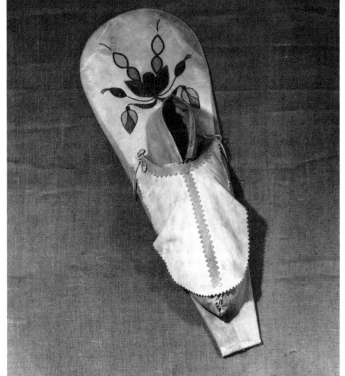

Cat. 196

Cat. 197

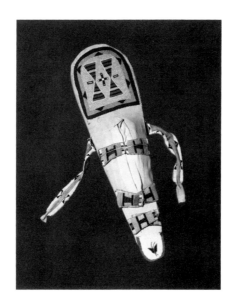

198. **Baby Carrier,** *Blackfeet*
37" long, 14" wide
Museum of the Plains Indian

The skin baby carrier has a geometric beaded design at the top and a buckskin bib covering the front. The design consists of a large, stepped diamond in the center of red and black alternating squares. A stepped pattern of green and red squares with a black border decorates either side. Around the hood are four red and black triangles. Near the top are two diagonal strips in a stepped pattern of red and black. The designs are set on a white field with a border of red and green alternating squares. (MPI 1113)

199. **Baby Carrier,** *Crow*
31" long, 8¼" wide
Museum of the Plains Indian

This muslin baby carrier is equipped with beaded leather bands sewn to the cloth. There are four main areas of beading: the base of the board, the head of the board, and two ties over the opening. The base is patterned with a butterfly sewn in blue beads with red and green outlining, with a strip of red cloth sewn around the edge. The two confining bands are similarly patterned in colors of mauve, green, white, yellow, and red. The upper part of the cradleboard contains a double-triangle design, beaded on a field of light blue with mauve borders. A red fabric strip lines the whole area. The stripes are green, navy blue, red, and yellow, and a Maltese cross of similar colors is placed between the two double triangles. (MPI 1100)

200. **Baby Carrier,** *Cheyenne (?)*
33" long, 12" wide
Museum of the Plains Indian

The hood of this baby carrier is of buckskin lined with orange cotton cloth. It is decorated with quillwork, beads, and fluffs. Designs of pyramid shapes are worked in blue, orange, yellow, and white on a field of red. The wrapped fringe and straps are red, yellow, orange, and green. Red quills cover the length of the hood, interrupted by red fluffs. The opening is decorated with beadwork in a pattern of white, dark blue, yellow, light blue, red, and green stripes. The bottom is of orange cloth, lined with grey felt. (MPI 1231)

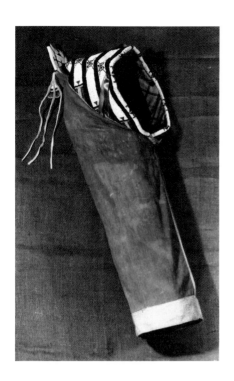

201. Baby Carrier, *Cheyenne*
37" long, 28" wide fully extended
Museum of the Plains Indian

This cloth-lined baby hood confines the beading to a parallelogram-shaped area encompassing the hood section only. The beading is green, blue, and red on white, with a geometric-striped pattern as the predominant design. The body of the carrier is red cloth, rimmed with white flannel-like fabric. The inside of the hood is plaid calico. There are leather beaded tassels — each with three fringes — hanging from the beaded headpiece. The hood is also decorated with three red ribbons sewn to the edge of the beaded section. (MPI 1236)

202. Baby Carrier, *Cheyenne*
14¹/₂" long frame, 26¹/₂" long hood
Museum of the Plains Indian

This baby carrier hood is fully beaded with a geometric figure and rows of six-pointed stars repeated on the sides. The figure consists of two stacked, stepped triangles in turquoise and light pink. The stars are alternately ochre and green at their points. The designs are done in lazy stitch on a white field. The carrier is mounted on a wooden frame with slats rising above the hood. The slats are decorated with a border of copper-headed tacks and ribbons, and red ribbons hang from the side of the hood. (MPI 1232)

203. Baby's Bonnet, *Cheyenne*
7" high, 5¹/₂" wide, folded
Museum of the Plains Indian

The surface of this baby bonnet is totally covered with beaded decoration. The background is dark blue, and the beading is divided into three sections. The border, composed of wine-red beads crossed at intervals with oblique white lines, continues uninterrupted. A strip of solid dark blue, followed by a line of periodic stepped-pyramid designs in green and white completes the motif and continues across the bonnet. The two panels are identical. Each consists of a cross-like design with inverted double-triangular ends executed in white, red, and silver. A central section contains a light blue and red windmill design bisected by a navy blue, single-bead design. The center panel, crossing the length of the bonnet, is made up of two Latin crosses with white arms, red central and end sections, and a small cluster of silver beads in the middle. The lining is of white muslin, as are the bonnet strings. (MPI 1149)

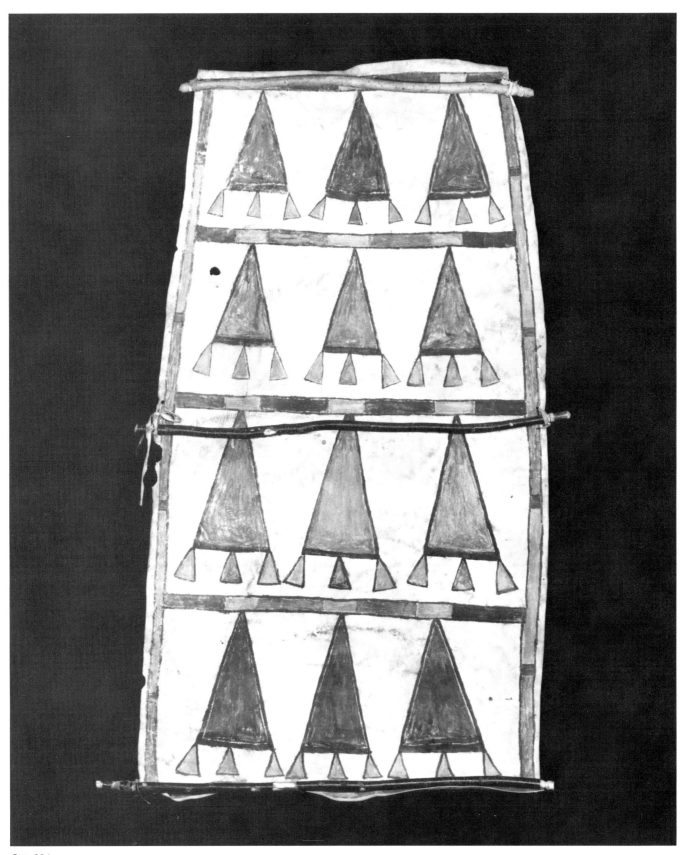

Cat. 204

Tipi Furnishings

Fig. 48 Tipi door on the Crow Reservation in 1909. *Photograph by Edward S. Curtis, courtesy of the National Anthropological Archives, Smithsonian Institution*

Painted Rawhide Tipi Door

Painted rawhide tipi doors are very rare in museum collections. Clark Wissler indicated that they were formerly in use among the Blackfeet but had become obsolete by the first decade of this century. He wrote, "So far as our information goes, a rawhide door shaped like and decorated after the manner of a parfleche was sometimes used; but the door curtain made of soft-dressed skins seems to have been the usual form . . . at present these curtains are made of wornout blankets or other cloth" (Wissler 1910:104).

A fine example of a painted rawhide door in the Hill Collection is Cat. 204, fashioned of a single piece of rawhide some 54 inches high and 30 inches at its widest point, with three stiffeners of chokecherry wood tied across the top, bottom, and midsection. Its striking decoration was achieved by the use of a few simple geometric forms — large and small triangles and narrow banded borders. Triangles with three smaller ones pendant from their bases are commonly seen in late nineteenth-century Crow beadwork. This door resembles so closely the painted hide door of a Crow tipi photographed by Edward S. Curtis in 1909 or earlier on the Crow Reservation that we might believe it to be the same door (Fig. 48). Certainly the photograph seems to confirm a Crow identification for this rare specimen. It also illustrates the appearance of the door in position on the outside of a tipi.

Willow Backrests

The largest pieces of tipi furniture among the nomadic tribes in buffalo days were the backrests composed of 125 or more peeled willow rods bound together, one over another, in a horizontal position with sinew cord. The length of the willow rods became gradually shorter as the backrest became higher, so that the piece has a triangular form with its base on the ground. Each backrest was supported by a tripod of poles. The great advantage of these backrests in the buffalo days was their light weight and portability. They could be easily rolled and carried on the travois when

Fig. 49 Blackfeet woman peeling bark from a pole intended for a backrest tripod. *Photograph by Walter McClintock, courtesy of the Western Americana Collection, The Beinecke Rare Book and Manuscript Library, Yale University*

camp was moved. A drawing of a backrest in place to form the bottom of a travois load as it was commonly transported by the Blackfeet appears in "The Horse in Blackfoot Indian Culture" (Ewers 1955:134–35).

After these Indians settled down on reservations and their log and frame houses were furnished with beds like those of the white people, they continued to use willow backrests in their tipis during summer encampments at Sun Dance time. Backrests were made by women in the spring, when the willows were easiest to peel.

Cat. 206 shows a backrest in which the ends of the willow rods are decorated with vertical bindings of buckskin. A buckskin pendant also hangs down in front of the upper portion of this ingenious willow mat. Both bindings and pendant are decorated with beadwork. The backrest resembles Blackfeet ones known to have been made during the early years of this century.

Cat. 205 offers a different view of a backrest in order to show the placement of the three poles that provide the support for a backrest. Women liked to decorate these tripods with simple geometric designs by removing small square, rectangular, or triangular sections of the bark with a sharp knife, as pictured by Walter McClintock in a photograph taken at the turn of the century (Fig. 49). The drawing for Cats. 207–213 illustrates geometric designs on the poles of several backrest tripods in the Hill Collection.

204. **Tipi Door,** *Crow*
● *54" long, 30" wide*
Museum of the Plains Indian

This rawhide tipi door is painted in
geometric patterns of green,
orange, and two shades of blue.
The design is divided into four
registers, each containing three
triangles in blue and green or dark
and light blue. Three small triangles
support each larger one. Three
chokecherry branches serve as
stiffeners. (MPI 1245)
Photo: page 180.

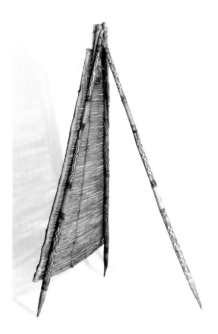

205. **Backrest,** *Blackfeet*
5'4" long, 1¼" diameter tripod
47" long, 9½" wide top,
30' wide bottom backrest
Northwest Area Foundation

These backrest poles are joined at
the top with a hide thong. Three
sets of checkerlike squares are cut
into the bark with yellow and blue
paint above and below each set.
The points are painted yellow. The
willow rod backrest is strung
together by sinew thongs forming a
truncated triangle. The outer edges
are covered with canvas, topped
with red flannel. (SMM 49–174)

206. **Backrest,** *Blackfeet*
59" long, 17¼" wide top,
38" wide bottom
Museum of the Plains Indian

This backrest is of stripped and
painted willow rods. Beaded leather
binds the sides. Alternating white
and red beads form rectangular
sections divided by two shades of
blue. A buckskin loop at the top is
decorated with two white beaded
rectangles with small blue and red
geometric designs. The lower edge
of the loop is edged with white
beads. The willow rods are painted
in horizontal stripes of orange, blue,
and red. (MPI 1246)

207. **Backrest Poles,** *Blackfeet*
5'1½" long, 1½" diameter
Northwest Area Foundation

These three poles are pointed at
one end and joined to one another
by a skin thong. The designs have
been cut into the poles.
(SMM 49–171)

208. **Backrest Poles,** *Blackfeet*
5'7" long, 1" diameter
Northwest Area Foundation

These three backrest poles are
decorated at the pointed end by a
series of simple triangular designs
cut into the bark. Above each
principal design area are three
circular rings within bark enclosures
that have been painted red.
(SMM 49–172)

209. **Backrest Poles,** *Blackfeet*
5' long, 1" diameter
Northwest Area Foundation

The design on these three poles is
cut in the bark in the form of
rectangular checkerlike bars. A
blue painted area on each end of
the design group is enclosed within
bark rings. (SMM 49–173)

210. **Backrest Poles,** *Blackfeet*
5'3½" long, 1½" diameter
Northwest Area Foundation

The bark has been cut on each of
the three poles in an identical
manner to form a series of
geometric designs. There is no
indication that these poles have
ever been painted. (SMM 49–175)

211. **Backrest Poles,** *Blackfeet*
5'4" long, 1" diameter
Northwest Area Foundation

Red painted rings at either end of
the cut bark design area decorate
each of the three poles in this
backrest. (SMM 49–177)

Cats. 207–213. The geometric designs on backrest poles are not necessarily shown to scale.
Drawing by Patricia Hemmis Osthus

212. **Backrest Poles,** *Blackfeet*
5'4" long, 1" diameter
Northwest Area Foundation

This set of poles is pointed at one
end. Although the designs are
similar, the poles may not all be
from the same set as two of the
poles have a thong hole at the
upper end while the third does not.
The third pole also differs in having
three carved design groups and in
its lack of the red and yellow paint
encircling the rings. (SMM 49–176)

213. **Backrest Poles,** *Blackfeet*
5'2" long, 1" diameter
Northwest Area Foundation

The design in these three poles is
cut in the form of an elongated
checkerboard pattern. The rings
that enclose the pattern area have
been painted red. (SMM 49–178)

Tools, Utensils, and Containers

Tools

The most essential tools in a buffalo-centered economy were the weapons used to kill the animals and prepare the hides. The flesher (Cat. 215) made from an elk bone and the scraper (Cat. 214) made from an elk antler were used to process the hides and make them ready for use as tipi covers, garments, containers, and the myriad of other objects required by the Plains Indian lifestyle.

The first step in hide preparation was to stretch the hide out hair side down and secure it to the ground with stakes — or attach it to a wooden frame with leather thongs. The flesher would then be repeatedly drawn across the hide, from one end to another, to remove all adhering fat and connecting tissue.

If the hide was to be tanned for use as a summer robe, parfleche, or other garment, the hair side would be removed. After a thorough soaking, the hide would be staked down again with the hair side up and the scraper would be drawn across the hide to remove the hair. Fig. 50 shows two women scraping and fleshing a hide that is staked to the ground.

Spoons

The Plains Indians carved spoons and ladles from the horns of bighorn sheep, buffalo, and later, cattle. The men were the carvers, and they began the work by soaking the horn in hot water, which made it pliable and easier to cut. Cat. 216 shows a buffalo-horn spoon decorated with beads and the carved head of a horse. Cat. 217, a Blackfeet cow-horn spoon, was obtained from Mrs. Takes Gun.

Wooden Bowls

Although white traders reported the use of wooden bowls by the Blackfeet for serving and eating foods during the early years of the nineteenth century, these native-made utensils tended to be replaced by wooden and metal ones of white manufacture as the century progressed. By the turn of the century, Clark Wissler was unable to collect an Indian-made wooden bowl from the Blackfeet. Even so, some older native-made bowls were preserved well into the present century as parts of ceremonial equipment accompanying medicine bundles, most especially the medicine pipe bundles of the Blackfeet.

Cat. 218 is a slightly cracked wooden bowl of an oval shape, 11 1/2 inches long by 8 inches wide. Its surface is covered with a reddish-brown paint, which probably indicates that it was once a part of a Blackfeet medicine bundle. This bowl appears to be of cottonwood, and it lacks the fine finish seen on many bowls of Sioux make in museum collections. Some Sioux bowls were also elaborated with ingeniously carved heads of animals or mythical creatures in human form rising above the rim on one side and facing the bowl cavity.

Bowl-making was women's work among the Blackfeet. A bowl was fashioned from a large burl from an ash or cottonwood tree. Ash was preferred because of its beautiful grain. The bowl-maker cut off a likely burl with an ax, carried it back to camp, and began to hollow it out with an ax. She finished the inside by carefully removing small chips from the surface with her metal-bladed skin scraping tool (Cat. 214). A careful worker smoothed the interior surface with a sand rock. She then removed the bark from the outside of the bowl with a knife. After allowing the bowl to dry in the sun, the maker greased the entire surface with animal fat. Finally she polished it to bring out the grain of the wood (Ewers 1945:58–59).

Fig. 50 Women scraping hides. *Photograph courtesy of W. H. Over Museum, University of South Dakota*

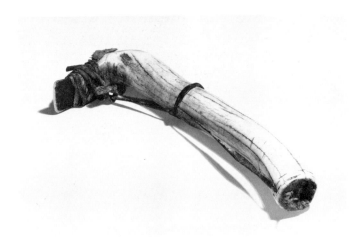

Cat. 214

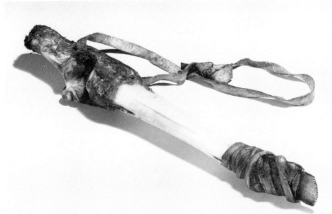

Cat. 215

Cat. 216

Cat. 217

214. **Scraper,** *Blackfeet*
12" long, 5½" wide
Northwest Area Foundation

The elk antler chosen to make this scraper has one remaining tine that projects at a right angle to the main antler in order to hold a smooth steel blade. A buckskin thong secures the blade and then loops around the center of the antler, extending upward to be knotted through a small hole in the hollow end. (SMM 1–869)

215. **Bone Flesher,** *Blackfeet*
16" long, 4" wide
Northwest Area Foundation

The flesher, made for removing tissue and flesh from animal hides, consists of a lower foreleg of an elk, with buckskin strips at the upper and lower ends. The strip at the upper end has a loop for wrapping around the wrist to insure stability in pulling or dragging the tool across the skin. A strip of hide, attached while wet and shrunken into place, secures a serrated steel blade to the bond at the lower end. A tag fastened to the flesher notes that it came from "Broadwater-Pepin Trading Co., Browning, Montana" and states that it was the property of "Short Face, a Blackfoot Indian." (SMM 1–868)

216. **Horn Spoon,** *Sioux*
10½" long, 3¾" wide
Northwest Area Foundation

This black bison-horn spoon has an elaborately decorated handle wrapped with cloth and strung beads. A red feather tassel is bound by a thin wire to the bowl end of the handle. A small carved-horn horse's head with red painted nostrils adorns the upper end of the handle. (SMM 49–193)

217. **Horn Spoon,** *Blackfeet*
10" long, 2½" wide
Northwest Area Foundation

This large, shallow spoon is made of cow horn and has a small thong attached to the handle. (SMM 49–192)

218. **Wooden Bowl,** *Blackfeet*
11½" long, 8" wide
Northwest Area Foundation

This slightly cracked, oval-shaped wooden bowl has been painted reddish-brown. (SMM 49–194)

Fig. 51 Brulé Sioux woman painting
parfleches. *Photograph by John
Anderson, courtesy of Jack R. Williams*

Painted Rawhide Containers

In the buffalo days, Northern Plains Indian women made containers of tough, long-wearing, waterproof rawhide for storing utilitarian and sacred articles as well as for use in transporting them when camp was moved. Containers intended to hold sacred objects were of different shapes from the others and were decorated with long, cut-rawhide fringes. Women painted the exposed surfaces of all these rawhide containers with colorful geometric patterns executed in native and/or trade colors.

After the buffalo were gone, the Indian women continued to make these containers from cattle rawhide obtained from the animals killed at the agency slaughterhouses to provide the beef issued to Indians by the government in their rations. A few older women with a high degree of Indian blood continued to process the cattle hides and make these containers as gifts to other Indians or for sale to non-Indian collectors.

The Parfleche

The most common form of painted rawhide container is known by the French word of *parfleche*. Mable Morrow, who has studied this type of container most thoroughly, defined the parfleche as "a folded and rectangular container made of buffalo or other large-animal hide which was used by the Indian people for storage and for packing of dried meat and other dried foods, blankets, clothing and other items" (Morrow 1975:25).

Each parfleche required nearly half of the hide of a buffalo or cow, and parfleches were generally made in matching pairs and transported with one on each side of a packhorse tied to the horns of the pack saddle. Their contents remained dry even when traveling in the hardest rain. Fig. 51 shows a Western Sioux woman painting a pair of parfleches on a hide stretched taut on the ground by a series of wooden pegs driven through the edge of the hide.

A Blackfeet woman made a parfleche by selecting "a hide with the hair on, whose inner side had been fleshed and scraped to an even thickness. She soaked the hide in water and while it was still damp, pegged it out on the ground hair side down. She knelt over the hide on her knees and began to paint on a portion of it the design composition she had in mind. She measured the lengths of the lines outlining the desired motifs precisely with peeled willow sticks of different lengths. Using these sticks as rulers, she drew the outlines of the forms with paint on a bone brush. Usually a single color was used for outlining all painted forms in the parfleche. Then she filled in the larger areas of the composition with other desired colors. She mixed the paints only with hot water, which caused it to sink into the damp hide and become permanently fixed after it had dried" (Ewers 1945:16).

Other Indian women used a gluelike sizing made from the juice of a cactus, the boiled tail of a beaver, or other liquid to cover the entire painted surface with a thin coating that made the paint shine and remain permanent. Women of other tribes employed the same or slightly different methods of making and painting parfleches (Morrow 1975:25–42).

Not until after the parfleche was painted was it cut to shape with a sharp knife, folded into its intended envelope-like shape, and the tie holes burned near the edges of the flaps with a very hot iron rod. A buffalo or cowhide was large enough to yield a pair of these containers with enough small pieces of rawhide left to make smaller pouches and soles for moccasins.

Cat. 223 pictures a pair of Sioux parfleches. They differ from the Blackfeet parfleche illustrated in Cat. 219 in their proportions as well as in the designs painted on their closing flaps. Blackfeet parfleches were shorter and proportionately wider than Sioux or Crow containers of this kind. A Crow parfleche is shown in Cat. 224. It differs from both Sioux and

Blackfeet parfleches in having a single pair of tie holes for closing the flaps with buckskin cords. The others have three sets of holes for this purpose.

During her study of the Indian parfleche in the 1940s, Morrow found many of these useful containers in the possessions of Indian women of tribes other than the ones who had made them. Not only were they widely diffused to other tribes of Plains Indians, but they were traded to other tribes in the Columbia Valley, west of the Rockies. Henry H. Spalding, a pioneer Christian missionary among the Nez Perce, wrote of his own trade of potatoes to Indians for some of these containers. An inventory of his mission at Lapwai in 1847 listed "42 Parfleches with hanging cords" (Drury 1958: 265, 363). Yet Francis Haines learned from Nez Perce informants during this century that the Nez Perce did not make the parfleche but obtained this article from their friends, the Crow, in exchange for the woven cornhusk bags they made so well (Haines 1955:38). A parfleche obtained from the Sioux in 1833 by Prince Maximilian is preserved in the Museum für Volkerkunde in Berlin. It bears a painted design very typical of the Cheyenne, suggesting that the container was of Cheyenne make, traded or given to the Sioux (Morrow 1975:78).

Indian testimony strongly suggests that the Indians of the Northern Plains did not make the parfleche until after they obtained the horse and after they acquired sharp metal knives from white traders (Ewers 1955: 115–16). The use of the parfleche by the Omaha for transporting dried meat on horseback as early as 1819 is suggested by Edwins James's observation that the Omaha used "quadrangular packages, each of a suitable size to attach conveniently to one side of the packsaddle of a horse" for this purpose (James 1823:I, 212).

Rawhide Work Case

Indian women of a number of Plains Indian tribes made workbags to hold their craft materials from two rectangular pieces of rawhide sewn together. An elliptical piece of soft-dressed skin formed the bottom, and an extension of soft skin formed a top that could be closed by a drawstring. Usually one side of the rawhide was painted so as to present the exposed surface when hung up inside a lodge or laid on the ground. Cat. 225 pictures a Sioux workbag bearing painted designs similar to those appearing on the pair of Sioux parfleches in Cat. 223.

Tubular Rawhide Case

The Blackfeet and their neighbors of the Northern Plains made rawhide cases in the form of long tubes closed at both ends to hold carefully wrapped and highly prized sacred objects — most especially feather bonnets. A good example of one of these cases, of Blackfeet origin, is illustrated in Cat. 226. It housed a straight-up bonnet.

The slightly tapering tube of rawhide is closed at each end by a cut rawhide disc tied to the main cylinder by rawhide cords passed through holes burned near the edges of both the tube and the end coverings. A long fringe of cut rawhide was suspended from the edge of the tube where it was fastened together. Generally the segment of the tube hidden from the eyes of the observer when it was transported on horseback or hung up in the owner's lodge was not painted. The design painted on the front is one commonly used by Blackfeet in decorating tubular cases of this kind — a central rhombus, flanked by very-broad-based triangles and connected at each end to smaller triangles.

Proof that this type of case was made and used long before the extermination of the buffalo on the Northern Plains appears in an illustration of one of them by Henry Rowe Schoolcraft in 1854. That author stated that the case was used to hold "an elaborate headdress of feathers," but he did not state its tribal origin (Schoolcraft 1854: 57–68).

Fig. 52 Rawhide cases, both tubular and side-fringed were used by Blackfeet Indians to hold sacred objects. This one is shown on a tripod behind a lodge in Sun Dance camp. *Photograph by Edward S. Curtis, courtesy of the National Anthropological Archives, Smithsonian Institution*

Side-fringed Rawhide Case

The Blackfeet and their neighbors made a smaller rawhide case of rectangular shape from a single piece of hide. This was folded twice to provide front and back with a closing flap over the top. It was then laced together at the sides with rawhide cords passing through holes burned near the edges of the rawhide. Cases of this kind, intended for holding sacred objects, were further decorated with long rawhide fringes. Only the exposed surface of the case was painted with geometric designs, much like those on a parfleche. An example of this type of case appears in Cat. 228. It probably is not of Blackfeet origin.

Doubtless these side-fringed cases were among the many kinds of "parchement bags" Prince Maximilian saw when he visited the Blackfeet camps near Fort McKenzie during the late summer of 1833. Certainly many of the fringed rawhide cases in museum collections have become so worn through long periods of exposure to the elements that the painted designs have become barely visible. It was customary to leave these containers of sacred objects outside on tripods behind the tipi during the daytime and to bring them inside at night. Edward Curtis photographed several fringed rawhide cases — of both the tubular and side-fringed varieties supported by a tripod — in the Piegan encampment on the Blackfeet Reservation in Montana in 1909 (Fig. 52). Even as recently as the 1940s, it was not uncommon to see these cases on tripods near the tipis in the annual Sun Dance encampments of the Piegan near the Museum of the Plains Indian on the Blackfeet Reservation.

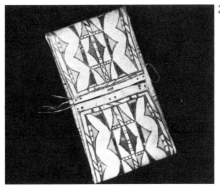

219. **Parfleche,** *Sioux*
57" long, 15½" high
Northwest Area Foundation

The parfleche container is shaped like a large painted envelope. The geometric patterns on the flaps are in yellow, red, blue, and green. (SMM 49–199)

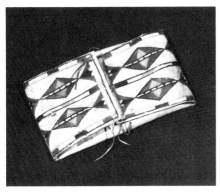

220. **Parfleche,** *Blackfeet*
23" long, 13" high
Northwest Area Foundation

This parfleche is decorated with triangles and rhomboids in red, blue, yellow, and green. (SMM 1–696)

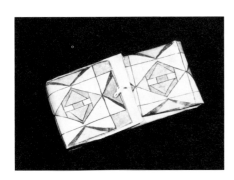

Cat. 221

221. **Parfleche,** *Northern Plains*
28" long, 13½" high
Museum of the Plains Indian

This painted parfleche is decorated with a geometric design in yellow, red, green, and blue. (MPI 1249)

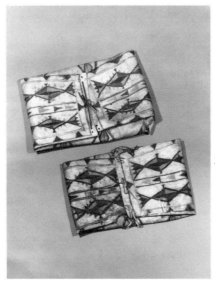

222. **Pair of Parfleches,** *Blackfeet*
22½" long, 14½" high
Museum of the Plains Indian

These parfleches differ slightly in size but are painted with the same design in green, red, yellow, and blue. (MPI 1251 and 1253)

Cat. 223

223. **Pair of Parfleches,** *Sioux*
22" long, 10½" high
Museum of the Plains Indian

These parfleches are decorated in red, yellow, blue, and green. (MPI 1250 and 1254)

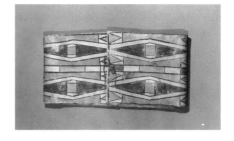

224. **Parfleche,** *Crow*
28" long, 13½" high
Museum of the Plains Indian

This parfleche is decorated only on the front with an orange, yellow, and green design of triangles and diamonds. The two front folding flaps are identical in design but slightly different in color. (MPI 1256)

225. **Rawhide Work Case,** *Sioux*
26" long, 10½" wide
Museum of the Plains Indian

This painted workbag has a buckskin extension bound with red strouding. (MPI 1255)

Cat. 226

Cat. 227

226. **Tubular Rawhide Case,** *Blackfeet*
23¹/₂" long, 21" long fringe
Northwest Area Foundation

This cylindrical bonnet case is
decorated by long hanging fringe
and a curvilinear design painted in
blue, yellow, green, and red.
(SMM 49–307)

227. **Fringed Rawhide Bag,** *Blackfeet*
9¹/₂" long, 9" wide
Northwest Area Foundation

This square bag is made of a
folded rectangular piece of rawhide
with long fringe sewn inside each
side seam. An overhanging flap
closing the bag is secured by two
tie thongs. An edging of blue and
orange with diamond and triangular
shapes is painted in orange
trimmed with red. A short carrying
strap is attached to the back.
(SMM 49–198)

Cat. 228

228. **Side-fringed Rawhide Case,**
Northern Plains
11³/₄" long, 11" wide
Museum of the Plains Indians

This painted and heavily fringed
square rawhide case is bound with
red strouding on the flap and sides.
There are white beads on the flap.
(MPI 1293)

Storage Bags

Beaded and quilled storage bags were referred to by some as "possible bags" since it was possible to store just about anything in them. Fashioned of soft skin, they, like the rawhide parfleches, were always made in pairs. Decoration ranged from quilled and beaded bands in lines to solidly beaded panels employing either the band or bar element, or to geometric designs featuring diamonds, triangles, hourglasses, rectangles, crosses, forked designs, and the like. Among the Sioux, the red lines on their bags were said to represent "the woman's trail" (Wissler 1904:242 seq.), while among the Arapahoe, the lines symbolized camp trails (Kroeber 1902:100 seq.). The edges and flaps of these storage bags were consistently ornamented with rectangular elements. Dyed horsehair or feather pendants bound with tin-can cones further decorated the edges and flaps. Possible bags were especially popular among the Sioux, Crow, Cheyenne, and Arapahoe, but they were not used by the Blackfeet.

Woven Bags

The Nez Perce so-called cornhusk bags were in fact more often made from Indian hemp (*Apocynum cannabium*). They were made by several of the tribes inhabiting the plateau country west of the plains. Here, false embroidery of colored yarn was applied over the weft to plain, twined basketry, thereby making the design. Invariably, the designs differ on each side. These flat, rectangular bags appear to have been extremely popular trade items, quite the fashionable thing to possess (Douglas 1935).

Dewclaw Bag

Cat. 273 illustrates an ingenious workbag of Blackfeet creation. It was made of four pieces of hide from the lower legs of an elk, hair side out, including the dewclaws, which served as decorative features. These were fitted and sewn together so that two pieces formed each side of the bag, shaped while the hide was still wet. As it dried, it formed a stiff bag with a rounded bottom. Cut buckskin fringes were added for decoration, and the soft buckskin flap at the top could be closed by means of a drawstring. These bags were used as workbags, during the latter years of the nineteenth century, primarily by older women. One of the bags was accessioned at the Smithsonian Institution in 1899. In more recent years, Blackfeet craftswomen have made some of these bags for sale to non-Indians. A variant of the Blackfeet elkskin bag is illustrated and described by Mable Morrow (1975:208–209).

Flat Pouch

A pouch that has no prototype in the culture of the buffalo days and was not typical of Northern Plains crafts in more recent times appears in Cat. 274. It illustrates the ingenuity Indians have long employed in remaking objects intended for other use. The large panel of geometric beadwork that decorates the exposed side of this flat pouch probably was derived from a woman's leggings of Assiniboine origin. The floral beadwork on the top flap of this pouch is in a different style — that of the Plains Cree or Metis.

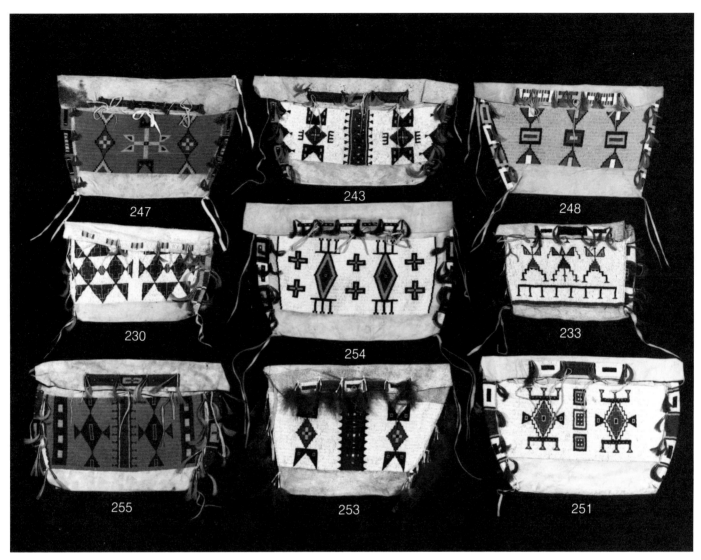

Possible Bags, *Group I. See Plates 18 and 19 and details this section.*

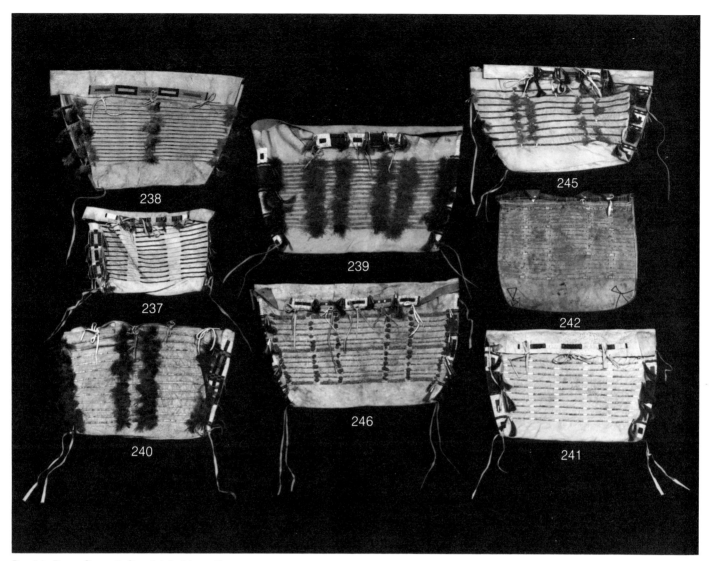

Possible Bags, *Group II. See details this section.*

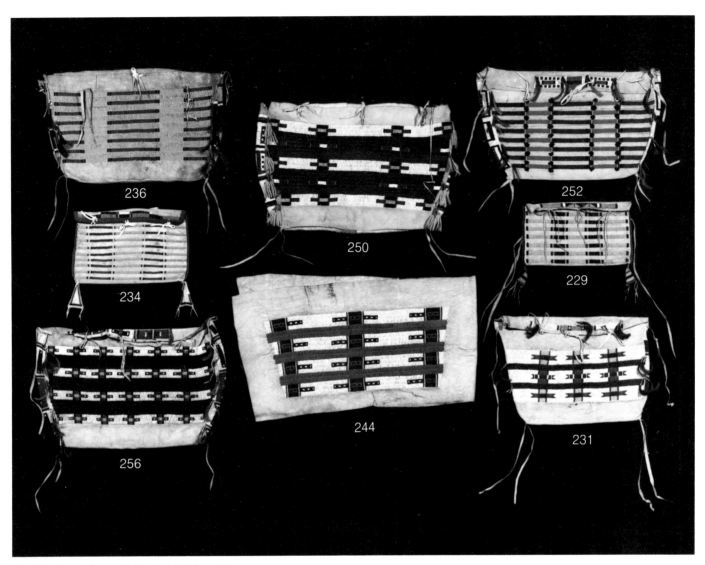

236

250

252

234

229

256

244

231

Possible Bags, *Group III. See details this section.*

196

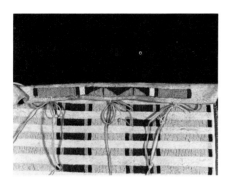

229. Possible Bags, *Crow*
12¼" long, 8¼" wide
Museum of the Plains Indian

These small bags are decorated with beaded stripes on the front and flap. The side is ornamented with red strouding and light blue beads. The stripes of light blue and green are divided by royal blue and pink. The flap has a band of three sections divided by royal blue and white. The outer sections are pink, and the center is green with two yellow triangles bisected by red. (MPI 1000a and b)

230. Possible Bags, *Sioux*
● *13" long, 17" wide*
Museum of the Plains Indian

The front beaded panels of these bags have repetitive patterns of diamonds and triangles in red, green, blue, and yellow on white. The side panel has a series of green, blue, yellow, and white rectangles. The front flap is a stripe of white, crossed with blue and yellow in a repeating pattern. (MPI 1001a and b)

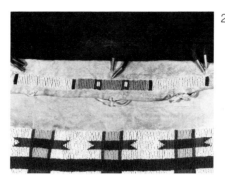

231. Possible Bags, *Sioux*
12½" long, 16½" wide
Museum of the Plains Indian

This pair of possible bags is decorated with beaded panels on the fronts, sides, and flaps. The front has five bars; three are white with three crosses in yellow, blue, green, and red. The remaining bars are royal blue. The side panels have five sections — two with green and three with royal blue and light blue rectangles. The sections are divided by red and yellow. The panel on the flap is white and light blue with two red and white stripes. (MPI 1002a and b)

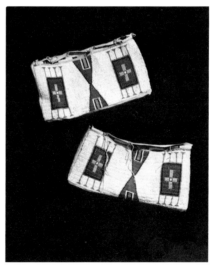

Cat. 232

232. Possible Bags, *Sioux*
10½" long, 18" wide
Museum of the Plains Indian

This pair of bags is decorated with beadwork on the front and upper lip. The front pattern has two inset rectangles symmetrically placed on either side of a large hourglass figure. The rectangles are in orange, blue, and green, with a blue and white cross and four top and bottom extensions. The hourglass is orange and blue, with a white, blue, and yellow rectangle in the center. The upper opening has the same colors on a white background (MPI 1003a and b)

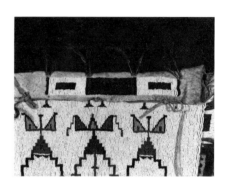

233. Possible Bag, *Sioux*
● *11½" long, 15½" wide*
Museum of the Plains Indian

This bag has beaded panels on the front, sides and flaps, with tin-cone dangles and red horsehair. The panels on the front has stepped pyramids with descending triangles in stepped line. The three figures are symmetrically placed on a white field over a horizontal line in dark blue, red, green, yellow, and light blue, with silver and brass faceted beads. The lower line is dark blue and the vertical lines end in red and brass bead triangles. The side panels have three rectangles of white and insets of green, yellow, and blue. The flap panel is composed of three white rectangles with insets of blue and green. (MPI 1004)

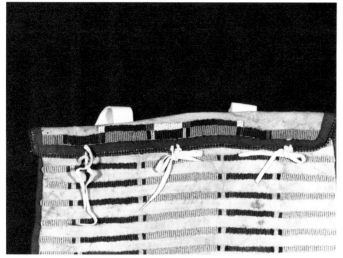

Cat. 234

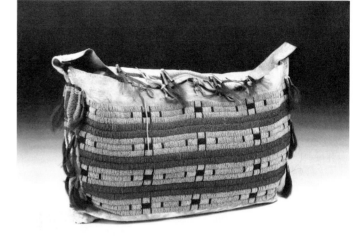

Cat. 235

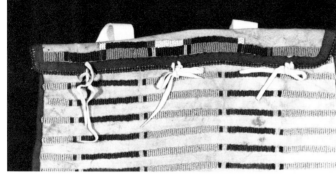

Cat. 236

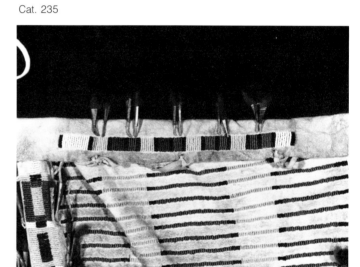

Cat. 237

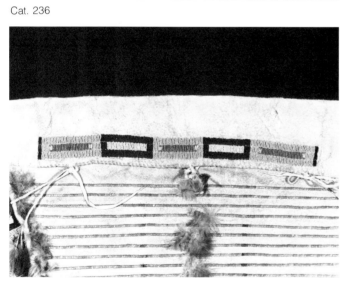

Cat. 238

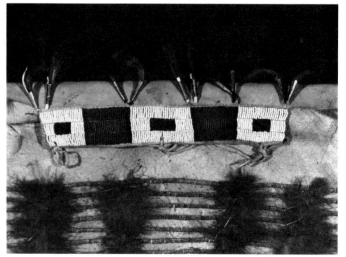

Cat. 239

234. **Possible Bag,** *Crow*
8" long, 13¼" wide
Museum of the Plains Indian

This small bag is decorated with beaded stripes of light blue, blue, yellow, red, and green. Red strouding edges the flap and side seam. The flap has a rectangular design of royal blue, green, lavender, yellow, red, and white. There is a line of green along the edge of the flap and two triangles with borders of light blue, pink, and royal blue. (MPI 1005)

235. **Possible Bag,** *Cheyenne*
13½" long, 20½" wide
Museum of the Plains Indian

This possible bag has beaded panels on the front, sides, and flap. Tin dangles with red horsehair are attached to the sides and flap. The design on the front is composed of six stripes, alternating light blue with dusky rose. The light blue stripes contain four crosses in blue and yellow. The three side panels are composed of rectangles of light blue with red insets and red with white insets. The flap contains outer rectangles of white with red insets and a center rectangle of light blue with a red inset. (MPI 1006)

236. **Possible Bag,** *Crow*
11¼" long, 20¾" wide
Museum of the Plains Indian

This bag has beaded bands of alternating red, yellow, dark blue, and light blue. The side panel is of rectangular blocks in light blue, aqua, red, green, yellow, and white. The flap has a beaded panel in light blue, dark blue, white, orange, and green. There are tin dangles with red horsehair on the sides. (MPI 1007)

237. **Possible Bag,** *Crow*
9½" long, 15½" wide
Museum of the Plains Indian

This possible bag is beaded in horizontal stripes. The colors alternate from dark blue to red or yellow. The side and flap panels are decorated in rectangles: white and blue, red and yellow, yellow and blue, and white and blue. The flap has a strip with solid blocks of white, yellow, green, and red. There are tin-cone dangles at the side and flap. (MPI 1008)

238. **Possible Bag,** *Cheyenne*
14" long, 22" wide
Museum of the Plains Indian

This possible bag is decorated with quillwork and beaded side panels. The flap has tin dangles. Purple feathers are attached to the sides and down the middle. The bag is covered with red quilled horizontal stripes. On either side of the feathers, the red lines are interrupted with a small section of purple quillwork. The side panels and the flap are beaded in a pattern of inset rectangles. The five rectangular boxes are light blue with insets of red with a yellow edge and dark blue with insets of yellow. (MPI 1009)

239. **Possible Bag,** *Cheyenne*
15½" long, 24½" wide
Museum of the Plains Indian

This possible bag is decorated with horizontal rows of red quillwork, divided by six columns of red feather fluffs. The beaded sides and flap are decorated with rectangles of white with dark blue insets and green with red insets. There are tin dangles with red horsehair on the flap and the sides. (MPI 1010)

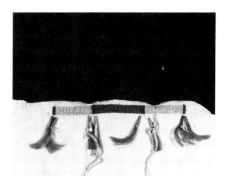

240. **Possible Bag,** *Cheyenne*
13" long, 20" wide
Museum of the Plains Indian

This possible bag is decorated with rows of red quillwork, a double row of red fluffs down the middle, and a row at each edge of the stripes. The beaded side panels have rectangles with alternating colors: white, green, yellow, light and dark blue, and red. The beaded flap panel consists of three rectangles of yellow and green divided by a royal blue stripe. Tin dangles with yellow horsehair are attached to the sides and flap. (MPI 1011)

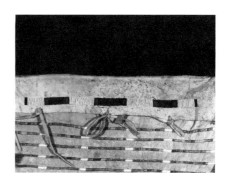

241. **Possible Bag,** *Sioux*
13" long, 19½" wide
Museum of the Plains Indian

This bag is decorated with red stripes of quillwork interrupted by white. The side panels are beaded in rectangles of white with royal blue, white with light blue and red edge, and green with red inset, separated by green and red or blue and yellow beads. The flap has alternating boxes of white and green separated with red and light blue or dark and light blue. Tin dangles with red horsehair are at the sides. (MPI 1012)

242. **Possible Bag,** *Cheyenne*
13½" long, 18½" wide
Museum of the Plains Indian

This possible bag has horizontal stripes of red quilling interrupted with green and white quills. The stripes are grouped in threes at the top and bottom and in pairs in the middle. There are three triangular projections on the flap for stringing the ties to close the bag. Light blue beadwork edges the flap. Along the back is beadwork in red, light blue, pink, dark blue, white, and yellow. (MPI 1013)

243. **Possible Bags,** *Sioux*
● *12½" long, 21½" wide*
Museum of the Plains Indian

This pair of bags has beaded panels on the front, sides, and flap. There are metal cone dangles with orange horsehair at the top of the beaded element and along the sides. The front panel has diamonds, stripes, and crosses in blue, green, pink, yellow, and red on white. The strips at the side and on the flap are in green, pink, and blue. (MPI 1014)

244. **Possible Bags,** *Cheyenne*
53" long, 14¼" wide
Museum of the Plains Indian

This long beaded buckskin "saddle cloth" was intended for two possible bags but was never completed. It is decorated with green and white stripes. These on the white field are rectangles with crosses in red and light blue. (MPI 1016)
Photo: page 196.

245. **Possible Bag,** *Cheyenne*
15" long, 22½" wide
Museum of the Plains Indian

This buckskin bag has horizontal striped red and white quillwork with red feather fluffs. Rectangular beaded decoration adorns the sides and flap. Tin dangles with red horsehair hang down the sides and on the flap. (MPI 1356a–b, II)

246. **Possible Bags,** *Cheyenne*
15" long, 22½" wide
Museum of the Plains Indian

This bag has horizontal stripes of red quillwork interspersed with white and yellow quills and bunches of red strouding. The horizontal stripes are in groups of three at the top, middle, and bottom, interspersed with single stripes. The beadwork on the sides and flap is patterned in five rectangles, of white with green and red insets and yellow with red and white insets. (MPI 1357a and b)

247. **Possible Bags,** *Cheyenne*
● *16" long, 21¾" wide*
Museum of the Plains Indian

This pair of bags has beadwork on the front, top of the flap, and at the sides. The front panel contains a cross terminating in triangles between two diamonds ending with triangles. The colors are green, yellow, red, and blue, on a pink field. The beaded strips on the ends and flap are striped, with blocks of color and crosses. There are metal cone dangles with red yarn fringe along the sides and on the flap. (MPI 1358a and b)

248. **Possible Bags,** *Sioux*
● *15" long, 22½" wide*
Museum of the Plains Indian

This pair of bags has beaded panels on the front, sides, and flap. Metal cone dangles with orange horsehair are on the flap and sides. The front panel has three rectangles connected to two stepped triangles with an inset of white. The side rectangles have insets of white and yellow with further insets of red and blue. Each rectangle is separated with a vertical blue line. The background is light blue with triangles outlined in dark blue. The strip on the flap is divided into three sections by white stripes. The outside sections have a white rectangular center divided by a red line and a border of red and yellow stripes. The center section is yellow with a green border. (MPI 1360)

249. **Possible Bags,** *Sioux*
13½" long, 20" wide
Museum of the Plains Indian

This pair has beaded panels on the front, side, and flap. The center is red, blue, yellow, green, and light blue with a red cross. The side panels have alternating colors of red, white, blue, and yellow. The flap contains the same pattern. Metal cones are attached to the flap and sides. (MPI 1359a and b)

Cat. 242

Cat. 243

Cat. 245

Cat. 246

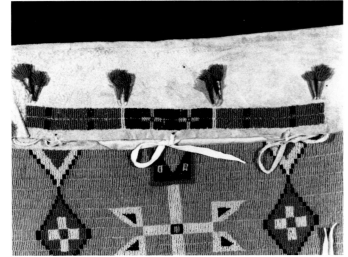

Cat. 247

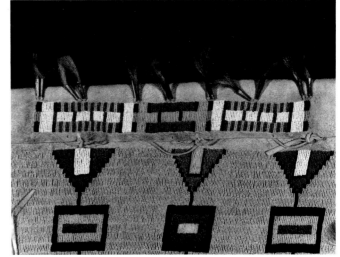

Cat. 248

250. **Possible Bags,** *Sioux*
15" long, 22½" wide
Museum of the Plains Indian

These bags have five bands, three composed of narrow white stripes with evenly spaced crosses of dark blue, red, yellow, and two of wide stripes with red, dark blue, and white on aqua. The side panels have three rectangles decorated with an H pattern; two show the H in white with the void in orange and white, and one shows the H in orange with the void in white. The patterns are divided by stripes of white, orange, and blue. Tin dangles with pink yarn hang along the sides. The bags are closed by ties at the sides. (MPI 1361a and b) *Photo: page 196.*

251. **Possible Bags,** *Sioux*
● *15¼" long, 22" wide*
Museum of the Plains Indian

This pair of bags is decorated with beaded panels on the front, sides, and flaps, and tin-cone dangles with red horsehair. The front panel has a symmetrical design of a diamond in red, yellow, light blue, white and dark blue surrounded by a dark blue stepped line terminating in triangles on the sides in dark blue, white, and red. Two of the figures are divided by three rectangles. The center figure is red, white, and green. The side panels consist of a strip of five squares of white with an inset of blue, green, and red. Each is separated by a triple stripe of red, yellow, and blue. The flap is decorated by three rectangles with inset boxes of white with blue, and green with red. A triple line of red, yellow, and blue separates each. Each has a canvas back and flap, while the exterior decorated side is of rawhide. (MPI 1362a and b)

252. **Possible Bags,** *Cheyenne*
13" long, 21" wide
Museum of the Plains Indian

This pair of bags has beading on the front, sides, and flap. There are tin dangles with orange-dyed horsehair on the sides and flap. The front consists of stripes of beadwork in alternating sections of green and orange, separated by blue, red, and white. Spots of red strouding are at evenly spaced intervals. The side panels have three inset rectangles: two have a white border with blue, white, green, and red inset. The center rectangle is white with a blue and white inset. The flap also has three inset rectangles; the outer two have borders of red and white with an interior of green and blue. The central rectangle, separated from the ends by a red and then a white stripe, consists of three rectangles in green, red, and green. (MPI 1363a and b)

253. **Possible Bags,** *Crow*
● *15" long, 21½" wide*
Museum of the Plains Indian

This pair of bags has beaded panels on the front, sides, and flap. There are metal cone dangles with red-dyed fluffs on the flap and sides. The front panel consists of a white field with diamonds topped by a double triangle. On either side of the diamond is a red vertical stripe with three green and white crosses and a row of triangles along the edges of the beaded stripe. The diamonds have a red border and a green interior with a yellow and blue inset. The triangles are blue with inset squares of yellow and red. On the side panel is a series of rectangles. The flap has five rectangles with insets divided by a blue and yellow stripe alternating from white with blue center to green with red center. (MPI 1364a and b)

254. **Possible Bags,** *Sioux*
● *13" long, 21" wide*
Museum of the Plains Indian

This pair of bags is beaded on the front, sides, and flap. There are tin cones with red horsehair on the side and flap. The front beaded panel has two large diamonds with a cross bar at the top and bottom with three vertical lines. The diamonds are blue, yellow, and red with a small green and yellow cross in the center, on white. At each side are crosses in green, yellow, and red. The side panels have three large rectangles in green, yellow, blue, and white, divided by a strip of red. The interior rectangle is white, green, and pink. The flap strip is set of five rectangles in white, green, and pink, and yellow, blue, and pink. Red strouding borders the flap. (MPI 1365a and b)

255. **Possible Bags,** *Crow*
● *15" long, 21½" wide*
Museum of the Plains Indian

This pair of bags has beaded panels on the front, sides, and flap, and tin-cone dangles tied with orange horsehair. The front panel is decorated with symmetrically placed diamonds of dark blue beads with an inset rectangle of yellow and red beads. Small, dark blue triangles are at each point; inset rectangles of red and green are on the side. The bottom and top rectangles are yellow and red. The two diamonds are separated by a vertical green stripe with inset red rectangles with borders of yellow and blue. The side panels are a series of rectangles: two small ones at each end and three large ones in the center. The outer two are green with inset panels of red. The inner panel is blue and yellow with inset red crosses. The flap repeats this pattern. (MPI 1366a and b)

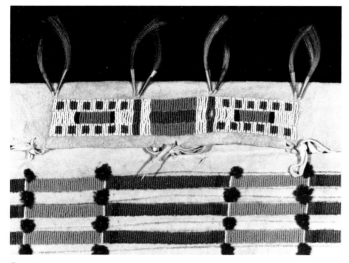

Cat. 252

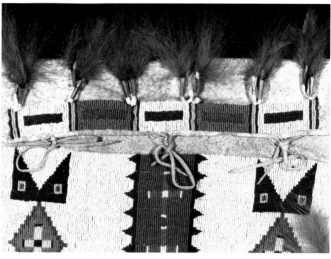

Cat. 253

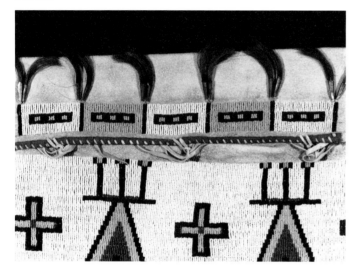

Cat. 254

Cat. 255

Cat. 256

256. **Possible Bags,** *Sioux*
14" long, 22" wide
Museum of the Plains Indian

These bags are beaded on the front, sides, and flap. The design has repetitive registers of white stripes with crosses of red, green, blue, and yellow and a wide stripe of dark blue. The side panels have five rectangles of dark blue with white inset, white with dark blue inset, and green with red inset. The flap has three rectangles of green with insets of red and white and white with an inset of dark blue and white, separated by red, yellow, and blue. Metal-cone dangles with red horsehair hang at the sides.
(MPI 1367a and b)

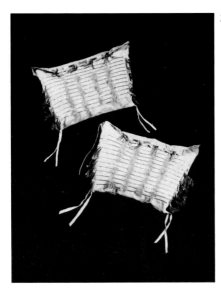

257. Possible Bags, *Sioux*
14" long, 21 1/2" wide
Northwest Area Foundation

In these bags, the entire front piece of soft hide is covered with horizontal red quill stripes and with red feathers, regularly spaced in each row. Each side of the bags is covered with a rectangular pattern of beadwork in yellow, green, and blue. Small tin cylinders and tufts of red horsehair are attached to the flap and sides. (SMM 49–195)

Cat. 258

258. Possible Bags, *Sioux*
11 1/2" long, 18" wide
Northwest Area Foundation

These identical soft hide bags carry the same beaded geometric decoration on the outside or flapside, while the inner side is undecorated. Cylindrical metal tinklers are attached by horsehair pendants to the sides. There is no decoration on the cover flap aside from three thongs that serve as fasteners.
(SMM 1–784 and 1–785)

259. Fiber Bag, *Nez Perce*
13 1/2" long, 8" diameter
Museum of the Plains Indian

This cylindrical bag displays a diamond pattern in red and black yarn woven over the warp. Commercial cloth and an inverted S in black border the upper edge. (MPI 986)

260. Fiber Bag, *Nez Perce*
16 1/2" long, 8" diameter
Museum of the Plains Indian

This cylindrical bag has geometric patterns in three shades of cornhusk woven over three shades of brown twine. The designs are sawtooth and diagonal striping. The rim of the bag is covered with commercial cloth secured with twine. (MPI 987)

261. Fiber Bag, *Nez Perce*
● *18" long, 14" wide*
Museum of the Plains Indian

This bag is woven from native hemp and cornhusks. The pattern decorating the bag consists of multicolored V shapes offset in each row to form a herringbone pattern. The dyed cornhusk decoration is red, green, blue-green, purple, and yellow. Rows of colored hourglass figures in green, red, purple, black, yellow, and orange-dyed cornhusks adorn the opposite side. (MPI 988)

262. Fiber Bag, *Nez Perce*
● *22" long, 16" wide*
Museum of the Plains Indian

This bag is woven of cotton string decorated with yarn. The pattern on one side is a series of herringbone stripes in alternating colors of olive-green and red, light green and scarlet red, and olive and light green. The other side has a series of red diamonds outlined in green and red, and of green outlined in green and red, with two small crosses. (MPI 989)

263. Fiber Bag, *Nez Perce*
● *17" long, 15 1/2" wide*
Museum of the Plains Indian

This woven hemp bag has designs in commercial yarn on one side and in dyed cornhusk on the other. One side has a repetitive motif of dark green triangles, pink double triangles, and blue, black, and red rectangles. The other side is a series of stepped pyramids in green and red cornhusks. There are three shades of tan in the body of the bag. (MPI 990)

Cat. 260

264. **Fiber Bag,** *Nez Perce*
- *18" long, 14½" wide*
Museum of the Plains Indian

This bag is of hemp and cornhusks. The bottom and top are of darker hemp. The decoration is of dyed cornhusk, consisting of four and one-half multicolored rectangles, each divided by an X. The X is yellow in the top row, with the side triangles in pink and the top and bottom in blue. In the second row the X is pink with the side triangles in green and the top and bottom in yellow. There is a projection on the top and bottom of each rectangle in either green or pink. The reverse has the same pattern of rectangles, striped and with triangular projections. The stripes are either yellow and green or pink and green. (MPI 991)

265. **Fiber Bag,** *Nez Perce*
- *18" long, 14½" wide*
Museum of the Plains Indian

This woven bag is of native hemp and cornhusks. The hemp is a darker shade of brown on the bottom. The geometric designs are in red, green, and blue-dyed cornhusk with bits of yarn overlay at the top. The pattern contains three diamonds with a stepped outline in each of the four and one-half rows. The reverse has two large yellow crosses outlined in green, with small green and red diamonds. (MPI 992)

266. **Fiber Bag,** *Nez Perce*
- *19" long, 14½" wide*
Museum of the Plains Indian

This bag has a hemp warp and cornhusk weft. The bottom and rim are of hemp and are darker than the body. The dyed cornhusk decoration consists of grey stepped diamonds with insets of yellow and green. On the reverse are two columns of diamonds with jagged red outlines and green, yellow, and purple interiors. The red decoration is of cotton string. (MPI 993)

267. **Fiber Bag,** *Nez Perce*
- *21" long, 16" wide*
Museum of the Plains Indian

This woven hemp bag has a cotton drawstring at the top. The body consists of two shades of tan; the darker is at the top and bottom. The geometric patterns on one side are Vs with triangles in red, green, and yellow; on the other side they are pink, red, purple, and green. (MPI 994)

268. **Fiber Bag,** *Nez Perce*
- *19" long, 14" wide*
Museum of the Plains Indian

This woven hemp bag has stepped-cross patterns using black, orange, and green yarn on one side, yellow and black on the other side. A black cross is inscribed with an orange diamond. On the upper and lower rows, a green cross is inscribed in the diamond. In the middle three rows are various hourglass shapes in black inside a diamond. The hide thongs tie at the top. Two shades of brown are used in the body. (MPI 995)

269. **Fiber Bag,** *Nez Perce*
- *16" long, 12½" wide*
Museum of the Plains Indian

This woven hemp bag is decorated with commercial yarn. On one side the patterns are repetitive. In two columns there are four registers: three consist of purple squares with two inset orange rectangles; two are of green diamonds with red crosses. The patterns on the other side are inverted Ls in alternating colors of blue and yellow. (MPI 996)

270. **Fiber Bag,** *Nez Perce*
- *20" long, 16" wide*
Museum of the Plains Indian

This bag is woven with hemp as the warp and cornhusk as the weft. The upper and lower portions have hemp as the weft, giving it a different color and texture from the body. The decoration is in bright red, green, blue, and black yarn. The designs are geometric and are arranged in four rows, the lower two repeating the patterns of the upper row. The motif in the first row is a blue diamond with red dots and a back rectangle in the center. The second row has a diamond of blue, natural, and green squares inscribed in a red stepped pattern. Each design is repeated three times. The reverse consists of four rows of stepped diamonds in alternating rows of pink and red. A strip of hide serves as a drawstring. (MPI 997)

271. **Fiber Bag,** *Nez Perce*
- *16" long, 12½" wide*
Museum of the Plains Indian

This woven bag is of hemp and cornhusks. The patterns are in dyed cornhusk. On one side, the designs are multicolored Vs in a herringbone pattern of red, green, blue-green, purple, and yellow. On the other side are rows of hourglass figures in green, red, purple, black, yellow, and orange. (MPI 998)

272. **Fiber Bag,** *Nez Perce*
- *18" long, 13" wide*
Museum of the Plains Indian

This bag has a hemp bottom and top and cornhusk body. The decoration is of dyed cornhusk in pink, aqua, light blue, yellow, purple, and orange. The pattern is a series of diamonds and triangles in two columns. The reverse consists of trapezoids in purple and orange. There is a double stripe of orange around the top. (MPI 999)

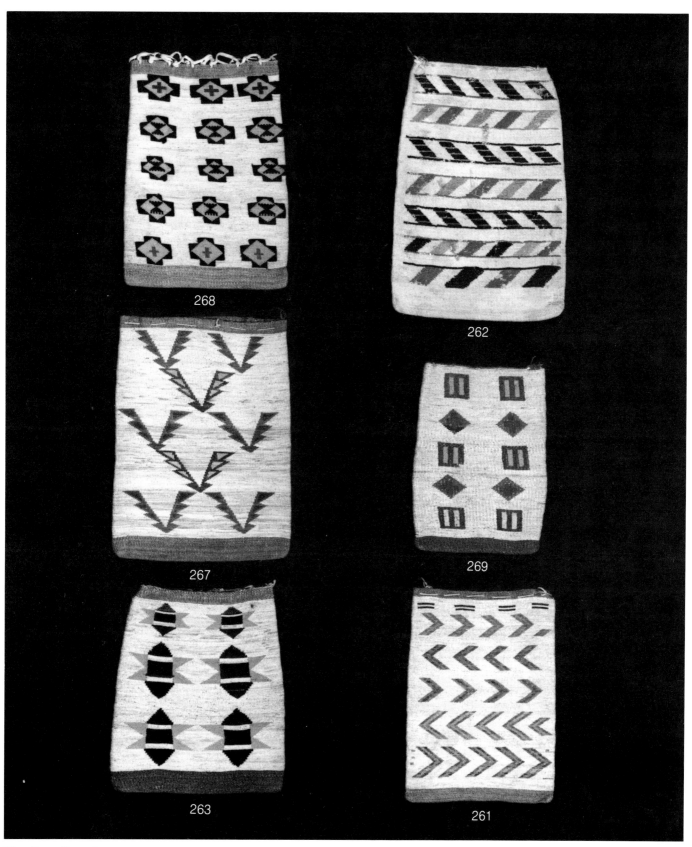

268

262

267

269

263

261

Fiber Bags, *Group I*

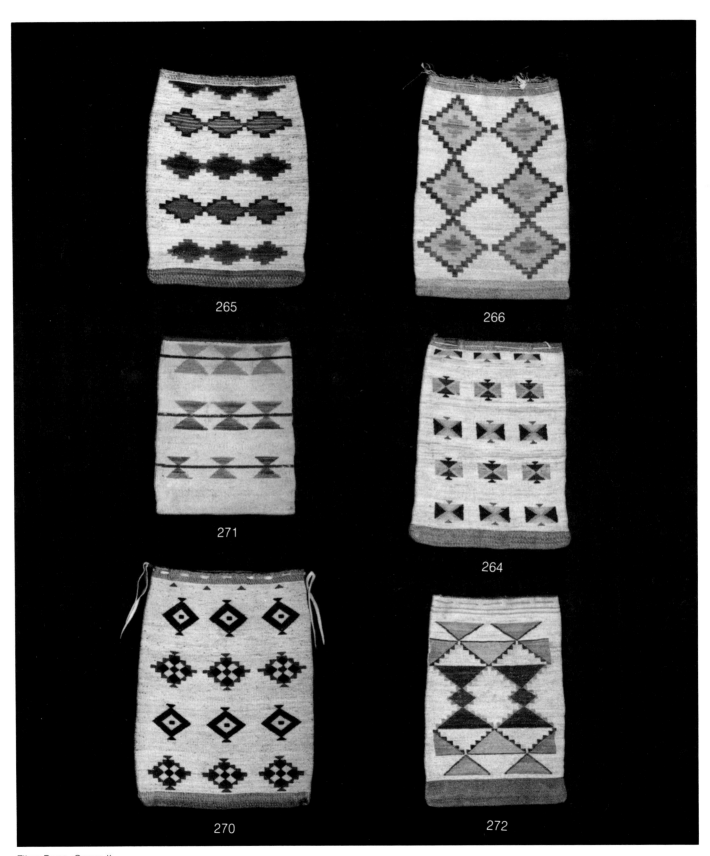

265

266

271

264

270

272

Fiber Bags, *Group II*

274. **Flat Pouch,** *Northern Plains*
10¼" long, 9½" wide
Museum of the Plains Indian

This beaded handbag is made from a woman's legging. The front is beaded with geometric designs on a light blue background. The patterns, composed of stepped pyramids and lines in red, dark blue, and yellow, are separated by a row of alternating blue and yellow rectangles. The borders are in red, blue, and yellow. The sides employ a different shade of light blue and red. The flap is decorated with a floral design in green, red, lavender, light blue, dark blue, yellow, and slate grey. There is a border of light blue, red, and dark blue beads around the flap. The handle is of copper-colored tubular beads strung at either side of a light blue strip, edged with red. Fringe hangs from the bottom. (MPI 1148)

273. **Dewclaw Bag,** *Blackfeet*
13¾" long, 13" wide
Museum of the Plains Indian

This bag is made of the lower portions of elk legs. There is buckskin fringe at the top and the bottom. Light blue beads edge the skin and the fringe. (MPI 1295)

Cat. 274

Horse Gear

The tribes of the Northern Plains recognized that the saddles and other articles of riding gear made by whites were stronger and more practical than those they made themselves. These people continued to make the more picturesque of their articles of riding gear for occasional use and display in Fourth of July parades and at other gatherings when traditional crafts were exhibited, such as at the Calgary Stampede and the Crow Fair, well within the present century.

Edwin T. Denig, a very observant trader who had known the tribes of this region since the 1830s, wrote in 1856: "Now the Blackfeet and Crow nations perceive at once the convenience and utility of European articles, especially portions of clothing, horse gear and other things. They readily throw aside the cord and use a bridle for a horse's mouth, and will pay well for a saddle" (Denig 1961:95). Even so, the Crow, renowned for their status as the richest in horses of all tribes of this region, continued to take pride in their skill in making handsome, high-horned women's saddles, colorful horse collars of distinctive design, and other decorative pieces of horse gear that enhanced their appearance on horseback in parades and on festive occasions. The women's saddles and horse collars made by the Crow were also coveted by neighboring tribes, including the Blackfeet. The Sioux were especially skilled in making beaded saddle blankets, some of which reached the Blackfeet. At the same time, Blackfeet women created decorated martingales and cruppers, which they beaded in colorful floral designs for use on their own horses.

Horse Collar

Cat. 276 shows an example of the very colorful horse collar developed by the Crow for decorating women's horses ridden in parades and on other occasions. Trader Edwin T. Denig may have been referring to this type of horse gear in use among the Crow prior to 1854 when he mentioned the "scarlet collars" on the horses of a Crow camp on the march (Denig 1961: 158). The Crow horse collar of the reservation period was most commonly made of red flannel and beaded spectacularly in designs that included those tall isosceles triangles so typical of Crow work. In the 1920s William Wildschut observed that no Crow woman would consider her riding horse fit to take part in a parade unless it wore on of these beaded collars (Plate 2 in Wildschut and Ewers 1959:26–27).

Woman's High-horned Saddle

Cat. 277 shows a woman's saddle of the Crow style. It is an old form among the Crow and Shoshone Indians, fashioned of a wooden frame covered with rawhide. Alfred Jacob Miller, the American artist who traveled the Overland Trail to the mountain men's rendezvous in the Rocky Mountains in 1837, pictured a number of Indian women riding saddles of this type — with very high pommels and cantles and large flattened extensions, fore and aft, on the tops. Two Crow saddles of this style in the Smithsonian Institution collections were acquired before 1870, some years before the buffalo were exterminated and the Crow settled on reservations (Ewers 1955:85–91).

A characteristic feature of Crow women's saddles is the attachment of a triangular beaded pendant to the outer edges of the circular top extensions of both pommel and cantle. Many of these Crow saddles also were equipped with elaborately beaded stirrups of the form illustrated in our example. This form appears to have been derived from a Spanish prototype of colonial times.

Cat. 275

275. **Bridle,** *Sioux*
21" long, 16" wide
Museum of the Plains Indian

The bridle of canvas straps is decorated with quill-wrapped rawhide. The quills are dyed red, yellow, white, and turquoise and are worked in geometric patterns. The brow band consists of many quill-wrapped, 3" strips attached to the canvas at the top. At the bottom of the quills are tin dangles with red fluffs. There is a red cloth rosette in the center of the nose band. (MPI 1301) *Photo: page 211.*

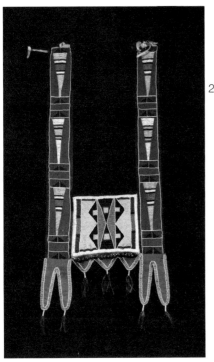

276. **Horse Collar,** *Crow*
● *37" long, 17" wide*
Museum of the Plains Indian

This horse collar has red strouding, beaded patterns, and is bound with black cotton cloth. The patterns are in diamonds and stripes in royal blue, green-yellow, light blue, red, orange, and white, on either side of a square panel with beadwork in green, light blue, pink, yellow, white, red, and royal blue. Triangular pieces of red strouding, beige cotton edged with white beads, and red and blue strouding form the fringe. There are small brass hawk bells along the lower edge of the square. (MPI 1306)

277. **Woman's Saddle,** *Crow*
21" long, 13" high
Museum of the Plains Indian

This wooden saddle is covered with skin and canvas. There is decorative beadwork on the pommel, cantle, and stirrups. Pink, blue, yellow, and green beads edge both pommel and cantle. The pommel has rectangular pendants of red, yellow, green, and blue beads. On the cantle, beadwork pendants consist of a red diamond with blue and yellow triangles at top and bottom. These are edged with red and green strouding and white beads. The stirrups are decorated on the sides and the base. Attached to the base is a rectangular panel outlined in white with a lower border of green and red strouding. (MPI 1257)

278. **Saddle,** *Northern Plains*
17" long, 8" high
Northwest Area Foundation

This saddle has a low bow frame of wood. The side bars are of straight pieces of wood; the pommel and cantle are high and arched outward at the top. There is a tiny prong under the pommel for the attachment of a quirt or rope. The tops of the pommel and cantle are edged with brass tacks with a skin fringe. The entire frame is covered with hide. A double canvas girth with stirrups is attached. (SMM 49–241)

279. **Saddle,** *Blackfeet*
19" sidebars,
9" high pommel and cantle
Northwest Area Foundation

This saddle retains its cloth pad, girth, and one stirrup. A series of brass-headed nails rims the end bows and front edges of the pommel and cantle. An attached tag indicates it may have come from the Broadwater-Pepin Trading Company in Browning, Montana, and that it may have belonged to Short Face, a Blackfeet Indian. (SMM 49–239)

212

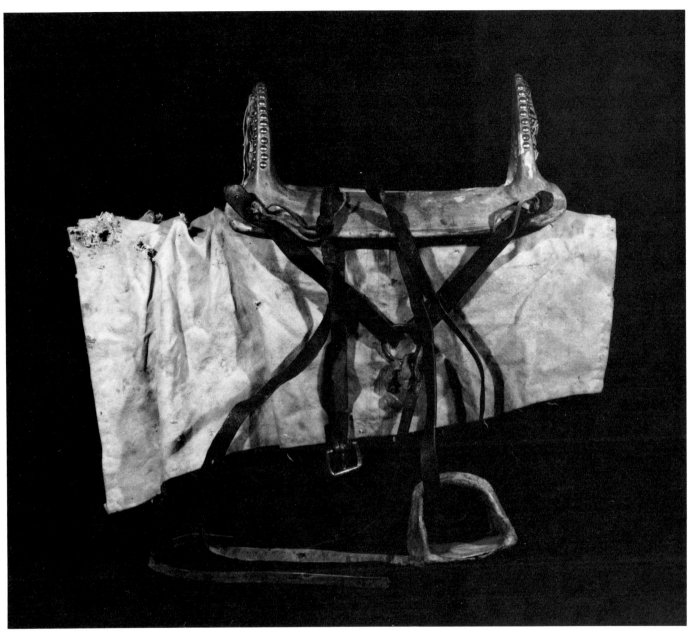

Cat. 279

Fig. 53 Woman on horse with horse collar.
*Photograph courtesy of Burlington
Northern Railroad*

Saddle Blankets

At least as early as the mid-nineteenth century, Western Sioux women were making saddle blankets composed of a central rectangle of skin or cloth, bordered on all sides by broad bands decorated with quillwork or beadwork. One of these, probably of Brulé origin, in the Warren Collection at the Smithsonian Institution was collected in 1855. Sioux women continued to make saddle blankets in this pattern long after their people settled on reservations. Cat. 283 portrays one of these blankets in a folded position as it would appear when placed on a horse's back before the saddle was added. The borders of this piece are decorated with narrow rows of porcupine quillwork, but the use of basket beads in the decoration of the fringes indicates that this saddle blanket was made, or at least reworked, no earlier than the 1890s.

The beaded saddle blanket in Cat. 280 may be somewhat older. The central rectangle of buckskin and the simple, blocky designs in the beadwork borders are reminiscent of those found in Sioux beadwork of the 1880s or earlier.

Martingales and Cruppers

Photographs taken about 1900 of Blackfeet Indian women on horseback, ready to take part in Fourth of July or other parades, show their horses decorated with martingales and cruppers very much like those pictured in Cat. 286 and Cat. 291. Older Indians stated during the 1940s that in their youth these items of horse gear were decorated with geometric designs "something like parfleche designs" (Ewers 1945:53–55). But by the turn of the century floral designs combined with graceful double curves were favored in the decoration of these articles. The beading was applied to red or black strouding backed with strong cotton cloth, with small brass bells attached to the fringes to make a tinkling noise when on parade. Cat. 290 shows a well-preserved martingale. Cat. 288 is a little more elaborate and is known to have been purchased from the Broadwater-Pepin Trading

Company in Browning before 1920. The martingale passed in front of the horse's neck and was tied to the woman's saddle at each end.

The Blackfeet crupper — tied to the rear of a woman's saddle at each end — passed under the horse's tail. A good example of a crupper of about the same age as the martingale just considered appears in Cat. 292. Its broad surface, which was placed over the horse's rump, is covered with red flannel on which there are floral beadwork designs. Even though they may have been made by full-blooded women, these martingales and cruppers of the early-twentieth-century Blackfeet probably were derived from Metis prototypes.

Double Saddlebag

Double saddlebags made of soft skin were to be thrown over a horse's back. By hanging a pocket on each side of the animal, the weight was distributed evenly. These have been made by the tribes of the Northern Plains since the buffalo days. Even so, the fur trader Charles Larpenteur, who saw these bags in use among the tribes of the region before the mid-nineteenth century, implied that this form of saddlebag was copied from the whites (Larpenteur 1898:67). Indians applied a large panel of decoration at each end of the bag and added long-cut fringes to hang down at each side. The Blackfeet thought these fringes should be long enough to fall below the horse's belly when the bag was in place. At the turn of the century, the Blackfeet employed floral and double-curve designs — much like those used on their martingales and cruppers — to decorate their saddlebags (Fig. 64 in Ewers 1945). However, the Sioux preferred geometric designs such as those they used in beading on other large, flat surfaces. A good example of a Sioux double saddlebag appears in Cat. 293.

Cat. 280

280. **Saddle Blanket,** *Sioux*
51" long, 24½" wide
Museum of the Plains Indian

This saddle blanket is decorated
with bells, beads, and painted
yellow fringe. The beading borders
the edge. The design is composed
of elements in sequence. At the
ends of the blanket are two
rectangular stripes of blue and light
blue beads on white. The next
element is a green cross with a red
center and blue and yellow accents.
A third element is a rectangular box
with a red border, a green frame
inside, and a navy blue and yellow
frame within the two. (MPI 1018)

281. **Saddle Blanket,** *Sioux*
60" long, 32" wide
Museum of the Plains Indian

This canvas saddle blanket is
decorated with beaded strips of
buckskin, with red, yellow, and blue
ribbons, brass bells, and sequins.
The beadwork is on a white field
with geometric patterns in mauve,
green, royal blue, silver, and
brass-plated faceted beads. An
American flag pattern is repeated
several times. This consists of red
and white stripes, a blue field, and
flagpole; silver faceted beads form
four crosses in the blue field. The
stand is green, orange, and light
blue. (MPI 1020) *No photo.*

282. **Saddle Blanket,** *Northern Plains*
49" long, 32" wide
Museum of the Plains Indian

This blanket of black wool has a
running floral design of white, dark
turquoise, pink, rose, yellow, and
green beads. Tin dangles hang
from either end of the panel.
(MPI 1088)

283. **Saddle Blanket,** *Sioux*
55½" long, 26" wide
Museum of the Plains Indian

This blanket of cotton cloth and
buckskin has stripes of quillwork, in
red, green, and yellow. The stripes
are periodically crossed by a
parallel row of red, downy feathers.
The quillwork between rows is
green. The blanket has a border of
red ribbon and fringed corners
ornamented with bells and yellow
ribbon. (MPI 1380)

Cat. 283

Cat. 284

Cat. 285

284. **Saddle Blanket,** *Sioux (?)*
44" long, 13" wide
Museum of the Plains Indian

This blanket is of elkhide, with a square beaded panel at each end connected by a beaded strip of light blue with red, green, yellow, and blue crosses. There is fringe at either end and fringe at the back. Red lines with white double triangles at the top and bottom and blue spots are at center; a red, white, and blue cross is in each corner. (MPI 1377)

285. **Saddle Cloth,** *Sioux*
52" long, 15" wide
Museum of the Plains Indian

This canvas cloth has four beaded buckskin bands. A repetitive pattern on a white background includes a green, red, and blue diamond with a blue E on either end, and side triangles. A red line flanked by a double triangle of green is the border. At the ends are brass bells, skin fringe strung with amber, and aqua basket beads. (MPI 1388)

286. **Martingale,** *Blackfeet*
47" long, 7" wide
Northwest Area Foundation

This martingale is of bead-decorated red flannel material backed by canvas and trimmed with black cloth. Each end of the decoration is reinforced by a small concealed stick. Fringe strung with large colored beads hangs from the lower edge. Each fringe thong terminates with a small bell. An attached tag indicates it may have come from the Broadwater-Pepin Trading Company, Browning, Montana. (SMM 49–245)

287. **Martingale,** *Blackfeet*
44½" long, 6¼" wide
Northwest Area Foundation

This red flannel martingale has a light canvas backing lined with white cotton cloth. Floral decoration adorns the red flannel. The lower edge is covered with beaded fringe ending in clear basket beads. An attached tag indicates it may have come from the Broadwater-Pepin Trading Company, Browning, Montana. (SMM 49–246)

Cat. 286

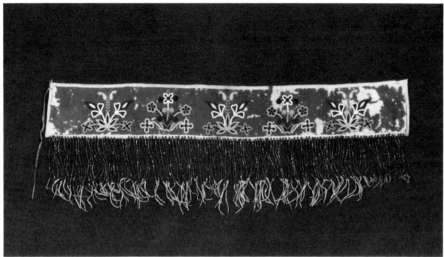

Cat. 287

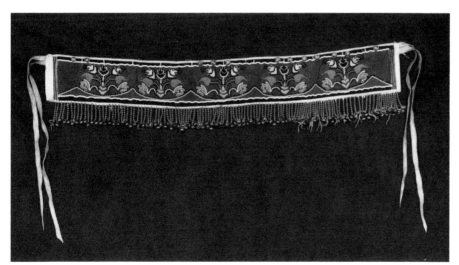

Cat. 288

288. **Martingale,** *Blackfeet*
49" long, 6¹/₂" wide
Northwest Area Foundation

This red flannel cloth, used for horse decoration, is backed by white cotton material. Floral beadwork covers the martingale and a heavy beaded fringe with metal beaded tinklers hangs from the full width. An attached label indicates this item may have come from the Broadwater-Pepin Trading Company, Browning, Montana. (SMM 49–289)

289. **Martingale,** *Blackfeet*
46" long, 6¹/₂" wide
Museum of the Plains Indian

This martingale has a floral bead pattern on a backing of red strouding bordered by a strip of black strouding on the bottom. Colors include white, light blue, orange, lavender, turquoise, black, rose, light green, translucent lavender, pink, yellow-green, and clear. A blue fabric border with a small floral pattern encompasses the martingale. Skin fringe strung with pink and green basket beads terminates with brass bells at the lower edge. (MPI 1087)

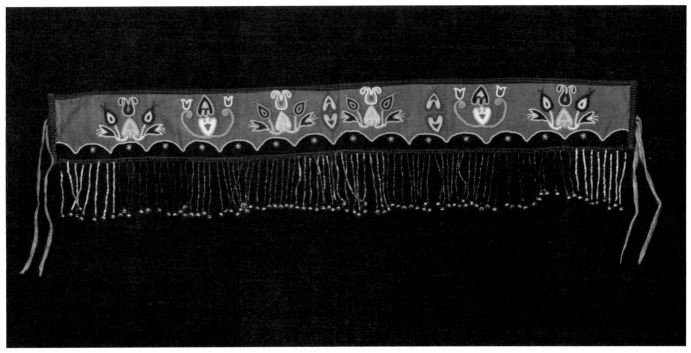

Cat. 290

Cat. 291

Cat. 292

Cat. 293

290. **Martingale,** *Blackfeet*
  ● *52" long, 7¹/₄" wide*
  Museum of the Plains Indian

This martingale has a background of red strouding with a lower border of black, lined with red calico. Beaded floral patterns are in white, yellow, green, pink, light blue, royal blue, light pink, aqua, and orange-yellow. The scalloped lower border has yellow beads and stars. Gold- and turquoise-colored bead fringe ends with brass hawk bells. (MPI 1089)

291. **Crupper,** *Blackfeet*
  36" long, 10" wide
  Northwest Area Foundation

The two canvas-backed red flannel pieces in this crupper are identically decorated and are joined at the bottom with a canvas strip. Navy blue flannel cloth is accented by white beadwork and five brass army-type buttons. Leather and flannel strips hang from the sides, with a metal tinkler at of each red flannel tassel. (SMM 49–244)

292. **Crupper,** *Blackfeet*
  27" long, 9" wide
  Northwest Area Foundation

This crupper consists of two pieces of rawhide joined together by a stout piece of skin and decorated by attached pieces of red flannel cloth with floral beadwork in identical patterns. The lower edges are fringed with hide strips and red flannel strips. (SMM 49–328)

293. **Double Saddlebag,** *Sioux*
  68" long, 12¹/₂" wide
  Museum of the Plains Indian

This elkskin saddlebag, lined with cotton cloth, is fringed at the bottom. Side panels are beaded in patterns of boxes, arrows, diamonds, and crosses in red, dark blue, yellow, and green on white. A large diamond with a red and yellow cross inset in the center of the panel has a double green, blue, and red triangle at each end. The corners have green, red, yellow, and blue insets. On either side of the large green and blue triangle are arrow motifs in red and blue. (MPI 1378)

Weapons and Warfare

Painted War Histories

Warriors have been a favorite subject in the graphic art of the men in the tribes living on the northwestern Plains since prehistoric times. Prehistoric artists painted or incised upon rock walls isolated figures of standing warriors carrying huge shields and primitive shock weapons. By early historic times, warriors on horseback carrying firearms began to appear in the rock art. Stuart and Betty Conner of Billings have examined and recorded the rock art at many scattered sites on the Montana High Plains. They have recognized a general trend "from front view motionless pictures of people to animated side view, realistic art" (Conner and Conner 1971:12).

John Ewers's studies of Indian paintings and drawings on the skin surfaces of buffalo robes and later upon paper and cloth supplied them by whites, covering the period since 1800, have also noted this trend. They indicate that it accelerated after the Indians of this region gained firsthand knowledge of the very realistic portraits of Indians and scenes in Indian life created by George Catlin and Karl Bodmer who visited the tribes of the upper Missouri a century and a half ago (1832–1834) (Ewers 1939; 1968).

The Blackfeet tended to be conservative in adopting a realistic style. Unlike the Sioux and the Crow, they clung to representing warriors and horses in a simple pictorial shorthand that lacked both action and realistic detail until after the buffalo were gone and these Indians were settled upon reservations. Some Blackfeet men continued to employ old-style picture-writing in the early decades of the twentieth century (Ewers 1983).

After the intertribal wars ended during the 1880s, Blackfeet veterans of those conflicts continued to picture their most memorable war deeds. Some of them were painted on the inner surfaces of animal hides — deer, elk, or domesticated animals (horse or cowhide). But as the nineteenth century neared its closed, more and more of these paintings appeared upon muslin or canvas, which the Indians received from the United States government as part of their annuity payments or obtained in trade with white merchants on the reservation.

Muslin or light canvas came to be used for the traditional hide draught screens the Indians hung inside their canvas-covered tipis after the buffalo were gone. Women usually painted those tipi liners with geometric designs. But some of these items bore pictorial war records painted by men. A portion of one of these (Cat. 294) in the Louis W. Hill Collection is of special interest. The horses and men are more realistically rendered on this painted cloth than they were on painted skins. The horses' legs are paired and the men ride astride their horses. Not all of the episodes are war actions. There is a bear hunt at the upper left and a buffalo hunt on the lower right. These two were typical male activities of earlier years and both were fraught with considerable danger to Indian participants. A clear representation of the Crow-painted lodge of the Piegan (at the lower left) may be sufficient to assure us that this was a Blackfeet painting.

Knowledge of the prior existence of such Indian murals as those painted on muslin or light canvas probably led to the Great Northern Railway's sponsorship of the most elaborate Indian mural project ever attempted by the Blackfeet. This involved the painting of a large number of murals on canvas to decorate the public spaces of the three large hotels built to accommodate tourists on the east side of the Rockies in Glacier National Park. A description of Many Glacier Hotel, not long after its opening in 1915, mentioned "a huge 180 foot canvas mural painted by Medicine Owl and no less than eleven Blackfeet chiefs" as the *piece de resistance* in the decoration of that wilderness inn (Sheire 1970:199). At that time, the Blackfeet no longer had chiefs, but the Great Northern Railway persisted in using this word as an honorary title for elderly Blackfeet Indians.

294. **Tipi Liner,** *Blackfeet*
16' long, 52¹/₂" high
Northwest Area Foundation

This tipi liner depicts various deeds of bravery in battle and during buffalo and bear hunts. The light canvas cloth is covered with figures on horses, people, and tipis painted in blue, red, black, orange, yellow, and green tempera. (SMM 54–34)

During the 1920s the Glacier Park Hotel Company, a subsidiary of the Great Northern Railway, published a booklet, *Picture Writing by the Blackfeet Indians in Glacier Park Hotels,* listing and describing 42 panels of pictorial war records interpreting episodes in the lives of 25 prominent Blackfeet warriors, which were exhibited in the public spaces in the Glacier Park Hotel at East Glacier, the Going-to-the-Sun Chalets on upper St. Mary's Lake, and at Many Glacier Hotel. The introduction to this booklet states in part: "The pictures described herein were made in 1913 and 1914." The booklet described each mural in detail but illustrated only two of them — episodes in the lives of "Chief Black Boy" and of "Chief Big Moon."

Illustrations of these and seven other of the murals appeared in an article on these paintings titled "Picture Stories of the Blackfeet Indians" by Clark McAdams (1919). The author's captions dated six of these murals "1916," or two years later than did the introduction to the Great Northern's booklet. McAdams also credited Charles Griffin of the Great Northern Railway, who "has been for many years a friend of the Blackfeet," with having played an important part in initiating this mural project: "He took the canvas and paint to the old men and induced them to make the picture writings" (McAdams 1919:1).

After the Great Northern Railway built the Prince of Wales Hotel on Waterton Lake and opened it to the public in 1927, additional Blackfeet war histories were used to decorate the public spaces in that handsome building. A Hileman photograph taken in the lobby of that hotel shows a number of these Indian-painted murals in place about the year 1930 (Fig. 11).

Although three of these four park hotels are still open to the public, the Indian-painted murals are no longer in place; nor does the railway's archive bear evidence that these murals are extant. However, in the spring of 1982

295. **War Record Canvas A,** *Blackfeet*
50′ long, 49″ high
Burlington Northern Collection

This war record includes the stories of Arrow Top Knot and others. It is painted in primary colors on army canvas.

296. **War Record Canvas B,** *Blackfeet*
50′ long, 49″ high
Burlington Northern Collection

War Record Canvas B contains the narrative history of Three Calf and others. Powdered tempera paint, in solution, was applied to the army canvas with twig brushes in ochre, red, green, blue, and black.

Cat. 295 (Arrow Top Knot)

Cat. 296 (Three Calf)

224

Royal Hassrick and John Ewers, at the invitation of curator Ann Walton, examined another series of Blackfeet war histories painted on canvas in the collection of the Burlington Northern Railroad in St. Paul. This series (Cats. 295–298) pictured noteworthy achievements of a somewhat younger group of Blackfeet veterans of the intertribal wars, a few of whom were still living on the Blackfeet Reservation (adjoining Glacier National Park) in Montana, during the 1940s. Whether the paintings of this series were intended to replace some of the murals originally installed in the larger hotels in Glacier National Park is not certain. They may have been painted a little later than the others. Louis W. Hill, Jr., recalled having seen those canvases painted during the second decade of this century, that the Great Northern Railway provided the materials — primarily paints and canvas — and that large numbers of Indians were employed in the project at the same time during the summer season. Some of these panels may have been painted by the men whose deeds are pictured. Others probably were executed by younger Indians under the direction of the then-middle-aged veterans who provided verbal accounts of their war experiences (Walton 1982:57).

It is fortunate that among these well-preserved war histories there are a number of panels of unique historical and cultural significance. Among them are several murals interpreting the career of White Quiver (ca. 1858–1931), who was remembered by elderly Blackfeet in the 1940s as the most active and most successful Blackfeet horse raider of whom they had knowledge. John C. Ewers devoted a section of "The Horse in Blackfoot Indian Culture" (1955:191–93) to a discussion of White Quiver's outstanding record as a horse raider. He was most active in raiding the Crow camps because the Crow had killed his father, and he vowed vengeance against them. But he also raided the Cree, Gros Ventres, Assiniboine, and Sioux. Only the Flathead Indians, among neighboring tribes, were his friends.

As a boy, White Quiver began to join raiding parties and he became an experienced raider while still in his teens. He grew to be a tall man of marked physical stamina who could ride three days and nights without food or rest while driving captured horses home from enemy camps. The Crow called this dark-skinned enemy "the big Negro" and it was said that Crow mothers disciplined their crying children by saying, "Keep quiet. The Big Negro is out there. He will get you if you don't stop crying."

By the early years of the present century, Blackfeet painters of war histories took pains to set off one episode from others by lines, so as to make these picture writings more comprehensible to persons who were not accustomed to viewing Indian war histories — such as the tourists who visited the hotels in Glacier National Park. Even so, the artist who interpreted White Quiver's war record continued to work in the naive style of rendering horses — many with but two legs, one front and one back — that Blackfeet artists had employed in the buffalo days. However, human beings were rendered a bit more realistically than by earlier Blackfeet artists — with their heads and clothed bodies pictured in some detail.

In the panel illustrating some of the achievements of the renowned raider, White Quiver, (Cat. 297a, next page), the artist identifies that hero by his pictorial signature — a full figure of a warrior with a white-painted quiver above his head. To the left of that is a vertical row of inverted U-shapes representing 21 raids against enemies in which White Quiver had participated. In each of the episodes pictured on this panel (as well as in his pictographic signature) White Quiver is identified by a single red feather pendant from the back of his head. Indian informants in the 1940s recalled that White Quiver's war medicine was a single feather given to him from the medicine bundle of Under Bull. The episodes pictured in this panel also confirm informants' testimony to the effect that White Quiver as a leader of war parties insisted upon taking the greatest risks himself when his parties

Cat. 297a (White Quiver)

297. **War Record Canvas C,** *Blackfeet*
● *50' long, 49" high*
Burlington Northern Collection

The story of White Quiver, the most
successful Indian horse rider, is told
in this pictographic record canvas
with tempera, crayon, and extensive
use of black outline (see Cats. 297a
and b, Plate 5, and cover
illustration). The story of Green-
Grass-Bull is told on another section
of the same canvas (see Cat. 297c).

Cat. 297b (White Quiver)

reached enemy camps. He would enter the camp alone, cut loose the most valuable horses picketed near their owners' tipis, lead them out of camp, and turn them over to others of his party to hold while he reentered the camp to obtain more choice horses. He also opened enemy corrals and took the best-looking horses. Rides-at-the-Door, who said he had accompanied White Quiver on eight raiding expeditions, remembered that on one of them White Quiver captured a large sorrel horse that later became renowned as a winning racer among the Blackfeet under the name of Big Sorrel. Probably the artist intended to picture White Quiver's taking of Big Sorrel from a Crow corral in the episode shown to the right of the center and near the bottom of this panel.

The Blackfeet prized mules because of their strength and stamina in transporting heavy loads. Those three long-eared animals White Quiver is releasing from a corral at the left of the center look like mules, known to the Blackfeet as "big ears." The three episodes at the top of this panel show White Quiver and his fellow raiders driving larger numbers of horses. One of the reasons for White Quiver's popularity as a raid leader was his liberality in sharing the horses he took from the enemy with other members of his party. Another reason was his generosity in giving away many of the animals he claimed as his share after the raiders reached home.

Another broad segment of canvas devoted to White Quiver's war record interprets pictorially another well-remembered aspect of his unorthodox conduct of raiding parties (Cat. 297b). Traditionally Blackfeet raiders set out on foot to take horses from enemy camps. A foot war party is pictured on the march in the episode at the upper right. Each of the ten men carries a gun over one shoulder and a pack on his back. The pack, supported by a strap across the wearer's breast, contained those articles most needed on a dangerous, lengthy trip to an enemy camp to capture horses — extra moccasins, an awl, and sinew thread for use in moccasin repair, one or more long rawhide ropes for catching, leading, or riding captured horses, a small pipe and tobacco for smoking at rest stops along the way, and the man's personal war medicine to wear when he went into action after the enemy camp was reached. The last item was usually something small and light in weight to be worn in the hair or around the warrior's neck.

It usually required sixteen to twenty days for a Blackfeet war party to reach the Crow camps south of the Yellowstone on foot. This rate of movement was to slow for the hyperactive raider, White Quiver. He preferred to lead parties on horseback to capture horses from enemy tribes. Mounted warriors could cover twice the distance foot war parties could travel each day. However, as they neared enemy country, mounted men had to proceed with greater caution for they were more conspicuous than men on foot. In either case, the Blackfeet preferred a dawn attack in capturing horses from enemy camps.

The other episodes in this segment of the canvas may have been intended to convey the varied sizes of raiding parties White Quiver led — ranging from no more than three men (bottom center) to as many as 10 or 12 (in other episodes). Older Indians in the 1940s, who knew White Quiver's war record, told of his preference for small parties. He rarely led expeditions composed of more than a dozen warriors. Some of his small parties succeeded in capturing more than a half-dozen horses per man and driving them home safely without being overtaken by the enemy.

The same painted canvas in the Burlington Northern Collection includes a number of episodes in the war record of the Piegan Indian Green-Grass-Bull (ca. 1862–1951), a man who was remembered by his contemporaries for his skill in painting war histories and as a craftsman who made pipes and dog travois. Probably Green-Grass-Bull himself painted the episodes in Cat. 297 from his experiences as a warrior. His pictographic signature

Cat. 297c (Green-Grass-Bull)

appears within the small rectangular frame at the upper center — in the form of a man shown beneath a buffalo bull standing in green grass (Cat. 297c, above).

Indians and whites who knew Green-Grass-Bull recall his fondness for dogs. In his older years he was often seen walking the streets of Browning, followed or surrounded by a number of dogs of different breeds. Probably it was this interest in dogs that caused Green-Grass-Bull to include two episodes interpreting the role of dogs in intertribal warfare in his paintings. The scene at the upper left appears to picture a defensive action in which barking dogs have alerted the men of the camp to a threatened enemy raid, and the men of the camp are coming out shooting. Within the rectangular outline at the far upper right the artist pictured three dogs confronting two men who were trying to steal picketed horses. Both the Blackfeet and their enemies relied upon their dogs to waken them in case of a night or dawn raid on their camps. Yet successful raiders were skilled in preventing the enemies' dogs from barking. Sometimes they threw pieces of meat to the dogs to keep them quiet. Or, if a dog barked, they retreated, and after a period of quiet, approached the camp from another direction (Ewers 1955: 176–93, 207–208). It is interesting to note that although Green-Grass-Bull pictured dogs in action, most of his horses are rendered in the traditional Blackfeet style — in static poses and with a single leg at front and at back.

In the Hill Collection there are some paintings on hide by Indians of the Northern Plains in which warriors on horseback are portrayed in profile but in greater details and more realistic action than was customary in traditional Blackfeet picture writing. On one tribally unidentified painted hide (details, Cats. 299a, b, c), a number of warriors are pictured astride running horses in which the horses' legs are rendered more realistically but in rocking-horse posture — with front legs extended forward and both rear legs backward. This was a stance much favored by Sioux, Cheyenne, and some Crow graphic artists in picturing actions in warfare with other Indian tribes or white during the last half of the nineteenth century. It was not a Blackfeet style. Presumably, then, this hide was not painted by the Blackfeet.

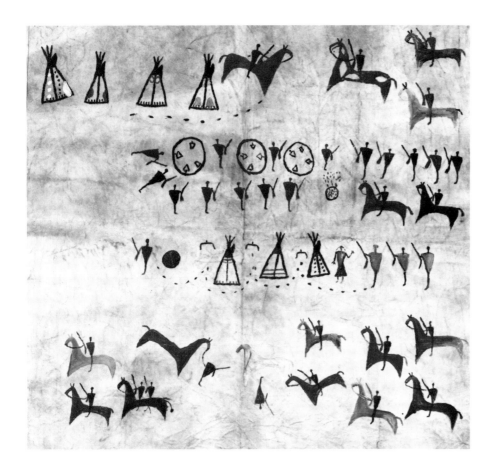

Cat. 299a

Cat. 299b

Cat. 299c

298. **War Record Canvas D,** *Plains (?)*
49" square
Burlington Northern Collection

This canvas is quite unlike the other three, both in size and style. The subject matter seems to be war and horse-stealing; however there are no identifying "heroes."

299. **Horsehide Robes,** *Plains*
8' long, 2½' high, plus 7½' long, 3' high
Northwest Area Foundation

This robe of three stitched sections has white horsehair still attached to the outside. The inner side is decorated with eight male figures in war regalia on horses galloping at full tilt. The pictures are painted in yellow, blue, red, and black with great attention to costume detail. (SMM 54-26)

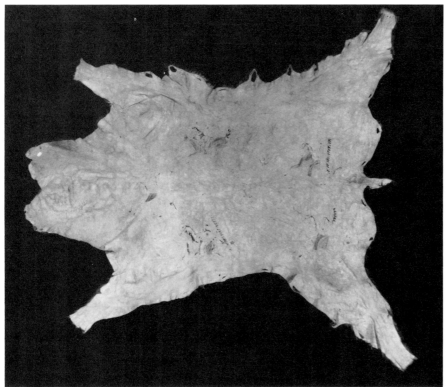

Cat. 300

300. **Calfskin Robe,** *Plains*
Approx. 4' long, 2¹/₂' wide
Northwest Area Foundation

This tanned calfskin robe has hair left on the outer surface. Painted figures, including five men on horseback, two deer, a bird, and a snake, are in black, red, and blue. (SMM 54–27)

301. **Bison Robe,** *Cheyenne (?)*
89" long, 71" wide
Museum of the Plains Indian

This painted robe depicts a series of events. Across the upper third is a scene of a bison hunt and one of wolves hunting a pronghorn and elk. Below this is a battle scene with warriors on horses and on foot and a tipi. At the bottom is a village scene with warriors wearing feather bonnets and carrying feathered shields, two men smoking pipes, a woman with an ax, a dog, and several horses. The bison are painted black and grey, the antelope and elk are yellow and black, the larger wolf is grey, and the smaller wolf yellow with spots. The horses and the warriors are painted green, yellow, red, and blue. The tipis are yellow. (MPI 1263)

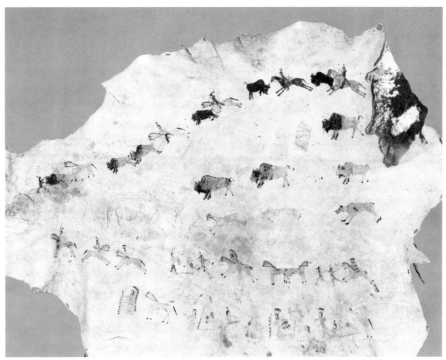

Cat. 301

230

Gun Cases

While originally gun cases may have served to keep the powder dry, in reservation days they were strictly showpieces for display in parades. Crow women on horseback, dressed in their finest regalia, often carried their husbands' weapons. It was then that gun cases became important parts of the paraphernalia.

Scabbards

European knives were among the earliest and most desirable items of trade, and Indians were quick to fashion sheaths in which to carry them. Men found knives essential not only in skinning and butchering but also as weapons in warfare. Women used smaller knives in food preparation, in the tailoring of clothing, and in the making of domestic wares.

Cat. 307 is a Crow man's scabbard of rawhide decorated with beads and brass upholstery tacks. The inverted U-shaped figures may symbolize horses' hooves, indicating the number of horses the owner captured on a particular occasion. The triangular aperture serves as a slit through which the belt is passed. Cat. 305 is a Blackfeet example of a man's scabbard further ornamented with tin-can cones.

Women's knife sheaths were worn suspended from the belt by strings of skin. Cat. 306 shows a Crow woman's beaded scabbard.

Decorated Sword Scabbard

In the buffalo days it was the Crow woman's duty to carry her husband's lance or sword on her horse when camp was moved, and this custom survived into the twentieth century when these formerly useful weapons were prized as status symbols and relics of the days of intertribal warfare. They were displayed by wives in parades or at the Crow Fair. The handsomely decorated rawhide scabbard may have been unique to the Crow. In his description of the decoration of a Crow woman's horse when camp was moved during the 1850s, Denig stated that the husband's sword, "if he has one, is tied along the side and hangs down," but he did not mention a scabbard. The husband carried his gun "in readiness for any attack however sudden" (Denig 1961:158.)

A fine example of one of the Crow scabbards of the reservation period appears in Cat. 308. It is made in a form resembling that of a short-handled spade, consisting of two pieces of heavy rawhide sewn together with buckskin cord and edged with red flannel. The narrow handlelike portion is painted with tall triangles and transverse bars, and it has two beaded cloth pendants attached to it. The spade shape is covered with red flannel, which is beaded elaborately and has a long-cut fringe. On parade the scabbard was oriented so that the handle of the weapon was downward and the spade shape with its long fringe protruded backward and upward (Fig. 35 in Wildshut and Ewers 1959:32–33; Galante 1980:64–73).

Bandoliers

Bandoliers were formerly used for carrying shot and firearm equipment. They became decorative items of apparel. Found throughout the Eastern Woodlands and beyond the Great Lakes, bandoliers were popular as far west as the Plains Cree and Plains Ojibway tribes. They were highly prized items of trade throughout the Northern Plains. Sitting Bull, the Sioux leader, posed in one for a photograph (Fig. 39).

302. Four Arrows, *Blackfeet*
27" long average
Museum of the Plains Indian

These arrows have triangular-shaped metal points and red shafts. Small feathers attached at the base of the fletching are dyed red on two of the arrows and purple on the other two. The fletching is made of variegated feathers. (MPI 1210)

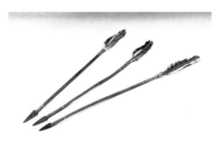

303. Set of Three Arrows, *Blackfeet*
26", 23½", and 23½" long
Museum of the Plains Indian

This set of arrows has metal points bound with sinew. They are fletched with owl feathers attached with sinew. The fletched ends are painted red. (MPI 1209)

304. Bow and Quiver Case, *Blackfeet*
33" long
Museum of the Plains Indian

This quiver and bow case is made of two attached cylinders of buckskin. The bow case is decorated with beadwork and fringe on the top and bottom. Red strouding binds the openings. At both top and bottom a beaded stepped pyramid is broken vertically in the middle with a strip of white and dark blue. The pyramid is dark blue, ochre, and turquoise on white. (MPI 1224)

Cat. 305

305. Knife Scabbard, *Blackfeet*
12" long, 4" wide
Museum of the Plains Indian

This scabbard of red-painted rawhide has a beaded band on tanned hide at the top and along the curved edge. The top pattern consists of two dark red stepped pyramids surmounted with crosses with black borders. Tin dangles are strung on hide with blue faceted beads. The curved edge is white with three triangles outlined in blue. Triangles on the ends are red with black centers; the middle one is light blue with black. Six brass tacks line the inside edge. (MPI 1022)

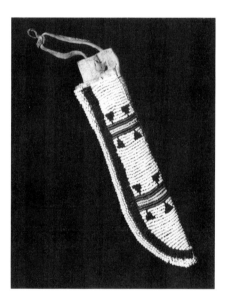

306. Woman's Knife Sheath. *Crow*
6¾" long, 1⅞" wide
Museum of the Plains Indian

This knife sheath is decorated with white, royal blue, light blue, and burgundy beads. The rounded edge is white with a royal blue border. The pattern, triple stripes of burgundy and light blue with triangles of royal blue at the apex, is repeated on a white field. (MPI 1025)

307. Knife Scabbard, *Crow*
10¹/₂" long, 3³/₄" wide
Museum of the Plains Indian

This scabbard is of rawhide decorated with beads at the top and along the curved edge as well as with brass tacks. The beadwork at the top is divided into four sections by a vertical yellow strip with a red cross and a horizontal strip of pink and blue. There is an inverted dark blue U against a light blue field in each quadrant. There is also a border of white with blue, red, and green. The curved edge is in strips of light blue, dark blue, red, and green. (MPI 1285)

Cat. 308

308. Lance Case, *Crow*
● *42" long, 7" wide*
Museum of the Plains Indian

This case is made of a parfleche painted in blue triangles with yellow and blue lines and bound with red and blue strouding. There are two pendants of beaded buckskin with red and green strouding and buckskin fringe. The beaded sections are triangles of blue, ochre, red, and green on a light blue field. The tip is beaded with stacked triangles on a pink background. (MPI 1289)

309. Gun Case, *Crow*
38" long, 6¹/₂" wide
Northwest Area Foundation

This elaborate hide gun case has geometric beaded patterns and strips of red blanket cloth bordering the side seam and beaded end panels. The buckskin fringe is quite long and very thick. (SMM 1–766)

310. Gun Case, *Blackfeet*
43" long, 7" wide
Northwest Area Foundation

This very long gun case is made of several pieces of hide. It is decorated by long fringe and two sections of beadwork. (SMM 49–200)

311. Gun Case, *Blackfeet*
43" long, 6¹/₄" wide
Northwest Area Foundation

This gun case is made of three separate pieces of hide. An intricately beaded panel adorns each end. Fringe decoration and red flannel edging further enhance the effect. (SMM 49–201)

Photos for Cats. 309–314
are on pages 234–35.

312. Gun Case, *Blackfeet*
40" long, 7" wide
Northwest Area Foundation

A light blue beaded background with triangles and diamonds of pink, blue, and red decorates both ends of this case. The fringe is longest and heaviest at the bottom, but it also runs along the top and length of the seam. (SMM 49–202)

313. Gun Case, *Crow*
43" long, 6¹/₂" wide
Museum of the Plains Indian

This gun case is of canvas with beaded panels at the ends. Long fringe extends from the ends and along the base. Red strouding is sewn to the seams and laced to the fringe on the small end. Red hourglass figures set in a light blue field are outlined in blue with small blue triangles topped with a yellow line. The intermediate space is green. A white border surrounds each panel. (MPI 1252)

314. Gun Case, *Crow*
43" long, 7" wide
Museum of the Plains Indian

The gun case is decorated with twisted fringe at the side and ends. The beaded panel at the narrow end has an hourglass design in pink beads with red strouding. Red and green strouding with yellow and blue beads border the seam with two diagonal stripes of blue beads done in lazy stitch. The wider panel is divided into rectangular sections filled with red, yellow, light and dark blue, and green beads in stripes and triangles with a white border. Red strouding fills three large rectangles. (MPI 1349)

Cat. 309

Cat. 310

Cat. 311

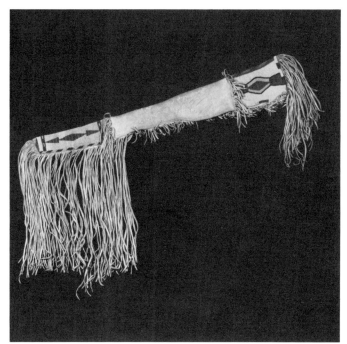

Cat. 312

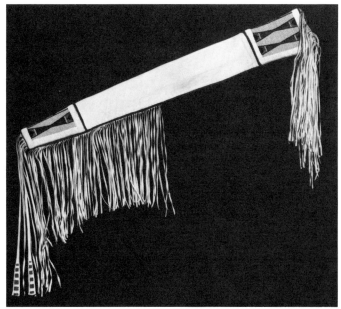

Cat. 313

Cat. 314

Cat. 315

Cat. 316

315. **Gun Case,** *Blackfeet*
42¹/₂" long, 7¹/₂" wide
Museum of the Plains Indian

This buckskin gun case has long
fringe at either end and panels of
beadwork and red strouding. The
fringe is edged with red strouding
laced through slotted buckskin. The
beaded panels are white with large
yellow diamonds bordered in red on
one side and diamonds with light
blue centers on the other. The field
is bordered by royal blue edged
with white beads. (MPI 1350)

316. **Gun Case,** *Blackfeet*
39¹/₂" long, 7¹/₄" wide
Museum of the Plains Indian

This gun case has beaded panels
and long fringe at each end. The
beads are in geometric patterns in
dark blue, red, and green, on a
light blue field. The borders of each
beaded panel are turquoise with
dark blue and yellow in a zigzag
pattern, edged with red strouding
and white beads. (MPI 1353)

317. **Bandolier,** *Cree, Ojibway*
46" long, 7¹/₄" wide
Museum of the Plains Indian

The pocket section of this beaded
bandolier has a design of vines and
leaves in blue, navy blue, green,
and red beads on white. The panel
is edged by a lattice design in
beadwork on beige cotton fabric
and by an orange strip rimming the
entire object. The base of the
pocket is sewn with a pattern calico
strip, beaded decoration, and yarn
tassels. The large beads are
alternating clear green and solid
blue. Above the pocket is a beaded
floral design in light green, yellow,
pink and white on blue fabric. The
straps have a floral design in the
same color plus forest green.
(MPI 1093)

Cat. 317

236

Pipes and Smoking Equipment

Tobacco Pipes

Since prehistoric times the Indians of the Northern Plains have smoked tobacco in stone pipe bowls attached to long wooden stems. In historic times, pipes were smoked for pleasure as well as in ceremonies and by women as well as by men. Pipe-making was a specialized craft, and most pipe-makers fashioned them both for their own use and for sale or barter with other Indians. Some of them sold pipes to non-Indian collectors. In the Hill Collection there are four styles of pipe bowls made and used by Indians of this region in historic times:

The Straight Pipe

Indian tradition and archaeological evidence affirm that the oldest form of pipe bowl in this region is the one Indians have called the "straight pipe." It is so called because the bowl is in the form of a straight tube to be attached to and in line with a long wooden stem for smoking. A good example of the straight pipe appears in Cat. 318. It is only 3½ inches long, of rather bulbous outline with a round collar at the stem end. Its blackened surface was intentionally produced by greasing it and placing it over a buckbrush fire, then polishing it with a piece of skin or cloth after its surface turned black. Straight pipes of this bulbous form have been found archaeologically in Montana, were seen by Lewis and Clark in 1805–1806 among the Indians of the region, and have been preserved into the twentieth century as part of the ceremonial equipment in some Blackfeet medicine bundles (Plate 20 in Ewers 1963:34–39).

The Modified Micmac Pipe

Anthropologists term the most common type of pipe bowl made and used by the Blackfeet during the last century and a half the "modified Micmac pipe" because it closely resembles the form of pipe made by the Micmac Indians of Nova Scotia. Its basic form is that of an acorn-shaped tobacco chamber atop a heavy, blocky base. This form of pipe may have been brought westward by Indian canoemen and hunters in the expansion of the fur trade by Montreal: through the Great Lakes and up the Saskatchewan River to the Blackfeet country near the Rocky Mountains during the late decades of the eighteenth century. We know that Prince Maximilian saw and collected pipes of this form among the Blackfeet in 1833. A few Blackfeet Indians were still making these modified Micmac-style pipe bowls more than a century later, using stone from local quarries on Blackfeet reservations in Montana and Alberta. They preferred a calcareous shale of fine-grained texture that could be easily worked with a knife and saw and would withstand heat without cracking. They used the same process for blackening the surfaces of these pipes as had been used in coloring the straight pipes. The Blackfeet used pipes of this form in pleasure smoking as well as ceremonially (Ewers 1963:39ff).

Three modified Micmac-style pipes are illustrated here. Cat. 319 and Cat. 320 are men's pipes. Cat. 321 may have been smoked by a woman. Some Blackfeet women used modified Micmac-style pipes in a somewhat smaller size than was smoked by men. Women also used a pipe of elbow shape. In their pleasure smoking, women used a short wooden stem of rosewood about 6 inches long and undecorated. The pipes illustrated here could have been made during the early decades of this century.

The Siouan Calumet

Pipe bowls made from the red stone quarried at a well-known site in present-day southwestern Minnesota have been very popular among the tribes of the Northern Plains for more than a century and a half. This stone is known as "catlinite" after the American artist, George Catlin, who visited that quarry in 1836 and pictured both it and numerous pipes fashioned from that stone in his accounts of his travels (Catlin 1841). One of those illustrations portrays Bull's Back Fat, head chief of the Blood tribe of Blackfeet (whom he met at Fort Union on the upper Missouri in 1832), holding a Siouan calumet in his hand (Fig. 11 in Catlin 1841:I). Probably that chief obtained that pipe ready-made from a Siouan source. At the beginning of this century, Clark Wissler observed that among the Blackfeet "pipe bowls of red catlinite are often seen but . . . are brought in by gift or barter" (Wissler 1910:83).

The form of the Siouan calumet changed some over the years. In Catlin's time, the sides of the upright portion of the bowl flared outward, but in most pipes made since the mid-nineteenth century, the sides of the tobacco chamber are vertical. Many pipes of the latter form are still made by Eastern Sioux Indians who are permitted to quarry the stone from this historic site, now preserved as Pipestone National Monument.

A "Siouan calumet" of catlinite in the shape most popular for more than a century, preserved in the Hill Collection, appears in Cat. 324.

The Effigy Pipe

Some pipe-makers among the tribes of the Northern Plains became very skilled in carving the stone bowls in miniature likenesses of human beings or animals found in their territory. The Sioux were most skillful in creating these effigy pipes. One of their favorite subjects was the head of the male bighorn or mountain sheep. Different carvers rendered the eyes, ears, and muzzles of these animals differently, but all took pains to emphasize the characteristic that gave these animals their name in the Indian sign language as well as in English — their huge, curving horns. Some carvers were quite content to portray these horns very realistically while omitting or greatly simplifying the other features of the animal's head.

Cat. 329 is a good example of a bighorn effigy pipe carved in catlinite with the head facing forward at the angle of an L-shaped bowl. This was surely the work of a Sioux carver even though it may have been collected among the Blackfeet.

Pipe Stems

Bowls were fitted to long, wooden stems for smoking. The traditional Blackfeet stem was of willow or ash, round in cross-section, and generally undecorated (Cat. 327). Sioux stems were of ash worked to a broad, oval shape in cross-section, often elaborately wrapped with braided quillwork for part of the length, beginning at the mouth piece (Cat. 331). The Blackfeet preferred their own stems for ceremonial smoking, but some Blackfeet acquired Sioux-style stems for pleasure smoking. In Catlin's portrait (preserved in the Smithsonian Institution) of Bull's Back Fat at Fort Union in the summer of 1832, the chief holds a handsomely quilled Sioux-style stem (Ewers 1965:77).

Pipe-makers took great care in boring the holes in stems for the passage of the smoke. The section of tree branch selected for the stem was cut, dried in the sun, then heated over a fire and bent perfectly straight. The maker took a piece of heavy wire about a yard long that had been heated red hot. He prayed that the wire would pass straight through the center of the stem. Burning out the side and ruining the stem was considered bad luck for the maker. If the wire passed straight through the center, the maker finished the stem's exterior by smoothing it with sand rock (Ewers 1945:58).

Tobacco Cutting Board

The Blackfeet grew their own tobacco in small plots for use in ceremonial smoking, but most of them came to prefer the white trader's milder tobacco. By the time the Blackfeet were on reservations only the Siksika (the northernmost of the three Blackfeet tribes) in Canada continued to plant the traditional sacred tobacco.

In 1877 the United States government provided 2,000 pounds of tobacco to the Blackfeet of Montana. The supplier had to meet set specifications: "The tobacco must be navy plug, light color, made of leaf, and sweetened only enough for preservation." By the 1930s the Indians still preferred pipe tobacco in plug form from merchants on the reservation. They preferred the brand whose label pictured a horse, which they called "horse tobacco."

The Blackfeet used a flat, wooden board on which to cut the plugs and mix the cut tobacco with the dried leaves of the bearberry for smoking. This was most commonly a sawed section of pine board an inch thick and about a foot wide. The board was usually painted a dark color and decorated with a border of brass tacks.

Less typical but unusually well-documented is the Blackfeet tobacco cutting board shown in Cat. 332, which belonged to Mountain Chief, son of the Piegan chief also known as Mountain Chief, who was a signer of the first Blackfeet treaty with the United States in 1855. The younger Mountain Chief was himself a veteran of intertribal wars and the oldest Indian on the reservation at the time of his death in 1941. He traded the board to the Broadwater-Pepin Trading Company in Browning, from which it was purchased for the Hill Collection before it closed operation on the Blackfeet Reservation in 1920.

Tobacco Bags

Among the Sioux, highly ornamented tobacco bags were originally badges of office carried by the *Wakincuzas* or "Pipe Owners." These men were appointed by the *Naces* or "Tribal Councilmen" (Hassrick 1964:27) with the responsibility for setting disputes, selecting new campsites, and carrying the village fire. It is not known when or where these tobacco bags originated, but it is interesting to note that in all the paintings of Plains Indians observed by Catlin and Bodmer in 1833 and 1834, none appear — even though pipes are much in evidence.

On the other hand, Catlin illustrates (1841:I, 272) three pouches. About them he writes: "Of pipes and the custom of smoking, I have already spoken; and I then said, that the Indians used several substitutes for tobacco, which they call *K'nick-K'neck.* For the carrying of this delicious weed or bark, and the preserving of its flavour, the women construct various curious pouches of otter, beaver, or other skins, which are ingeniously ornamented with porcupine quills and beads, and generally carried hanging across the left arm, containing a quantity of the precious narcotic, with flint and steel, and spunk, for lighting the pipe." Bodmer, too, pictures a similar "white skunk tobacco pouch" (Thomas and Ronneldfeldt 1976: 232).

In a painting, *Group of Piegan Indians* by John Mix Stanley, executed in 1867 (Plate VIII in Kinietz 1942), the figure in the right foreground is holding what is obviously a tobacco bag. Stanley had visited the Piegan in 1853 where he made sketches that were the basis of later works.

In a photograph taken at Fort Laramie in 1868 by Alexander Gardner (Vestal 1948:135) of Sioux and Cheyenne, there is an unidentified man holding a tobacco bag. Photographs of headmen and dignitaries taken in the 1870s (particularly of Sioux, Cheyenne, and Arapahoe) abound with pipes and tobacco bags.

Of the 23 tobacco bags in the collection, eight are tentatively identified as Crow, eight as Sioux, four as Blackfeet, two as Assiniboine, and one as Kutenai. The high percentage of Sioux bags in a collection accumulated in a large part outside their territory suggests that they were a popular item of gift or trade.

Tobacco bags, frequently tied to the pipe at the juncture of the stem and the bowl, contained not only Indian tobacco (a mixture of *kinnikin-nick,* red willow bark, and tobacco), but a pipe tamper and lighting material. The pipe, too, was occasionally stored in the bag. Even when the stem was detached from the bowl, part of the stem frequently protruded from the opening at the top.

The typical bag was rectangular in shape and made of soft tanned leather, usually deerskin. The upper one-half to two-thirds of the bag was usually undecorated, save for ornamentation along the seam and around the opening. The lower third was solidly decorated with quillwork or beads. At the base of the bag were attached cut rawhide strips, covered with quillwork to which was sewn long deerskin fringe (Wissler 1910). The bags varied in length, but averaged about 36 inches. In general, the seam along the side was off center and since it was embellished with beads of quills, it appeared to have been designed to be the front of the bag. Tie strings were frequently attached to the back. The large beaded panel at the lower third of the bag, commonly displaying geometric designs, appears on both sides, but the front always differs from the back either in design or color or both. Apparently no one thought to inquire why each side should consistently be different from the other.

One photograph (Fig. 25) shows White Calf, last head chief of the Piegans, holding his tobacco bag. The absence of quilled slats is not uncommon among the Blackfeet pouches.

Cat. 341 and Cat. 335 show two Sioux quilled tobacco bags. While each exhibit simple and early design motifs, from their condition they would appear to have been made no earlier than the turn of the century. Furthermore, quilling does not lend itself to the intricacies of late Sioux design. Cat. 336, attributed to the Sioux, also exhibits bold, geometric forms and may well have been in use in the 1870s. Cat. 338 and Cat. 340 are typical Sioux bags of the late period. Iron Shell, hereditary Brulé Sioux chief, is shown with a similar late-style tobacco bag as he posed for his photograph in 1936 (Hassrick 1964:220D).

Cat. 339 is a Crow example. Not only the outlining of the design motifs, but also the use of light blue and yellow beads attest to its tribal identity. Cat. 337 has been tentatively identified as Assiniboine, essentially because the placement of the design elements is unique and the scalloped mouth is common among the more northerly tribes. Cat. 333 is a Blackfeet bag. The mouth is fashioned with four large flaps of scallops while the base lacks the quilled slats found on bags of the Sioux, Cheyenne, Arapahoe, and Crow.

While identified as a Kutenai bag, these three-sided pouches were in use among the Plains Cree and Plains Ojibway and are also ascribed to the Metis or mixed-blood Indians of the Red River region (Cat. 342).

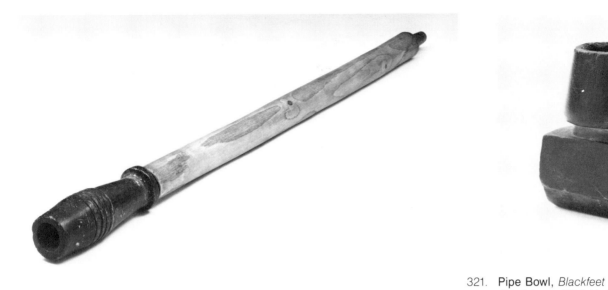

318. **Pipe,** *Northern Plains*
17" long stem, 3¹/₂" long bowl
Museum of the Plains Indian

This straight pipe is made of blackstone with a wooden stem. (MPI 1165a and b)

319. **Pipe Bowl,** *Blackfeet*
1⁵/₈" long, 2⁵/₈" high
Northwest Area Foundation

This Micmac-style stone pipe is decorated at the base with etched rectangular criss-crossing. The color of the stone is dark orange. (SMM 49–42)

320. **Pipe Bowl,** *unspecified tribe*
3" long, 3³/₄" high, ¹⁵/₁₆" hole
Northwest Area Foundation

This Micmac-style stone pipe bowl is of a reddish-orange stone. (SMM 49–38)

321. **Pipe Bowl,** *Blackfeet*
1³/₁₆" long, 1³/₄" high
Northwest Area Foundation

This small woman's pipe is of blackstone and would have been used for recreational, rather than ceremonial, smoking. (SMM 49–39)

322. **Pipe Bowl and Stem,** *Blackfeet*
14¹/₂" long stem,
2" long, 1¹/₄" high bowl
Museum of the Plains Indian

This small blackstone elbow pipe bowl has an unpeeled wooden stem. (MPI 1162a and b)

328. **Tomahawk-style Pipe,** *Plains*
16³/₁₆" long, 7³/₁₆" long head
Northwest Area Foundation

This brass tomahawk-style pipe is fitted with a plain hardwood stem. (SMM 49–44)

329. **Effigy Pipe,** *Sioux*
14¹/₂" long stem,
4³/₄" long, 3¹/₂" high bowl
Museum of the Plains Indian

This pipe is of carved catlinite with a wooden stem. The bowl is an elbow type with a carved effigy of a Rocky Mountain sheep head at the end. (MPI 1163a and b)

330. **Effigy Pipe,** *Plains*
14¹/₂" long total
2¹/₂" long, 1⁵/₈" high bowl
Museum of the Plains Indian

This effigy pipe bowl of catlinite displays a small figure facing the smoker. The stem is of bamboo. (MPI 1166)

323. **Pipe,** *Sioux or Assiniboine*
11¹/₂" long stem,
1¹/₄" long, 1³/₈" high bowl
Museum of the Plains Indian

This small elbow pipe has a bowl of catlinite with a plain wooden stem. (MPI 1161a and b)

326. **Calumet Pipe Bowl**
5¹/₈" long, 1¹/₈" high
Northwest Area Foundation

This pipe bowl with a projecting stem is of light orange moderately polished calinite. (SMM 49–279)

331. **Pipe Stem,** *Sioux*
22" long
Northwest Area Foundation

This flat type wooden pipe stem is decorated with colored quillwork in a pyramidal pattern. Colored horsehair is added. The bowl is Cat. 326. (SMM 49–47 and 49–279)

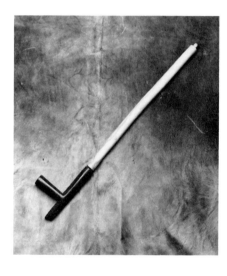

332. **Tobacco Cutting Board,** *Blackfeet*
12¹/₂" diameter
Northwest Area Foundation

This crudely cut circular board was repaired on the top by attaching two metal strips with nails. A double circle of brass nails adorns the edge. A small center hole facilitates emptying cut tobacco into a pipe. The bottom shows "Soo-e-pick-Cis-che-mot" in pencil. Attached by a skin thong is a sales tag from the Broadwater-Pepin Trading Company, Browning, Montana, listing ownership as "from Mountain Chief called Big Brave, a Blackfoot Indian." (SMM 49–61)

324. **Pipe Bowl,** *Northern Plains*
7¹/₂" long, 3³/₈" high
Northwest Area Foundation

This T-shaped pipe bowl has a dark red stripe running through the orange stone of the body. (SMM 49–33)

325. **Pipe Bowl,** *Plains*
7" long, 2⁷/₈" high
Northwest Area Foundation

This pipe bowl of reddish-orange stone has parallel rings at the top of the bowl, at the joint of the bowl, and at the stem end. (SMM 49–277) *No photo.*

327. **Pipe and Stem,** *Blackfeet*
7¹/₂" long bowl
Northwest Area Foundation

The stem is of wood. The bowl is Cat. 324. (SMM 49–282 and 49–33)

Cat. 328

Cat. 329

Cat. 330

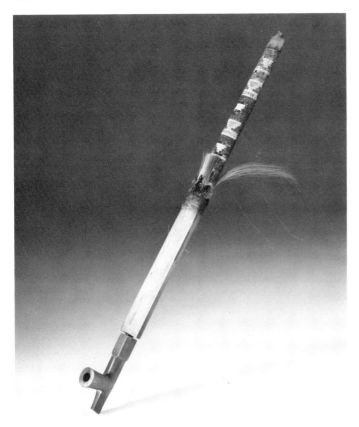

Cat. 331

Cat. 332

Cat. 334a

334. **Tobacco Bag,** *Sioux*
36" long, 6" wide
Northwest Area Foundation

This bag has four sections: a top of soft leather, a smaller section covered with beadwork in a geometric pattern, quill-wrapped hide slats, and long fringe. (SMM 49–57)

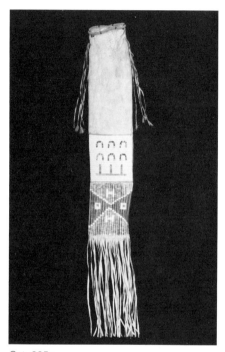

Cat. 335a

333. **Tobacco Bag,** *Blackfeet*
27½" long, 6" wide
Museum of the Plains Indian

This bag is beaded on one side only with a square panel in dark red, green, orange, blue, and white on red. The bag is edged with beaded strips in green and dark blue and has long, undecorated fringe at the bottom. The thong ties are edged with copper-colored beads. (MPI 1099)

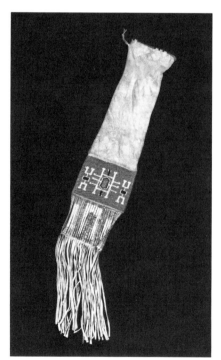

Cat. 334b

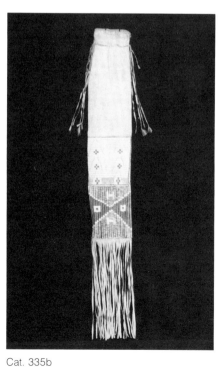

Cat. 335b

335. **Tobacco Bag,** *Sioux*
46" long, 6" wide
Northwest Area Foundation

This bag of tanned hide has orange and blue beads at the lip. There are quilled panels on each side at the lower third of the bag. One consists of a panel of yellow with two rows of inverted U-shapes above an E. The patterns are in purple. The other panel is a faded purple with two columns of yellow, stacked pyramids with blue and red crosses and a pink stripe at the base. Rawhide fringe below the panels is quill-wrapped with geometric patterns: a red hourglass with white and purple squares. The remaining field is purple with white forms. The drawstrings are wrapped with red quills and have purple horsehair tips. (SMM 49–58)

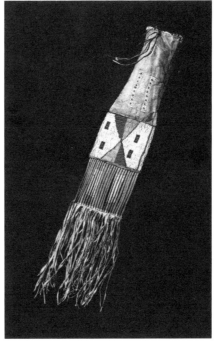

Cat. 336b

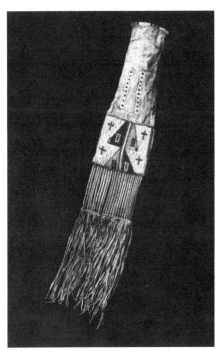

Cat. 336a

336. **Tobacco Bag,** *Sioux*
32" long, 5" wide
Northwest Area Foundation

This highly decorated bag has beadwork at the top of the soft hide section, just above the double thong closing, as well as two decorated sections on the body. Orange quillwork covers the slats leading to heavy fringe at the bottom. (SMM 49–59)

337. **Tobacco Bag,** *Assiniboine (?)*
34" long, 7" wide
Northwest Area Foundation

This four-section bag has several minor variations on the standard type. The upper part of the bag is in two pieces, each rectangular in shape and sewed together along both edges. The beaded portion is attached to the bottom. Quill-covered slats and a separate fringe section complete the bag. (SMM 49–60)

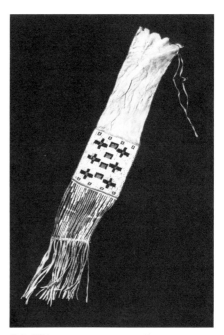

Cat. 337a

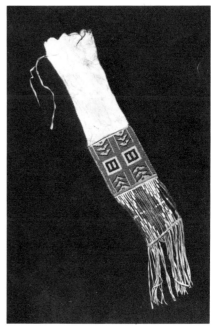

Cat. 337b

245

Cat. 338a

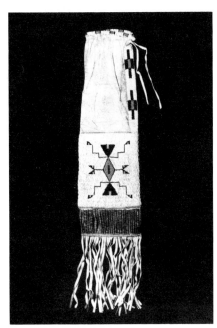

Cat. 338b

338. **Tobacco Bag,** *Sioux*
34" long, 7¼" wide
Museum of the Plains Indian

This bag is decorated with beads in various geometric figures and motifs of dark blue, light blue, red, and yellow on white. The beading at the mouth is in white, dark blue, light blue, and red. Quilled slats are cardinal red. (MPI 1309)

Cat. 339a

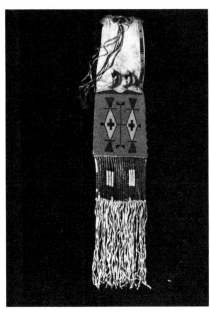

Cat. 339b

339. **Tobacco Bag,** *Crow*
36" long, 7½" wide
Museum of the Plains Indian

This bag is beaded on its upper portion. There are solid beaded panels with different designs on either side of the bag. One side shows two connected diamond shapes outlined in blue, with red triangles attached on each end. The field is light blue. The interior of the diamond is yellow, with a cross of red and blue checkers. There is a light blue field on the reverse side of the bag, with a series of triangles in yellow, green, and red with blue accents. The axis of the design is two identical squares in red with yellow centers. A wavy band of green around the top of the design panels is outlined in red. There are two horsehair dangles with red-quilled stems and red-dyed horsehair and two slim beaded extensions, in light blue, navy blue, red, green, and white. The slats at the bottom are quilled in red with two designs of purple bordered squares with yellow interiors and pink centers. The buckskin fringe is ornamented with blue beads. (MPI 1315)

340. **Tobacco Bag,** *Sioux*
23" long, 7" wide
Museum of the Plains Indian

This bag has rolled beading around the mouth and beaded strips on either side of the neck. The colors on either side of the bag are the same, with different designs. The beading is in blue, green, red, and white. The slats are quilled in pink and white. A single fringe element is attached to each slat. (MPI 1317)

Cat. 340a

Cat. 340b

Cat. 341a

Cat. 341b

341. **Tobacco Bag,** *Sioux*
23" long, 6¹/₄" wide
Museum of the Plains Indian

This quilled buckskin bag is decorated overall with quillwork, excluding the end fringes. The quilled slats have a pattern of white stepped pyramids edged with purple, on a red background. The lower panels are quilled. One side has solid quilling throughout on a red background. The pattern consists of a double inverse stepped pyramid, and the bulk of the design is carried out in turquoise and gold colors. The images oppose each other over a central bar. There are yellow inserts, edged with turquoise, along the edges. The other side has narrow quilled strips in red with small gold inserts. The top of this section is quilled with three diamond forms in red, orange, and purple. Above these are red feather dangles. There are quilled ties on either side of the bag, in red, turquoise, green, and white. A similar band of quilling edges the mouth, and there is a narrow edge in green beads.
(MPI 1314)

342. **Tobacco Bag,** *Kutenai*
17" long, 4¹/₄" wide
Museum of the Plains Indian

This bag is made of three beaded triangular sections with fringing at the seams. The identical sections are decorated in twining patterns. The beading is in blue, light blue, red, green, pink, and yellow. The top of the bag is serrated.
(MPI 1098)

Musical Instruments

The principal musical instruments found among the Plains Indians were the rattle, drum, flute, and whistle. Drums and rattles were used as accompaniment to singing both by singers at ceremonial dances and by shamans in their incantations while curing the sick. Formerly in the possession of Short Face, a Blackfeet Indian, Cat. 348 shows a shaman's rattle made from a bison scrotum and its painted parfleche case. Cat. 343 pictures a Crow hand drum decorated with a green dragonfly and embellished with eagle feathers (Plate 19 in Catlin 1913:I) portrayed a Blackfeet shaman holding a similar hand drum as part of his paraphernalia. Cat. 345 shows an eagle bone whistle supported by a beaded necklace. Such whistles were sounded by participants in the Sun Dance as well as on the warpath (Hassrick 1964:81).

344. **Drum and Drum Supports,**
● *Blackfeet*
21 1/2" diameter, 10" high drum
Museum of the Plains Indian
26" long drum supports
Northwest Area Foundation

343. **Hand Drum,** *Crow*
16" diameter, 3" high
Museum of the Plains Indian

This hand drum is laced to a wooden frame. The head is painted yellow with a red circle toward the center with a green dragonfly. The sides are painted red. There is a hide thong with two spotted eagle feathers and four Venetian trade beads. (MPI 1240)

This large, double-headed Grass Dance drum was made from a cut-down section of a barrel by lacing the skin heads together with rawhide. A faint red earth design is painted on the head. There are four handles of twisted rawhide protruding from the side. (MPI 1244)

The four drum supports were made by wrapping a piece of wet hide around a long, thin, rounded sapling. The handle is entirely wrapped with red cloth covered by pink yarn. Beads are wound tightly around the hide covering. Feathers and colored yarn mixed with red feathers hang from the tips. (SMM 49–268)

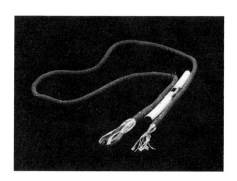

345. **Whistle,** *Northern Plains*
5¾" long
Northwest Area Foundation

This eagle-wing bone whistle has a red and green beaded cord fastened to the whistle with sinew. (SMM 1–871)

346. **Rawhide Rattle,** *Blackfeet*
11½" long
Northwest Area Foundation

This seamed rattle is of heavy rawhide attached to a wooden handle. The bulbous section was shaped by wetting the skin and filling it with shot. The shot was removed when the hide was dry and shaken out before the handle was attached. (SMM 1–653)

347. **Rattle,** *Blackfeet*
10" long, 12" diameter
Private collection, St. Paul

Fish Wolf Robe had the enviable reputation of being the best Blackfeet dancer for many years during the first half of this century. After his death in the 1970s, his wife presented his colorful dance rattle to a friend of the family, who placed it in his private collection. Intricate geometric designs of blue, grey, and red are painted against either yellow or black background colors. Thick black lines are used to separate the design element and to serve as bands surrounding the dried-gourd, wooden-handled rattle.

348. **Medicine Rattle and Rawhide Medicine Case,** *Blackfeet*
12½" long, 3½" wide case
9" long rattle
Northwest Area Foundation

This reddish-brown painted rawhide rattle has a painted cylindrical rawhide ceremonial case cut on a slight taper, rolled, and fastened by a single thong passing in and out of punched holes. The two disc ends and main case are painted in geometric designs in yellow, red, green, and blue. An attached tag reads: "From Short Face, A Blackfeet Indian. The rattle is used in the dances by Brave Dogs and Big Beavers." (SMM 49–306)

Religious Objects

Ritual objects, made to aid man in his efforts to persuade the powers that control the universe, varied to some degree among High Plains Indian tribes. Some things were held in common, such as small tied medicine bundles, totem animals, and vision-seeking. Religious objects could be particularly efficacious to just one person, for example, Wades-in-the-Water's dream shirt (Cat. 82). The items that follow illustrate the variety of sacred objects.

Cat. 349

349. **Horse Mask,** *Sioux*
18½" long, 17" wide
Museum of the Plains Indian

This colorful horse mask of buckskin is decorated with quills and beadwork. The upper half has a design of red stripes. There are two pairs of holes: the upper pair is for the horse's ears; the lower pair, bound with black cotton cloth, is for the eyes. The lower half of the mask is covered with a panel of quillwork in a starburst design in orange, red, yellow, white, and purple. Both sides are fringed, while the bottom is bound with beads in strips of white, yellow, blue, and red.
(MPI 1302)

350. **Necklace**, *Blackfeet*
15" long
Museum of the Plains Indian

This necklace of porcelain disc
beads, with French brass beads
interspersed, is strung on a
buckskin thong. A medicine pouch
with light blue and white beads is
attached. (MPI 1290)

351. **Medicine Bag**, *Blackfeet*
14" long, 9" wide
Museum of the Plains Indian

This smoke-tanned bag contains
four medicine pouches and five
pouches are attached to the
outside. The outside pouches are
painted red and are wrapped with
white quill. There is fringe along the
side seams. Three of the inner bags
are made of buckskin. (MPI 1183)

Cat. 353a

Cat. 353b

353. Ghost Dance Dress, *Pawnee*
● *36" long, 22" wide*
Museum of the Plains Indian

This ochre-colored dress has fringe on the shoulders, under the sleeves, and at the hem. The bottom of the dress, including the fringe, is painted blue-green. The front shows a male figure in a long feather bonnet, standing next to a green bow and arrow, and a crescent moon and pipe. The headdress has yellow and blue feathers; the pipe is green and blue. Above the paintings are long-haired figures, wearing long dresses of yellow and red. One wears a long feather bonnet and the other holds a pipe. A five-pointed star rises above the latter's head, with a yellow-green crescent to the left. The figure with the headdress has a yellow face, painted patterns on the shoulder, and a blue and yellow tipi on each sleeve. The neck is edged with dark blue ribbon and white beads. Seven large tadpoles with tails outlined in green, a pair of crossed pipes in blue, and a blue bird on a triangular flap at the neck decorate the other side. (MPI 1396)

352. Otter Medicine Bag, *Northern Plains*
47" long, 8" wide
Northwest Area Foundation

This medicine bag is made from a complete otterskin with quillwork and tin dangles applied to the inset of the long tail and on the four paws. Seven brass bells with quillwork and dangles are attached by decorated thongs, arranged in a circle on the central dorsal surface. A small medicine bag is attached to the neck. Metal buttons have been placed in the eye sockets. (SMM 1–782)

Acknowledgements

The authors thank the following people for their contributions to this project:

Margaret Ewers and Barbara Hassrick for research help, especially in the Browning phase.
Terry Saario, Judith Healey, John Taylor, and Irving Clark of the Northwest Area Foundation; Monica Taylor for assistance in the foundation archives.
Loretta Pepion and Wilbur Black Weasel of the Museum of the Plains Indian.
The staff of the Science Museum of Minnesota, especially Lou Casagrande and Melissa Stoddart for research help and Jean Madsen and Gretchen Anderson for conservation of the collection on exhibit.
Pat Stafford and the staff of Burlington Northern Railroad.
Jeanne Perrin for typing and retyping the manuscript.
An anonymous St. Paul donor.
Matt Walton for constant encouragement.